MW00562828

WAR STORIES

WAR STORIES

PARIS TO V-E DAY

ROBERT O. BABCOCK

RAYMOND —
Thanks for your
service in USMC,
Semper Fi!
Bob Babcock

DEEDS PUBLISHING | ATLANTA, GEORGIA

Most of the material in this book is a subset of stories previously published in 2006 by Deeds Publishing in *War Stories: Utah Beach to Pleiku* by Robert O. Babcock.

Disclaimer - No claim is made as to the historical accuracy of the stories in this book. They are as accurate as memories faded by thirty to thirty-five years can make them, but this is not intended to be a history book that will stand the test of historical scholars. It is the military experiences of 4th Infantry Division veterans as each GI remembers it.

Published by Deeds Publishing
Marietta, GA
www.deedspublishing.com

Printed in the United States of America

Library of Congress Cataloging-in-Publications Data is available upon request

ISBN 978-1-941165-08-9

Books are available in quantity for promotional or premium use. For information, write Deeds Publishing, PO Box 682212, Marietta, GA 30068 or info@deedspublishing.com.

Design and layout by Mark Babcock

First edition 2014

10 9 8 7 6 5 4 3 2 1

This book is dedicated to all past, present, and future veterans of the 4th Infantry Division, especially those who made the supreme sacrifice in defense of our American way of life, and their families.

TABLE OF CONTENTS

Introduction

This book is one of a series of three that are subsets of the book, *War Stories: Utah Beach to Pleiku,* first published in 2001. That book was my effort to preserve the stories of 4th Infantry Division veterans who had served in World War II, the Cold War, and in Vietnam. Thanks to the input of the 4ID veterans and their family members, that book turned out to be over 725 pages long—much larger than most people want to buy and read.

In this 70th anniversary year of D-Day, the liberation of Paris, the breaching of the Siegfried Line, the Battle of the Hurtgen Forest, the Battle of the Bulge, the fight across Germany, and V-E Day in World War II, we decided to republish that book into two World War II and one Vietnam volumes—available in both paperback and e-book. Although the large version is still available in paperback format, we believe our readers will enjoy these smaller volumes as they read or re-read the exploits of Soldiers of the 4th Infantry Division.

As you read the stories, you will see that some stories show the author as deceased. That was the status as of 2000 when the book was first written. Since then, sadly, many more, if not most, of the WWII contributors to these stories are now gone—but their stories live on.

When I first started attending annual reunions of the National 4th Infantry Division Association in 1990, the highlight of each reunion was sitting with WWII vets and listening for hours to the stories of their exploits in Europe. As I anticipated each year sitting down again with a specific veteran whose stories had captivated me the year before, I found that all too often I would ask about where he was, only to find out that he had died, and his stories died with him.

When I became president of the National 4th Infantry Division Association in 1998-2000, one of my primary missions I set for myself was to preserve the stories of 4ID veterans so they would be available long past the time that our veterans went on to their heavenly rewards.

I am currently working on *War Stories II,* adding more World War II, Cold War, and Vietnam stories, and including sections on the 4th Infantry Division's actions in Iraq and Afghanistan. That book will be published once I have enough stories to make it viable. All who served in any capacity with the 4th Infantry Division are encouraged to send me their stories.

As you read this 70th anniversary commemorative edition, reflect back on those members of "the greatest generation" who cared enough to not only fight and defeat the Nazi threat to the world, but also cared enough to write down their memories so future generations could learn from their experiences. I challenge all veterans of all eras to do the same—and make sure your family, your unit, and others you care about have access to your stories. If you need help doing that, feel free to contact this author at info@deedspublishing.com.

Ten percent of all profits of this book will be donated to the National 4th Infantry Division Association to help perpetuate its almost 100 years helping the veterans and family members of those who served in that great division—Steadfast and Loyal,

Bob Babcock, May 2014
President and Historian, National 4th Infantry Division Association
Company B, 1st Battalion, 22nd Infantry Regiment
4th Infantry Division, Vietnam 1966-1967

The Siegfried Line to The Hürtgen Forest
September, October, November 1944

While others celebrated the liberation of Paris, the 4th Infantry Division continued their relentless attack on the retreating German army, crossing France and into Belgium. Just seventeen days after liberating Paris, a patrol from the 4th Infantry Division became the first allied unit to cross the Siegfried Line and enter the German homeland. Fighting continued in the Siegfried Line through the month of September until the Allied supply shortages caused them to fall back into Belgium in early October. Patrols kept contact with the Germans until early November when the Division was alerted to move to a place most had never heard of—the Hürtgen Forest.

By early December, no 4th Infantry Division veteran who entered the Hürtgen Forest would ever be able to forget it. The 4th Infantry Division's bloodiest battle of WWII was fought in November and early December in the "hellhole" known as the Hürtgen Forest.

Chronology of the 4th Infantry Division, 29 August 1944 through 3 December 1944.

Courtesy of Robert S. Rush, Ph.D.

29 August. V Corps, leaving Fr 2nd Armd Div behind in Paris, drives NE with 4th Div to Mitry Mory-Le Plessis area.

30 August. V Corps continues pursuit of enemy north-eastward, passing 28th div through Fr 2nd Armd Div to advance abreast 4th Div.

31 August. V Corps passes 5th Armd Div through 28th and 4th Divs and continues NE with all three.

1 September. 4th Div, motorized and reinf by CCA of 5th Armd Div, takes the lead, thrusting to vicinity of Chauny.

4 September. 4th Div continues mopping up in old zone.

5 September. 102nd Cav Gp screens assembly of 4th Div NW of Mézières

6 September. 4th Inf and 5th Armd Divs move forward from the Meuse, 4th on left reaching Bièvre and 5th Armd overrunning Sedan.

7 September. 4th Div continues E on N flank of corps toward St. Hubert.

8 September. V Corps, with 4th Div on N and 28th on S, meets strongeeerr rear guard opposition as it continues E to positions generally between Jemelle and Margut.

10 September. In V Corps area, 4th Div reaches general line Regne-Bastogne. 12 September. 4th Div advances toward St. Vith against light resistance.

13 September. In V Corps area, forward elements of 4th Div assemble near the Schnee Eifel at Radscheid and Bleialf.

14 September. Siegfried Line: 4th Div penetrates West Wall in the Schnee Eifel; 12th Inf cuts Schnee Eifel highway and drives NE along it, taking Hill 698; 22nd reaches crest of Schnee Eifel ridge and gets one bn on E slopes overlooking Hontheim.

15 September. Siegfried Line: 8th Inf goes into action on N flank of 4th Div but is unable to advance; 12th drives NE along Schnee Eifel highway, taking strongpoints at crossroads 655; dangerous gap exists between it and 22nd Inf; 22nd, ordered to take Brandscheid before continuing main drive undergoes enemy counterattack near Hontheim and does not advance.

16 September. Siegfried Line: 12th Inf of 4th Div makes fruitless and costly efforts to push NE for the next few days; 8th Inf enters center of line and drives down E slopes of the Schnee Eifel hampered more by terrain than enemy; 22nd Inf is still unable to take Brandscheid but gains hill on outskirts, and elements of regt take important hill on Bleialf-Prüm highway about midway between Meisert and Sellerich.

17 September. Siegfried Line: 4th Div, after further costly efforts to get to E edge of the Schnee Eifel forest and to take Brandscheid, almost succeeding in each case, calls off offensive and passes to aggressive defense.

19 September. Schnee Eifel: In V Corps area, 1st Bn of 12th Inf, 4th Div, falls back a little under counterattack SW along Schnee Eifel highway; later regains former positions and some ground beyond.

4 October. Schnee Eifel: V Corps changes target date for West Wall offensive to 10 October; directs 28th and 4th Divs to reconnoiter in force to E beginning on 6 October.

7 October. Schnee Eifel: In V Corps area, 28th and 4th Divs advance to line of departure for West Wall offensive.

6 November. Hürtgen: In US First Army's VII Corps area, 4th Div, moving from V Corps zone to Zweifall area, is ordered to release 12th Inf, which under command of 28th Inf, V Corps, is to begin relief of elements of 28th Div at once. Relief of 109th Inf by 12th Inf of 4th Div cannot be accomplished on night 6-7 as planned.

7 November. Hürtgen: 12th Inf, 4th Div, relieves 109th Inf on N flank N of Germeter.

10 November. Hürtgen: In VII Corps area, 12th Inf, which reverts to 4th Div from attachment to 28th Div of V Corps, undergoes a determined counterattack on plateau SW of Hürtgen that engulfs 2 cos and forces remnants back to S third of plateau. Because of weakened state of the regt, CCR of 5th Armd Div is attached to Corps.

12 November. Hürtgen: Two cos of 12th Inf, 4th Div, break through to the isolated forces on plateau SW of Hürtgen, but they too become encircled.

15 November. Hürtgen: 12th Inf of 4th Div breaks through to the 4 encircled cos on plateau SW of Hürtgen and withdraws them, but by now the regt holds only S edge of the plateau.

16 November. Hürtgen: 4th Div, reinf by CCR of 5th Armd Div, attacks on broad front in Hürtgen Forest at scene of earlier battles in effort to break through between Schevenhütte and Hürtgen, making main effort on left in order to support 1st Div; elements of 8th Inf on N and 22nd Inf in center make extremely slow progress against well organized positions within the forest, 12th Inf can scarcely move on plateau SW of Hürtgen.

17 November. Hürtgen: Enemy continues to contain efforts of 4th Div to advance through Hürtgen Forest.

18 November. Hürtgen: 4th Div advances in Hürtgen Forest, where 8th Inf, in 1000 yard drive, penetrates outer defenses of approach to Düren and 22nd reaches positions astride road leading E to Grosshau, but gap exists between the regts.

19 November. Hürtgen: 4th Div suspends eastward attacks in order to consolidate and try to close gaps between 8th and 22nd Regts. Boundary between VII and V Corps is shifted N above Hürtgen so that the 2 corps can coordinate operations to clear Hürtgen-Grosshau area.

20 November. Hürtgen: 4th Div, beset with supply problems, narrows gap within its line somewhat. During 5 days of fighting in Hürtgen Forest, the div has gained only 1 ½ miles, and that at high cost.

21 November. Hürtgen: 121st Inf of 8th Div attacks through 12th Inf of 4th Div (VII Corps) on plateau SW of Hürtgen, where enemy has checked previous efforts to advance.

22 November. Hürtgen: Renewing attacks in Hürtgen Forest, 4th Div's 8th and 22nd Regts feint eastward while slipping elements around enemy; forward elements of 8th Inf reach heights at Gut Schwarzenbroich, the first objective, while advance force of 22nd reaches positions 700 yards W of Grosshau; depleted 12th Inf begins attack to secure right flank of 22nd and advances very slowly.

23 November. Hürtgen: Forward elements of 8th Inf, 4th Div, are driving steadily NE in Hürtgen Forest while other elements battle enemy at Gut Schwarzenbroich; 22nd Inf remains near Grosshau but does not risk an attack.

25 November. Hürtgen: 8th Inf, 4th Div, reaches positions a little more than a mile from the edge of Hürtgen Forest; in conjunction with CCR, 5th Armed Div (V Corps) 22nd Inf attacks toward Grosshau but cannot take it; 4th Div suspends attacks for several days after this.

26 November. Hürtgen: 4th Div consolidates positions in Hürtgen Forest; 12th Inf at last gets into position N and W of Hürtgen to protect S flank of 22nd Inf.

27 November. Hürtgen: 4th Div continues to consolidate and improve positions in Hürtgen Forest; elements of V Corps relieve 12th Inf near Hürtgen.

28 November. Hürtgen: In center of 4th Div zone, 12th Inf begins attack to close gap between 8th and 22nd Regts in Hürtgen Forest.

29 November. Hürtgen: 4th Div renews attack all along line in Hürtgen Forest and finds that enemy has strengthened his defenses during lull in fighting 8th Inf makes negligible progress toward road center at E of forest; 12th Inf closes gap between 8th and 22nd, in frontal and flanking attacks supported by armor, takes Grosshau and cuts road to Gey.

30 November. Hürtgen: 8th Inf, 4th Div, continues costly efforts to get through Hürtgen Forest; 12th, advancing more than 1000 yards, reaches edge of woods W of Gey, but is too weak to attack the village; 22nd reinf by bn of 5th Armd Div [46th AIB] attempts to secure Grosshau clearing and forest between Grosshau and Gey in order to swing NE toward Düren; some elements reach edge of woods overlooking Gey, but rest of force suffers heavily while trying to come abreast.

1 December. Hürtgen: 8th Inf, 4th Div, still trying in vain to get out of Hürtgen Forest, has gained less than 1000 yards during 3 days of hard fighting, 22nd Inf, committing its reserves, finally emerges to establish thin line along woods overlooking Gey. Gen Collins orders attack halted. Since 16 November, 4th Div has made maximum gain of a little more than 3 miles at exceedingly high cost.

2 December. Hürtgen: 22nd Inf, 4th Div, repels counterattack from Gey with help of arty.

3 December. Hürtgen: 330th Regt, 83d Div, from VIII Corps sector begins relief of 4th Div, which is eventually to move to Luxembourg. The usually inactive German Air Force appears in strength in afternoon, about 60 ME 109s attacking without causing serious damage and at a cost of at least 19 shot down.

John Dowdy, CO, 1-22 Infantry—1944

A Tribute to One of America's Finest Combat Leaders— Killed in Action in the Siegfried Line on 16 September 1944

"He was a fountain of strength at which all men might drink."

In the two hundred year history of the 22nd Infantry Regiment, John Dowdy was one of the most aggressive, yet charismatic, commanders that 1st Battalion and the 22nd Infantry Regiment has ever seen. He led his men always from the front, never expecting them to do anything he was not prepared to do himself. He inspired courage in his Battalion, motivating his Soldiers to continue pressing on in the face of extreme hardships, regrouping them after costly setbacks from the enemy, and instilling in them the dedication to ultimate victory which was the essence of his fighting spirit.

Thanks to the efforts of his cousin, Karen Scott, and to 1-22 Infantry's webmaster, Michael Belis, his story has come to light, to ensure that he will never be forgotten.

Karen wrote: "Such an American story—who would guess that a little kid growing up in the boonies, with his overalls hanging down, would someday rally his troops on a ridge in France, turn the tide of the battle, take the objective, and clear the way to Cherbourg?"

John Dowdy served his entire military career with the 22nd Infantry. Though details of that career are sketchy and incomplete, the following is an historical sketch of one of the most dynamic leaders the Regiment has ever seen. In thirty-eight total days of combat, John Dowdy received the Distinguished Service Cross, two Silver Star Medals, two Purple Heart medals, and the Combat Infantryman's Badge.

John Dowdy entered the US Army from the University of Georgia on June 15, 1939 as a 2nd Lieutenant in the 22nd Infantry. On February 25, 1941 he was promoted to 1st Lieutenant. On February 1, 1942 he received a promotion to Captain, becoming, at the age of 23, one of the youngest Captains and Company Commanders in the Army at that time. On August 16, 1943, he was promoted to Major and served on the Regimental Staff of the 22nd Infantry's Commander, Colonel Hervey Tribolet.

Sometime in late 1943, prior to the Regiment sailing overseas in January of 1944, Dowdy was made Executive Officer of the 2nd Battalion. On D-Day he came ashore on Utah Beach with 2nd Battalion in the second wave of the landings. On June 8, 1944 (D-Day plus two), he was given command of 1st Battalion, relieving LTC Sewell Brumby, who had been wounded.

Dowdy took 1st Battalion inland from the beach area as the 22nd Infantry became the right flank of the 4th Division's point of attack. The Regiment's mission was to reduce the enemy strongpoints along the beaches and destroy the heavily fortified batteries several miles inland. Positioned on the high ground between Dodainville and Azeville were two German battery forts, one at Azeville and the other at Crisbecq. Each fort consisted of four massive concrete blockhouses containing the artillery batteries, the guns at Crisbecq being 210mm long barreled monsters. The Crisbecq battery was one of the most powerful coastal battery forts of the entire German Atlantic Wall. Both forts were protected by interconnected trenches, pillboxes, barbed wire, and automatic weapons.

For four days the Regiment battled fierce German resistance in the attempt to take these forts, while suffering heavy casualties in the process. Azeville and Crisbecq were taken, as were Ste. Marcouf and Ozeville. The last major strongpoint on the way to Cherbourg was the heavily fortified high ground of the Quineville ridge. On June 14 the 22nd Infantry and one Battalion of the 39th Infantry attacked this high ground with tank support. Dowdy took 1st Battalion, with its supporting tanks of the 70th Tank Battalion, and captured the eastern part of the ridge, and another hill to the east of that. For his actions that day he was awarded the Distinguished Service Cross. The citation for that award read:

"For extraordinary heroism in action against the enemy on June 15, 1944 (sic). Fierce artillery, machinegun, mortar and small arms fire inflicted heavy casualties upon Lt. Col. Dowdy's command as it attacked high ground. One assault company, having lost all of its officers and most of its key non-commissioned officers, became completely demoralized;

withdrawal was imminent. Friendly tanks operating in support of the attack began to retreat. Realizing that his entire command was threatened with annihilation, Lt. Col. Dowdy, disregarding completely his own safety, moved afoot through a hail of fire and personally directed the fire of the tanks upon the enemy. Courageously he proceeded forward unfalteringly to the forward elements of his command. While under fire, he organized them for an attack. Lt. Col. Dowdy's exemplary actions spearheaded a devastating assault, which resulted in the capture of the strongly fortified position and more than 100 prisoners."

For the next several days the Regiment assembled and received replacements, and on June 19 began the drive toward Cherbourg. By June 22, 1st Battalion was holding high ground near Gonneville, on the extreme right flank of a three Division assault upon the fortress city. For six days the Regiment held the flank and prevented German forces from linking up with the city.

On the last day of continuous action, June 27, while leading his Battalion, Dowdy suffered serious shrapnel wounds to his right leg from enemy artillery. Refusing to be evacuated, he remained in command for 18 hours after being wounded, most likely until the surrender of all German forces east of Cherbourg, at 1330 hours on June 28. For his actions that day John Dowdy received the Silver Star and Purple Heart.

Dowdy spent the months of July and August in a hospital in England recovering from his wounds, and was promoted to Lieutenant Colonel on July 21, 1944. He rejoined the Regiment on September 1, 1944. Colonel Charles "Buck" Lanham was then in command of the 22nd, and Dowdy became part of Lanham's staff. During the three days of September 1-3, Dowdy became Lanham's "right-hand-man." In those three days the Regiment fought its way across more than 100 miles of France and Belgium, with Lanham and Dowdy directing its movements and operations.

On September 4 Dowdy resumed command of 1st Battalion. Lanham wrote of Dowdy:

When this fight was over I gave John back his battalion (1st Battalion) which had suffered heavily in his absence. Within twenty-four hours it was like a new outfit. John was everywhere and his courage, his strength, his spirit, and his personality ran like flame through the com-

mand. I think he was the greatest leader of men that I have ever seen, and I have spent a lifetime in the Army. And certainly no man has ever been more deeply loved by those he led and by those who had the high privilege of serving with him as fellow officers.

John was with us when we broke the Siegfried line on (Sept) 14th. The blow that he and his battalion struck that day will never be forgotten by our enemy. We ruptured the line on September 14th and on September 15th we continued the attack to widen the breach and to improve our positions. The fighting was bitter and the enemy was fanatical. The troops that opposed us were largely SS formations, the elite of the German Army, with orders from Hitler in person to fight to the death. And in large measure this is what they did.

On September 16th John and his battalion again took their objective—a critical hill in our zone. The enemy reaction was violent. He made repeated efforts to throw John from his hard-won position, but these were beaten off. He then resorted to violent artillery and mortar fire—this was probably the heaviest series of concentrations we have ever received. John ordered his battalion to dig in on the high ground for the night. He then began circulating among his troops; adjusting their positions, correcting their dispositions, placing his weapons in the most advantageous locations, joking with the men, reassuring them, seeing to their safety. He walked through the storm of shellfire as if he were walking down a street in his home town—calm, cool, completely composed, and without the slightest trace of hurry or excitement. He was a fountain of strength at which all-men might drink.

He made two complete circuits of his position, and still not satisfied that his men were adequately cared for, he began a third trip. He was perhaps halfway through when the fatal shell landed. He was killed instantly, and though it might well have been otherwise, his body was not mutilated. Only a fragment of the shell did the deadly work.

Charles B. MacDonald, in the book *The Siegfried Line Campaign* described the above action thus: "The only bright development on this part of the front came in the afternoon of 16 September when the 1st Battalion pushed out of the Pruem State Forest to seize a hill that commanded the Bleialf-Pruem highway a few hundred yards west of the German-held village of Sellerich. Even this achievement was marred by the loss from

German shelling of some thirty-five men wounded and eight killed, including the battalion commander, Lt. Col. John Dowdy." (p. 53)

For his leadership and bravery under fire, at the cost of his life on that September day, John Dowdy was awarded his second Silver Star and second Purple Heart. He was 26 years old when he died.

Regimental Chaplain Bill Boice wrote of Dowdy: "One of the finest officers of the regiment, Lt. Colonel John Dowdy had proved himself an able officer in combat again and again. His personal care for the troops under his command, his knowledge of military tactics, had saved lives and boosted morale."

Perhaps the best tribute to John Dowdy was written by Colonel "Buck" Lanham, in a personal letter to John's mother, Eva, when he wrote: "....I have seen many officers and many men go down. Each one, no matter how humble, has been a blow and a personal loss to me. But I say truthfully that never has a death so stunned me as that of John. And the Regiment shared that grief with me. John was worshipped by his battalion; it was a form of hero worship, and John was a hero and died a hero, in the true sense of that much abused word."

LTC John Dowdy was buried in the US Military Cemetery at Fosse, Belgium. For several years a Belgian family adopted the grave and kept it well looked after, making sure it always had fresh flowers. On April 8, 1949 LTC Dowdy's body was returned to the US and he now rests in the Dowdy plot in Tifton, Georgia.

Karen Scott's (John's cousin) dedication to preserving the memory of her ancestor insures that LTC Dowdy's legacy will always be remembered. Thanks to her, this important chapter has been written in the history of the 4th Infantry Division and the history of 1-22 Infantry. We also thank Michael Belis, 4ID Vietnam vet, for preserving this story, plus more, including pictures, in the website he runs for 1-22 Infantry, www.1-22infantry.org.

Robert Gast, Warsaw, IN
Companies B and C, 1st Battalion, 12th Infantry Regiment
The Tankers Shared

The so-called mad dash from Paris to the Siegfried Line was really not a dash. It was a combination of walking, riding trucks, and riding tanks. I thought that riding tanks was one of the most memorable experiences of the war. The officers and men of the armored unit attached to us were great people. They got a big kick out of waving good-bye to us when they closed the hatch. They were always willing to share some of the things they had that seemed like luxuries to us—things like their rations, a razor, and even a tooth brush.

Charles Hardin, Pinellas Park, FL
HQ, 3rd Battalion, 22nd Infantry Regiment

Didn't Blow Us All to Hell

Several months ago, you asked if anyone was on the first patrol into Germany. I believe I was. I was a jeep driver and I believe I drove the 3rd Battalion liaison officer on that patrol. I really didn't know our objective was to get a shovel full of German dirt. Later on we attacked the Siegfried Line in the identical area that we patrolled.

We didn't know the pillboxes were only a mile away as they were all covered with pine trees; there were open fields and then the pine trees. I think the town we went into was Brandscheid, Germany. I'm not sure. The patrol was uneventful, and I don't know why they didn't blow us all to hell.

Conrad "Frenchy" Adams, Gulfport, MS
Company E, 2nd Battalion, 8th Infantry Regiment

A Miracle in the Siegfried Line

As we went on towards Germany, we entered the Siegfried Line. One night, we were told to dig our foxhole near a fence. We started to dig and hit rocks. So my buddy and I backed up around ten feet and dug our foxhole. During the night, a German 88 hit exactly in the middle where we had been digging our foxhole. (Remember, I believe in miracles—that's another one.)

Robert Gast, Warsaw, IN
Companies B and C, 1st Battalion, 12th Infantry Regiment

An Unusual Thing Happened

My platoon was the second platoon from our battalion to enter the Siegfried Line. I was to contact the first platoon that had gone earlier and had not been heard from. We were very fortunate and stumbled onto a bunch of German soldiers that were caught completely by surprise. They surrendered without a shot being fired. This gave us the wrong idea as to what to expect from the enemy. One very unusual thing happened. We were dug in and tied down and here comes another battalion attacking through us. I thought, my God, what are they doing? It wasn't long before they came running back to us. Another strategic withdrawal. A young lieutenant jumped into my hole with me. It was Bud Reed, a guy I knew at Indiana University and a good friend of my sister and brother-in-law.

Morris L. Harvey (Deceased), Benton, KY
Company M, 3rd Battalion, 22nd Infantry Regiment

A Story Worth Preserving
As told to his son, Kerry Harvey

This is the story of my father's World War II combat experiences, told mostly in his own words. It is a story worth preserving. In those days, he was known as Private First Class Morris L. Harvey.

Morris: "After we left Paris, we started chasing the German Army again the rest of the way through France and most of Belgium. When we finally caught up with them, we couldn't let them go."

Kerry: Were there any battles during that time?

Morris: Like I said, there were one-day or two-day actions at a time. Then you would move again. My job was machine gunner on a lead jeep. My jeep was out front all the time to make sure nobody was ambushed. We were there to draw fire. If anybody was going to be ambushed it was going to be our jeep. It was kind of a nervous time. A time or two we got too far ahead and ran into Germans with nobody close enough to help. We would just have to turn tail and run and hope we got out all right. Finally, one day in September, our lieutenant said, "Hey Y'all, come up here, I want to show you something." I wasn't really interested in anything he had to show to me, but I didn't have much choice. I went up the hill, and he handed me his field glasses. I couldn't see anything but trees and the like for a while. Then I saw a lot of German pillboxes in a forti-fied line. That kind of made your heart drop. That was the Siegfried Line.

Kerry: What was the Siegfried Line?

Morris: That was a defensive line along the German border that was sup-posed to be impregnable. It was built out of concrete block, reinforced pillboxes, and they were about half buried in the ground. They were painted green like the woods, and they were hard to see. The 4th Infantry Division made the first breach in the Siegfried Line. We were on German soil and we were the first American troops across the German frontier.

Kerry: How did you manage to get across the Siegfried Line?

Morris: It was just a matter of taking one pillbox at a time. We soon found out you couldn't take them from the front. They all had a crossfire in front of them and we had to get through that.

Kerry: What do you mean crossfire?

Morris: One covered the other one. In front, you got fire from that pill-box, and then there was one on each side of you shooting at you from both sides. My job was to fire into that pillbox. (In and around it to keep any Germans pinned down and to keep their heads down while riflemen went in.)

We first tried blowing the steel doors off them with bangalore torpe-does. Sometimes that would work and sometimes it would not. We used satchel charges and everything. We would get around behind them and either kill them, run them off, or take prisoners. The riflemen got on top of the pillboxes. They couldn't hurt us when we were on top of them and we could throw hand grenades in the gun slits. We could eventually find something to blow the door off, but usually after a few hand grenades and a couple of explosions on the door, they would come out with their hands up.

Kerry: So, you were not on the jeep when doing that?

Morris: No. That was strictly on foot, packing that gun on your back.

Kerry: How was your gun set up? How many people did it take to serve the gun?

Morris: There were seven men in a machine gun squad. There was a first gunner, a second gunner, and five ammunition bearers. Their job was to keep ammunition to the gun. A belt of ammunition had 250 rounds, and every fourth round was a tracer. In my case—I don't know about other gunners—I never did use a sight. I used the tracer, and I had good depth perception. I could tell where I was shooting.

Kerry: You were the first gunner?

Morris: I was the first gunner.

Kerry: Do you remember who your second gunner was?

Morris: Some of them I never did even know by name; some of them didn't last long. I had several. I couldn't exactly say how many. I remember the first one because he was the first gunner when I joined the squad. When I joined the squad he moved to second gunner, and I moved in as first gunner. He had been an ammunition bearer, and he didn't know much about shooting the gun; I had been trained for that. He was from New York City, New York. He was hit and I got another one.

Kerry: So the second gunner would be the guy in the hole with you?

Morris: Yes. He was the guy who fed the belt into the gun. Ammunition bearers brought the ammunition up, and I think each one of them carried maybe four boxes, which was 1000 rounds. I could burn a belt in about a minute.

Kerry: How many second gunners did you have?

Morris: One kid I remember joined me on the Siegfried Line. We had stopped because we had run out of food and ammunition. Everything was in short supply, and we had to stop. We were down to about half-strength. About half of our battalion had been killed or wounded and we weren't getting replacements.

We weren't getting any kind of supplies. We just dug in there for a couple of weeks and we dug a good hole and put logs and dirt on top of it and just sort of set up housekeeping. Some of the guys got out behind the lines, and we killed some deer. That was the first venison I ever ate. We sent it back to the kitchen, and they cleaned them and made hot venison sandwiches and sent them up. That was in the Ardennes Forest. They decided they wanted us to take an "armored" town called Brandscheid, and we had to pour fire into that town. I didn't know the name of most of the towns, but I knew the name of that one because it was an armored town and we had a pretty good little fight over it.

Kerry: What does that mean, an armored town?

Morris: Well, it was just surrounded by pillboxes. There were pillboxes in it. We used chemical ordnance and dropped some phosphorous shells in there. A few months later after the American Army was kicked out of Brandscheid, I came back and helped take it a second time. It was still glowing from the phosphorous they had dropped. I imagine the Germans got a hot seat over that."

Harold Blackwell, Mesa, AZ
Battery A, 377th Anti-Aircraft Artillery Battalion

We Got Real Brave

My first battery CP in Germany was near Bleialf—actually we were in an abandoned pillbox complex. I had a Lieutenant Campbell, who was fluent in German, and the German phone line was still working. We were surprised to realize that we were on a party line and hearing German troop movement information. Lieutenant Campbell, who passed away this past year at age 88, listened carefully to the German orders and interjected counter commands at frequent intervals. This was typical GI sport, but it only lasted about fifteen minutes until the line went dead.

My jeep driver and I were on a short reconnaissance just north of Bleialf and heard noises like singing coming from a pillbox. We got real brave (or foolhardy), and crept up to the pillbox and tossed a grenade into an opening. We were doubly surprised to see about seven SS soldiers come tumbling out with their hands up. All seven had had a generous amount of Calvados or whatever. We covered them, disarmed them, and marched them in front of the jeep to the nearest prisoner of war compound. To this day, I still have a picture of the SS Lieutenant and his Luger and SS dagger.

P.S. I also was pleased to find my battery mentioned in Dr. Boice's history. Yes, we were attached to the 22nd Combat Team for eleven months. We got official credit for thirteen German planes shot down in the 22nd Infantry zone of operation. Of course, we thought we shot down a lot more. Ho-hum.

Emmett G. Ryan (Deceased), Apache Junction, AZ
Company B, 1st Battalion, 12th Infantry Regiment

Wounded in Action
As told to his daughter, Janice Bryson, Tolleson, Arizona

I was wounded twice during the European Campaign. The first time was at Mortain in August 1944. My wife has an article from the Arizona Republic in which I am quoted as saying to a reporter, "The Mortain fighting was the toughest part of the campaign. Large German Panzer Divisions were trying to split the Allied Armies by throwing everything at us."

I made the mistake of having the rear of my anatomy exposed to gunfire as I wasn't lying flat enough. Fortunately for me, my field glasses were in the way and the wound was not serious as the bullet was deflected. After resting about five days, I went back into the action. The medics weren't doing anything with the wound, and I couldn't sit down anyway. I figured I might as well be fighting.

The second time was a little more serious. Our unit was one of the first to smash into the Siegfried Line. I was leading my platoon through pillboxes and anit-tank obstacles when I was struck in the left shoulder with shrapnel. I walked back to the aid station, about a mile back. When I arrived, an officer asked for any wounded men who could sit up, to go as guards while taking the more seriously wounded back to a field hospital in a jeep. The Germans were trying to get back to Germany and would attack jeeps and steal them to drive back. I thought I was also going to the hospital, just acting as a guard along the way. It turned out we were going to another aid station. Patients were then being sent on to the hospital.

When we arrived at the camp, everyone was eating. One of the drivers from our Division recognized me and got me something to eat. I was really hurting by then and only wanted to rest. I looked for a tent and found one with no one else in there. I had no bed and no blankets. I was hurting so bad and it was so bitter cold. I just lay down in the empty tent. I should have found a tent with other people for warmth. I woke up the next day and went to eat breakfast. An officer came up to me and asked why I had blood all over me. I explained to him how I happened to be there at the camp. The officer told the MP to put me on the first ambulance going back to Bar Le Duc. A number of the wounded were being taken there. We stopped at a barracks somewhere along the way. There were about fifteen or twenty of us guys. We were given towels and told to go in and clean up. There was a pilot with us that had bad burns on one arm and shoulder from his plane catching fire. I had blood all over my back.

The pilot said, "If you wash my back, I'll wash yours."

It felt good to be clean for a change. For the seriously wounded guys, it was a true statement: If you made it to the aid stations, you would usually make it. The people there were real good.

I was operated on at Bar Le Duc and flown to England. Planes were dropping paratroopers and supplies into Holland. They would then land in other areas and take the wounded back. It wasn't a pleasant flight, I've never flown since. I was strapped onto a stretcher, and there were holes in the plane from anti-aircraft fire.

I spent three months in the hospital in Frome, England. When the Battle of the Bulge started, it wasn't long before all the NCOs and officers were sent back into action. I sure hated to go back. It hadn't bothered me on D-Day, but now I knew what it was really like. As we were heading into the battle area, I was afraid I wouldn't be assigned back to the 12th Infantry Regiment, so I hitched a ride over to them and rejoined the outfit.

Newspaper Article
Siegfried Line September 24, 1944

An interesting article found in the archives is the following story, written by Henry T. Gorrell. The title, "Atlantan on First Patrol in Germany," indicates it may be from an Atlanta paper.—Bob Babcock

With the Fourth Infantry Division in the Schnee Eifel, Sept 24 (Delayed) (UP)

The US Fourth Infantry Division, first American Army outfit to crack the Hindenburg Line at Meuse-Argonne in the last war and first to enter Paris in this one, also was first to penetrate Germany through the Siegfried Line in force, it was disclosed today.

Lieutenant C. M. Shugart, of Sioux City, IA, was the first United States infantry officer to lead a patrol in Nazi Germany, and three days later, the door to Germany was opened when Colonel Charles T. Lanham, a West Pointer from Washington, DC, led his 22nd Infantry Regiment in a gallant, daring charge through lines which had been considered impregnable.

Shugart's patrol crossed into Germany on September 11; Lanham's charge came on September 14. The men of the 4th Infantry Division might still be fighting hand-to-hand to breach the Siegfried Line had it not been for the tall, slim colonel's heroic dash.

Pinned Down

The 22nd Regiment had spearheaded a frontal attack against the formidable, sixfoot-thick Siegfried pillboxes, but they soon found themselves on top of the fortifications with only rifles, while Germans inside had machine guns. At his command post, Lanham received a report over his field telephone: "We are pinned down by heavy fire…tank destroyers are unable to make any progress."

Later came an even gloomier report. "I'm afraid the men are falling…"

This last report had followed direct hits on our infantry tanks and tank destroyers, leaving the foremost Doughboys temporarily unsupported. Then, the field telephone went dead.

Lanham dropped the telephone and rushed forward as far as he could in his staff car. Accompanied by four men, one a French volunteer, he left the car and ran up the wooded hillside with bullets and shrapnel clipping the ground around his feet.

Hollywood Spectacle

Soon Lanham was among the invading infantrymen, shouting and singing at the top of his lungs, waving his .45 in the air and calling out his men by name as he waved them forward. The reaction was instantaneous. If the colonel could wade into the Germans, so could all the rest of them, and there followed a Hollywood spectacle of troops rushing forward to battle, singing and shouting as they passed the colonel.

Bypassing their colonel, the men of the 22nd Infantry stormed through the last Nazi bunkers and were shortly masters of the topmost heights of Schnee Eifel. The Siegfried Line had been breached.

It now was the colonel's duty to rejoin the main body of his troops, and he retraced his steps, followed by the Frenchman and the three members of his staff. They were fired upon from a bypassed bunker at a range of twelve feet. The colonel was unhurt, but the young Frenchman fell, mortally wounded in the stomach. Lanham bent over the youth and the youth whispered, "I'm dying, sir, but I'm glad to be dying here within the Siegfried Line after fighting the Germans on the soil of Germany."

He died as five German Storm Troopers exited the nearby pillbox by a secret door and again fired on the little group. The Americans opened fire, killed three of them, and wounded two others as they attempted to flee. Then a tank destroyer moved up and blasted away the steel doors of the pillbox and twenty Germans marched out with their hands up.

Lanham returned to his command post. With him on the gallant dash were Captain Howard C. Blazzard of Phoenix, Arizona; Captain Robert C. McLean, of Shelbyville, Tennessee; and Sergeant James C. Smith, of Tullahoma, Tennessee. Lanham is a native of Washington, where his wife lives and where his father is commissioner of the District of Columbia.

Lanham's charge was preceded by the patrol penetration into Germany of Shugart, who led his eight men across the frontier early on the night of September 11.

Atlantan on Patrol

With Shugart were Sergeant Wallace W. Morton, of Indianapolis; Sergeant Paul C. Mercher of Kurtztown, Pennsylvania; Private First Class James C. Carney, of Taunton, MA; Private First Class Dennis O. Cain of 754 West Echo St NW, Atlanta; Private First Class Edward Reinert of St. Paul, Minnesota; Private First Class Arthur Peters, of Thoorp, Pennsylvania; Private First Class Joe A. Pachecosanto, of Domingo, New Mexico; and Private First Class Henry Weber, also of New Mexico.

The patrol's mission was to find a fording place across a river over which larger elements of the Fourth Division might follow.

Shugart beat a hasty retreat, but not before grabbing souvenirs, including a button off a German's coat and a helmet full of "sacred" Nazi soil, which he delivered to Major General Raymond O. Barton, of Ada, Oklahoma, commander of the Division.

Since the initial penetration, forward battalions of the Fourth, including one commanded by Lieutenant Colonel Charles Jackson, of Bell, California, have repelled successive German counterattacks aimed at recapturing Siegfried Line pillboxes in the Schnee Eifel where the Division opened the door to Germany proper about a week ago.

With Hemingway

This correspondent hit the Normandy Beach with the Fourth Division on D-Day and was one of three correspondents with it on the entry into Germany, after it had blazed the path of the First Army from Paris through Northern France and Belgium. Among the three correspondents was author Ernest Hemingway, who is believed to be the first correspondent to enter Germany. I compared notes with him and he convinced me that, with the Fourth Division, he entered Germany a full hour before tanks of an American armored division crossed the frontier at Rotgen in the vicinity of Aachen.

Among those who led the Fourth's assault troops into Germany were company commanders Lieutenant W. Wittkopf, of East St. Louis, IL; and Captain Glenn W. Thorne, of Morgantown, WV. The two were lead company commanders in Jackson's battalion, which effected the first complete breakthrough in the Siegfried Line where it was considered strongest, in the wooded heights of Schnee Eifel.

Bill Riiska, Winsted, CT
4th Reconnaissance Troop (Mechanized)

Liberating a Slave Camp

After Paris, the recon's job was to lead a task force that was heading toward Brussels. There was everything in the column but someone had to go first, and that was the recon. We followed close behind the retreating Germans wondering where they might choose to fight a delaying action. Many times we found ourselves bivouacking for the night in German rendezvous points. As soon as they found out that we were there, they didn't contest the fact. We destroyed a lot of German equipment and men in this fashion.

The Frenchman Lladislaw Francuz (Woidek) from Bretigny south of Paris was with us all this time until November 5. He rode in my jeep.

As we moved up into the woods on the border, the recon wasn't able to move about so freely. Late one afternoon, some engineers came up the hill to the cross roads. They set about putting aiming stakes with various colored ribbons beside the road. The next morning, at first light, we heard trucks grinding up the hill. They were loaded with rockets, and the stakes were their aiming points. When they were lined up someone pushed the button, and they were dispatched into Germany. When the firing was complete, the trucks took off as fast as possible back down the hill without waiting for their men. We had to stay there. When the first counter-battery shell exploded, three of us were standing against a tree. Corporal Czarnomski caught nine pieces of shrapnel in his back that would have hit me in the chest. Sergeant Nystrom was hit in the foot, and Corporal Shockey was hit in the head and chest. I was still standing there.

Sometime after Strasbourg, we liberated a slave camp for processing cement. Vladimir (Willie) Kutz, about sixteen years old, somehow or other joined our recon troop the same as Ladis (Woidek) Francuz did in August. Willie spoke Russian, Slavic languages, and German. He was very helpful. He didn't travel with me.

One incident I do remember was that it was very cold and wet in late March when we stopped at the edge of this German town and had to set up a perimeter. The house we chose was ideal. I went into the house, and it was full of women of various ages and states of pregnancy. When I asked them to vacate the house and to go to another house farther up the road, they set up such a weeping and wailing that I went out to the yard and told the guys we would sleep out in the yard.

Now I was the enemy. Willie asked if he could go into the house and talk to the women. I said yes and he went in. In a few minutes, all the women came out and paraded down the road to the next house. I asked him what he had said to them. He told me that he gave them three minutes to get out of the house or he would set fire to the house and shoot them as they came out the door.

The last we saw of "Willie" was when he headed east dressed in an American uniform, speaking Russian and driving a German Mercedes Command Car. The first Russian officer he met told him to forget that he had ever seen an American. Willie came to our National Convention in Cherry Hill.

Tom Reid, Marietta, GA
Cannon Company, 22nd Infantry Regiment and Company I, 3rd Battalion, 22nd Infantry Regiment

First Troops on German Soil

August 1944 for the 22nd Infantry ended with the triumphant entry into Paris on the 25th followed by a rapid chase of the retreating German Army through Northern France and into Belgium.

The 22nd Infantry entered Belgium early in September and pursued the Wehrmacht relentlessly. The advance was on the order of ten to twenty miles per day. Some days we were motorized for the larger part of the trip. Towns and villages became a blur as the Germans chose to retreat, hindering our advance by roadblocks such as fallen trees and blown bridges, rather than making a stand.

All of this took a toll on the normal order of things. Rations were K-rations—three boxes, each of a different outer color for breakfast, lunch, and dinner. The "heat" was on the supply echelons to get food, ammo, water, and supplies forward. They did it through prodigious effort and teamwork by all.

On September 11 the 22nd Infantry Regiment entered Germany, the first troops on German soil, and on September 14 we penetrated the Siegfried Line of pillboxes and dragons' teeth in the vicinity of Bleialf and Brandscheid, just over the German border.

I was a first lieutenant at the time, serving as a forward observer for Cannon Company. In the Regiment at that time there was a Cannon Company equipped with six 105mm short-barreled howitzers with a maximum range of 6500 yards. This gave the Regiment immediate access to some firepower in addition to the artillery, which was in direct support.

During this attack on the Siegfried Line I was mostly with Company I, 22nd Infantry, commanded by Captain Joe Samuels. He was still commanding the company after bringing it ashore on D-Day in Normandy some three months earlier.

Naturally, we had been moving much too fast for the bath units to catch up, and now that we were in the Siegfried Line, we were spread too thinly for units to rotate to the rear for baths or anything else.

September moved along, and in early October the 22nd moved northward to new positions. Thus, the month had come and gone, and my bath story for September 1944 is easy to tell—I didn't get one.

Peter Triolo, Pueblo, CO
HQ, 1st Battalion, 12th Infantry Regiment

You Won't Believe What We See

Large concrete underground bunkers and gun emplacements fortified the Siegfried Line. The bunkers were about twenty feet in diameter and ten feet deep in the ground. Only about two feet of concrete were above ground. They had one problem: they vented the bathrooms with a four-inch cast iron pipe. Rather than trying to capture them, we brought tanks up with steel blades and moved dirt over the top of the pillbox, covering it completely. Then we threw a string of dynamite down the pipe; that took care of the pillbox.

The second day we were on the Siegfried line, we got a call from one of our rifle companies on the radio. The message was, "Colonel Jackson, you won't believe what we see." There was a German officer with about fifty men marching up the road singing. They were a reserve unit that didn't even know we were there. Colonel Jackson ordered that we set a trap and capture them. When they brought the officer to headquarters, he demanded to know what we were doing in Germany. I'm sure we all laughed. They were sent back as prisoners.

Tom Reid, Marietta, GA
Cannon Company, 22nd Infantry Regiment and Company I,
3rd Battalion, 22nd Infantry Regiment

Ever Killed a Pig with a Wagon Spoke?

The time was mid-September 1944, and the 22nd Infantry Regiment was in the Schnee Eifel, a rugged group of hills along the Siegfried line of Germany. The 22nd Infantry was the first American unit to penetrate the Siegfried line and the Regiment held on, waiting for reinforcements and supplies—mainly gasoline, to catch up so the advance could continue.

As a forward observer in the Cannon Company, I was with Company I, commanded by Captain Joe Samuels of Orange, Virginia. For several days, elements of the company were in a farmyard where a pigsty housed one lone pig, left behind in the evacuation by the village inhabitants.

After weeks existing on K rations, this pig began to look pretty good. We could see visions of roasted pork, sausage patties and ribs. Little did we know these required processing, smoking, and curing of the meat, all of which took time and facilities that we did not have.

The first task was killing the pig. Shooting him would be the simplest method, but as we were temporarily in a static position, we didn't want to draw attention to our exposed position. Someone suggested bludgeoning him over the head with a stick or piece of stone. Never having experienced anything like this before, I volunteered to kill the pig. The handiest implement I saw was a wagon spoke in the farmyard.

And so, I set to work. Just cornering the pig and catching him was a feat in itself, but holding on to the wagon spoke at the same time required almost acrobatic skills. At age twenty-four, I was a lot stronger and more agile than I am today at eighty.

To make a long story short, I finally held on to the pig and got him into the corner where he couldn't get away. Then I started hitting him on the head with the weapon of choice; the wagon spoke. I couldn't believe how many times I had to hit him. Of course he was squealing loudly all of this time, thus creating far more noise than if we had dispatched him with one well-aimed rifle shot.

After what seemed like an eternity, the blows to the head finally killed him, although, I do not recommend this method to kill a pig. Someone cut him up and after a minimum of butchering; we roasted part of the pig over an open fire in the cellar of the farmhouse. It was good, but the payoff came that night and the next morning. Everybody who participated in the pig roast got sick, and to this day, I want to see all pork products cured, smoked, processed, and properly cooked. But back to the beginning. Have you ever killed a pig with a wagon spoke?

Earl Slater, Hendersonville, TN
Companies E and G, 2nd Battalion, 22nd Infantry Regiment

A Chilling Affair—Combat Bath
As told to his daughter, Anita Slater Capps

Most Americans consider a hot bath a necessity. It rates right up there with our daily bread. Compared to much of the world, we are bath obsessive. It is the prime directive of war that a hot bath is the first casualty of the civilized world. Therefore, to an American infantryman in combat, a hot bath is the ultimate luxury.

It is the second unwritten law of battle that infantrymen seldom know their exact location in relation to the rest of the planet. One foxhole with five inches of water in the bottom looks pretty much like the last one you crawled out of. I can only testify that this incident occurred in the European Theater of Operations, somewhere between Eupen and St. Vith, Belgium.

One chilly October day, word came around that bath facilities were available. All I knew was that somewhere about ten miles behind our lines lay the possibility of a hot bath and clean clothes. As supply sergeant for Company G, 2nd Battalion, 22nd Infantry Regiment, I had a jeep at my disposal. (It was our outfit's only motorized vehicle). Three of us ultimately piled into the jeep, and off we went. Eventually we located a huge tent set up in a big field right next to a stream. Wisps of steam wafted from every opening. Just inside, a hot bath awaited! We were jubilant at our good fortune. I, for one, had seen my last real shave and shower before I'd landed on Utah Beach on D-Day. The best I'd been able to do since then was a bit of a sponge bath at a creek. Most often, all that was available was a helmet full of cold water and a very bad razor. All attempts at cleanliness were pitiful indeed. Anyway, there was seldom time on the battlefront for such delicate considerations. And clean clothes? I had been in my uniform so long that I could scarcely remember how to get out of it, much less what it looked like when it was clean.

We eagerly ducked under the tent flap and were instantly enveloped in a heavenly vapor. We could scarcely see each other through the mist. The outside temperature was only 35 or 40 degrees, so all of that wonderful hot water was putting off enormous clouds of steam. This was scarcely a luxury accommodation. Plumbing was one big pipe that ran the length of the tent. It was studded with about forty closely spaced showerheads. The temperature of the water was set somewhere else. There were no controls for personal preference, but it seemed like the Hilton to us.

After being issued soap, razors, and the first real towels that we had seen in months, we quickly stripped off our overripe uniforms and dashed into that glorious flow of heated water. Everything was going great. We got all soaped up from head to foot and then jumped back under the shower to rinse off. The hot water was gone! The water was being pumped directly from the stream behind the tent into some kind of boiler system, and either the fire went out or we had simply used up the heated water supply.

Some of the men were stunned speechless at the unexpected icy shock of cold water, and, of course, some of them heated the air with an assortment of colorful language. There was a tent full of soapy men dashing in and out of one huge freezing shower bath. Myself, I ran under the water about six times before I got rid of the soap.

Once we were dry, things were really looking up again. We climbed into fresh uniforms. Then, somewhat reluctantly, we donned our still nasty field jackets and combat boots. This unexpected treat didn't extend quite as far as clean jackets and boots, but that was OK. We took that little setback in stride and headed for the jeep.

Jeep? Where was the jeep? Gone! Somebody stole our damned jeep! Now, those jeeps didn't have ignition keys, just a switch that you turned off and on. We stumbled around there for a while arguing about what to do.

At last, I said, "I'm going to steal us another jeep!"

We appropriated an unoccupied vehicle and returned to our unit. After that experience I swore that I wasn't going to take another damned bath before I left Europe! No matter—there was never another opportunity.

Bob Frisby, York, PA
Company A, 1st Battalion, 22nd Infantry Regiment

Naked GIs

Tom Reid's bath story reminded me of the only bath I had at one of the portable units set up by engineers. I think it was early October 1944. The length of time you had to get wet, soap up, and rinse has escaped me now, but it was short. We dried off and walked across some duckboards to a tent for clean clothes. About halfway across, one or two tracks with quad mounted 50s started firing nearby. None of us knew they were there until they started firing. For a second, a group of naked GIs were really caught off guard, with nowhere to put their hands and their faithful companion, the M-1 rifle, wasn't there. I don't think anyone hit the ground or mud, but I would imagine our facial expressions, if they could have been captured on film, would have made someone a lot of money.

John Worthman, (Deceased)
Medic, 22nd Infantry Regiment

Germans Retreat

Then we moved north and east to Riems. Often air cover would radio us of a German column on a road parallel to us. We would send troops in trucks across country and the air cover would strafe the column. Then we'd have a bit of fighting and many prisoners to guard and treat. Dead horses and ruined trucks had to be cleared; then back to our column and on to the city with a beautiful cathedral. It was a city of marvelous champagnes.

The move from Paris toward Germany was done with incredible speed, possibly because the Germans were in a retreat. It was orderly and planned, but still in full retreat. We were transported by trucking companies. On September 1 we headed north. Then came interesting names: Soissons, Crecy, Guise, and Valincienne. We went ninety miles and were in Belgium on September 3.

On September 13 we were in Germany near Urb and Groslangerfeld. We were low on gasoline and had to stop even though there was no organized resistance. Trucks and planes delivered what they could. We thought the 3rd Army tanks were getting the fuel while running around down south, and we were in Germany and otherwise ready to continue. Later we learned that they too, were in very short supply of gasoline.

On the way we passed some WWI trenches already well eroded and grasscovered. In Belgium there was cheering and waving from the civilians. In Germany there were looks of concern and disbelief and white flags from the windows. They didn't seem angry, just amazed. We were now at the Siegfried Line. It was formidable in appearance with essentially four lines of defense and up to thirty-five miles deep. Bunkers were well camouflaged, well fortified, and connected to each other by tunnels. Ditches, barbed wire in concertina rolls and concrete dragon's teeth tended to deflect the assault to places where the bunkermounted guns could crossfire. This was hard fighting again, but we were much more familiar with fortifications after Normandy. Now we concentrated on a bunker.

First, we used heavy small arms fire at all embrasures while flamethrowers and "pole-charge" men moved up. The flamethrowers then heated an embrasure. If it went well, the metal and cement exploded on the heated embrasure. If successful, the metal and cement yielded, and the bunker was breached. Then we pushed explosive charges through the breach to finish the bunker. As a result, bunkers lateral to it were exposed to flank fire and fell easily. We did this for three weeks and breached nearly the whole line. We felt certain we could have done so with adequate supplies.

We were limited again by lack of supply. We were too far from the supply areas in Normandy. We were also competing for supplies with the 3rd Army, which consumed fuel and ammunition faster than we—at least gasoline. On October 4 the 22nd Infantry was moved to a location near Bullingen. From then until mid-November we did some fighting, did a lot of patrolling to find German resistance pockets, had a wonderful opportunity to eat hot meals, got new clothing, and trained the regiment to its peak. It was cold at night and cool in the day. For a three-day period, we were near a small fast stream where I bathed daily. I never felt so clean. I had all my personal gear mud-free, and the aid stations were supplied fully. On November 16, we moved to the Hürtgen Forest.

Tallie Crocker, Mt. Pleasant, SC
HQ, 2nd Battalion, 12th Infantry Regiment

Hürtgen Forest

On November 6, 1944, the 12th Infantry Regiment was attached to the 28th Infantry Division, which was having a rough time in the Hürtgen Forest. The Germans had driven a salient in their lines and had essentially split their defense in half.

The 12th Infantry left for this assignment at 1745 hours for the 45-mile motor march to the location of the 28th Infantry Division. The weather was miserable with a cold rain falling. The original plan was for the regiment to go into a bivouac area and wait until morning for the relief of the 28th.

Colonel Luckett, the Regimental Commander, and his staff, along with Lieutenant Colonel Montelbano and the staff of the 2nd Battalion of the 12th Infantry, went ahead to meet with the staff of the 28th to get more information on the relief. I was S-3 (Operations Officer) of the 2nd Battalion.

When we reached the headquarters of the 28th, we were informed that the relief was to take place immediately, rather than the next morning, so there was no time for reconnaissance. Since we were operating with radios silenced, a messenger was sent to inform the columns that they were not to go into bivouac. At 4 A.M. on November 7, the relief began—in pouring rain, total darkness—and was not completed until midmorning.

The positions that were occupied by the 109th Infantry Regiment were along a salient that the Germans had driven into the 28th lines and were not always in the best place for fighting. The positions that were occupied by the 2nd Battalion of the 12th were along a firebreak and not passable by vehicles, so everything had to be hand carried.

There were dead bodies of the 109th all over the area. Since we had replacements who had not done any fighting, we had some of our troops who had combat experience move the frozen dead bodies, pile them in several spots, and hide them with boughs broken from the trees by artillery fire.

On November 10, there was a 500-yard gap between Company E and Companies F and G. The plan was for the 1st Battalion to attack at the deepest part of the German salient; Company E was to attack the edge of the salient, and Companies F and G were to attack their fronts. Shortly after the attacks began, the Germans stopped them and got behind F and G Companies. With Companies F and G were the Battalion CO, the S-3 (me), and an artillery observer with his radio operator. When we tried to send wounded people out, we discovered that we were surrounded by the Germans.

Every day we were subjected to an attack by the Germans. After each attack, we took stock of the .30 caliber ammo on hand for the machine guns, as well as for rifles. If we felt that we didn't have enough machine gun ammo for the next attack, we took ammo from the M-1 eight round clips and hand inserted it into the wet cloth machine gun belts or vice versa. We withstood an attack each day, with two attacks on one day.

I told the officer to fire, and assured him that we knew what we were doing.

When those tanks saw the white phosphorus, they left the area in a hurry.

On one occasion the Germans brought tanks within one hundred yards of our positions and yelled for us to surrender since they had us surrounded. The men yelled back, "F--k you," and we requested the artillery forward observer to request artillery fire, high explosive as well as white phosphorus in the area of the tanks. The artillery officer at the guns requested a repeat of the coordinates because of the nearness to our troops. I took the handset from the observer, told the officer to fire, and assured him that we knew what we were doing. When those tanks saw the white phosphorus, they left the area in a hurry.

The lack of food was quite a problem. We searched the packs of the dead 28th Infantry Division troops for food, and retrieved from the ground the "dog biscuits" and cheese that had been discarded by the troops. Our first-aid station, which was in large, log-covered holes, had a number of casualties to handle. We had a medic sergeant and aid men manning the aid station, and they really did an excellent job.

By the morning of the third day, November 12, only two of our radios had batteries with a little life left. Fortunately, the artillery radio worked until noon. We were finally left with our battalion radio, which couldn't reach our Battalion HQ. I knew that the 1st Battalion was closer to us than our Battalion CP. I remembered the channel number of their radio net because of a firefight we had taken part in with them in the Siegfried Line. When in a stagnant or offensive operation, we used call signs of Red, White, and Blue for the battalions. Also, when in a defensive situation, we used a three-day prearranged code. That code expired on our first day of isolation. I switched our radio to the 1st Battalion's channel and called, "Red from White," twice, with no response. I then called, "Red from White, come in Chuck." (Chuck Jackson, the 1st Battalion CO, and my brother-in-law).

His reply was, "Love from __," (I don't remember his code name now). But I still remember ours. His message was, "Bring all your loves to me."

We interpreted that to mean, "withdraw," but we wanted to make certain, so I replied, "I think I know what you mean, but want to be certain."

His reply was, "What do you do when you meet a girl with more than you have?" I later told Chuck that the reply should have been, "Attack!"

There was very little daylight left, so we assembled the two company commanders and discussed a withdrawal plan. We decided to withdraw to the location of the 3rd Battalion since it was a shorter distance (about six hundred yards). We also prayed for a foggy morning, but while we slept it snowed all night. When we got up it was to a bright sunny morning. For some reason the Germans had left during the night, and we lost only two men to mines during our withdrawal. When Chuck Jackson greeted me, he said, "I'm so glad to see you—I wondered what Mary would say if she found out that we were so close, and you didn't make it."

When we reached our Battalion Headquarters, Major General R. O. Barton, Division Commander, was standing outside to welcome us and to inform us that we were again in the 4th Infantry Division.

When I returned to the CP, I learned that I had trench foot and was evacuated two days later. I didn't return to the 12th Infantry Regiment until early February 1945, so I missed the German breakthrough. We had been told nothing about trench foot or its prevention, but when more casualties were being sustained from that problem than from the Germans, prevention was really enforced. Trench foot was encountered in WW I also—guess that's where the word "trench" came from.

Robert Gast, Warsaw, IN
Companies B and C, 1st Battalion, 12th Infantry Regiment

All Hell Broke Loose

I will never forget the first day that we entered the Hürtgen Forest. My platoon guide said to me, "Lieutenant, I don't like the smell of this." Those were his exact words. He went back to an aid station, and I never saw him again. In less than two weeks my platoon was gone, along with most of the line officers and men of the entire regiment. I only remember one day that we seemed to temporarily get the better of the enemy.

One afternoon we were getting nowhere trying to work our way forward in that treacherous forest. One of my men came to me and informed me that there was a road and a break in the forest on our left flank. We decided to deploy down the road, off to the side, and to keep complete silence. I sent two scouts out ahead, and my runner and I followed by about fifty yards. We had not gone very far when one of the scouts gave us the "down sign" and motioned me to come forward. I could not believe what I saw—a machine gun sticking out from a camouflaged foxhole. We walked quietly over and knocked the camouflage from the top of the hole. There at the bottom sat two German soldiers eating their rations. We not only took them prisoner, but we also captured a number of their platoon that we caught by surprise. Captain Witkoff, our company commander, came forward and established his CP. A forward observer came up to direct fire on the enemy. Unfortunately for all of us, he came up short, and the 105s came pouring in on us. At the same time, the Germans had zeroed in on our position and 88s began bursting in the trees above us. The casualties were terrible.

In Colonel Johnson's book, *The History of the 12th Infantry Regiment in WWII,* he devotes a number of paragraphs on the attempt to get to and relieve Companies F and G. I was the only line officer left in Company C when that final attempt was made. We had been almost wiped out by the constant shelling, and had made a withdrawal to regroup. I was in a hole with a group of soldiers when a voice called out, "Anyone in there?" Of course, we all came out. It was another lieutenant who was trying to round up enough men to open up a way to Companies F and G. We could locate maybe forty or fifty men. I'm not sure. I do know that he and I were the only officers. To make a long story short, we did manage to fight our way to Companies F and G. A lot of us were wounded, however, including myself, and ended up trapped along with the two companies of the 2nd Battalion.

I ended up in an "aid" hole with six or seven badly wounded men. Most of them were too bad to try to leave with the ill-fated attempt to evacuate the wounded. The next morning, at the crack of dawn, Colonel Sibert, about six or eight soldiers, twelve wounded men, and a number of German prisoners started the ill-fated escape. We walked right into a bunch of German soldiers. I was the first of the wounded, just behind a blinded GI. All hell broke loose. The mad dash back to where we started from is impossible to describe. I don't know how any of us made it. The next morning we left single file and used a different route. It was successful. We had only a few casualties from "Bouncing Betties."

Bob Berglund (Deceased), Defuniak Springs, FL
HQ Company, 3rd Battalion, 12th Infantry Regiment

Heavy Casualties

The 12th Infantry Regiment had moved into Germany's Hürtgen Forest to relieve the decimated 28th Infantry Division on the night of November 6, 1944, and had been in constant heavy combat there for seventeen days when this story begins.

On November 24, 1944, the 3rd Battalion HQ and aid station were located about a mile behind the front lines in a captured German pillbox. It seemed like a lot more than a mile going through that evergreen forest where trees left standing had all the limbs and most of the bark blown off. They almost looked like fields of giant toothpicks standing amid all the rubble. The Hürtgen Forest is the only place during the War in Europe that I can remember where the Germans had as much artillery and mortar fire as we did, and in the forest it was devastating.

Because of the heavy casualties and the difficulty of the terrain—hilly country, no roads, trees blown down "every which way," and many streams to cross—all the casualties had to be hand carried back to the battalion aid station. The battalion medical aid men were being worn out. Of course, the aid men were getting their share of casualties, too. So, on the morning of November 24, Battalion HQ Company asked for volunteers to help the medical aid men bring out the casualties from Company I, who were dug in on top of a hill about a mile from the battalion aid station. I was one of the volunteers. We had a guide from Company I to show us the way. By the time we got organized with the guide, it was early afternoon when we started out. We all had put on Red Cross armbands, and no one brought a weapon; we were supposed to be acting as medics. After about an hour of walking through the forest following the guide, he said he was lost and didn't know how to get to Company I.

The leaders of the group talked it over and decided to go back to battalion. In late November it gets dark early and they were afraid that if we kept going, we might walk right into the German lines since the guide had no idea where we were. In defense of the guide, the forest all looked the same to me, too. Of course, I had never been there before.

The next morning, November 25, we got a new guide and set out again. This time we got to Company I with no problem. We did hear some small arms fire off to our left just before we got to the company but didn't think too much about it. After all, we were on the front line. We started back around noon with two litter cases and several walking wounded. I was helping one of the walking wounded. The man I was helping wanted to bring his rifle, but I said, "No." We were all wearing Red Cross armbands and, if we didn't have any weapons and we did run into a German, he might let us pass.

When we started down the hill from where Company I was dug in, heading back to Battalion, we had two litter cases that were at the head of the column, with four litter bearers on each litter due to the rough terrain and the distance we had to go. Then came the walking wounded. There were about fifteen of us in the column. The head of the column had just reached the bottom of the hill where there was a small stream that had to be crossed when a German opened up on us with an automatic weapon. He just swept the column with automatic fire. I was hit in the right buttock. Of course, everyone hit the ground. I looked around, and I was right out in the open, but a short distance away there were three small trees with the ground mounded up around them. That looked like a lot better cover than where I was so I jumped up, ran to the trees, and dropped down behind them. When I moved, the German must have seen me because he sprayed the area again. This time I was hit in the left foot.

One of the litter cases was hit again when we were first fired on. He must have been in a lot of pain because he sat up on the litter and called for a medic. When he did, the German opened up on him again. This happened a couple of times; then he didn't sit up anymore. I was told this at the evacuation hospital by a witness. I heard the firing, but I didn't see it happen. I was keeping my head down. I also heard that the company had sent out a patrol and got to know what really happened to him. What I do know is that a couple of the guys at the end of the column nearest to Company I were able to get back to the company and get help. So, after we had been lying there not daring to move for about two hours, help came, and we finally got back to Battalion HQ. But instead of me helping the "walking wounded" get back, I was being helped back.

Henry "Hank" Strecker (Deceased)—Company C, 1-12 Infantry

Siegfried Line Experiences

Submitted by his daughter, Leslie Strecker Weisner

The third time I was hit was about the time Ward Means got wounded. C Company, First Battalion, 12th Regiment, with one platoon from A Company were attacking the Germans in the Hurtgen Forest. Snow was falling on the morning of November 11, 1944. F and G Companies, Second Battalion, 12th Regiment, were surrounded by Germans for about three days without food or medical supplies. It was do or die. Heavy weapons D Company set up two water-cooled .30 caliber machine guns and opened fire as we charged the Germans. We ran at them yelling, "Let 'em have it," as we fired our rifles. The Germans were completely caught off guard. I took one German prisoner out of a foxhole; the rest ran off into the woods.

I started telling the boys from F Company, lying in their foxholes, that we had broken through the German lines. They were overjoyed and some began to cry with extreme relief. I was out of water, so I started scooping up hands full of water out of holes torn in the ground by shell fragments. I felt like I owned that forest. The Germans started firing .88 mm armor piercing shells at us from a tank. The shells would hit the three to four inch thick pine tree trunks, snapping them off like toothpicks, three or four at a time. The tree trunks would snap in a cloud of steam-like vapor. I walked around like nothing could kill me. That feeling is very rare. Most of the time, you're groveling for a hole and praying you don't get hit. Also—shaking like a leaf.

It started getting dark and orders came up that we had to spend the night there. I started looking for a foxhole to crawl into. There was a dead German in a hole and I grabbed him by the boots and started to pull him out, but the cloying smell stopped me. I did not think I could cope with that odor all night.

Ray Litterst occupied the next hole I came to and Ray invited me to spend the night there. In the middle of the night, I woke up. Ice water was dripping down my neck and my feet were ice cold. I raised my head to look down at my feet. During the night it started to snow again and my boots were covered with snow.

The elements were taking their turn at giving us the works. At dawn, we awoke with nothing to eat. Ray had an extra bittersweet chocolate bar which he offered me. I appreciated this tremendously.

After about three hours, we received orders to withdraw from these positions. In the meantime, the Germans dropped a small mortar round on us and it hit in the pine trees overhead, sending a shower of snow down on us. The shrapnel hit no one. I thought to myself, this does not look good. They are probably zeroing in on us. As we moved on out, I saw a new BAR used as a support to hold up the front of a foxhole. I was tempted to change it for my old one, but second thoughts stopped me. Mine was tried and true.

As we moved on out, we had to pass through some cleared ground. As we suspected, we had given them four hours to set up their artillery. The German artillery gunners were second to none. All hell broke loose. By this time in my fighting career, I became an old hand at finding the nearest hole or whatever to crawl into. I found a hole with four other fellows in it. We were in there like sardines.

November 13th, suddenly I heard someone calling, "Help me fellow!" I immediately recognized the voice of Ward "Brownie" Means. I hesitated momentarily, thinking I'm relatively safe in this hole. But then you think, if that was me out there, I would want someone to help me. I scrambled out of the hole and ran over to where Brownie was lying in the snow.

There was an aid lieutenant with Ward, but that lieutenant wasn't much bigger than me. I only weighed about 135 pounds but the good Lord turned our bodies into steel. I put Ward's left arm over my shoulder and the lieutenant took his right. Ward was hit in the back and couldn't walk. His left hand had the forefinger tip and thumb blown off. Blood was running down the front of my raincoat. If someone saw you dragging someone at home here with a back injury like that, they would swear you were crazy. But the time was NOW.

Smoke was curling up out of the shell holes around us. We had to drag Ward over 200 yards of shell-ploughed ground with rounds falling all around us. Only by the grace of God did we make it. We put Ward on a litter and the aid men carried him back. The Germans shelled us for over an hour before they quit. They used zonal fire on us, not changing the settings on their guns.

I crawled into another hole with two aid men in it. The one aid man asked if I was hit. Ward's blood was on my coat and there were two holes in it. I said no. I opened my raincoat and fatigue shirt. I was wearing a German pistol I found in a farmyard back in Normandy. I had made a shoulder holster for it. A piece of shrapnel went through my coat and shirt, hit the pistol, tearing the holster and gouging the steel butt, and bounced out leaving two holes, two inches apart. I still have the pocket material out of the shirt, with the holes in it, which means nothing to anyone but my family and me. God had his hand over me again.

Robert Williamson, Lakeland, FL
Company F, 2nd Battalion, 12th Infantry Regiment

Three Days and Three Nights

We went at night by truck convoy and moved up and around Aachen. We stayed in a big forest called the "Hürtgen Forest," and got into the foxholes, which weren't very deep and weren't covered with logs when we got there. We had no blankets, and it was extremely cold. The next morning those Germans started sending over barrages and made it kind of hot for us all morning. Around 1000 hours we moved out farther into the forest where we relieved the 28th Infantry Division. When we relieved them, they had the men that had been killed piled up like cords of wood. The next morning the artillery started again and lasted through the day. The following morning we took off through the forest and hadn't gone more than three or four hundred yards when some of the men stepped on some "shoe mines" and "Bouncing Betties," which blew their legs off. There were so many in our paths that we couldn't get through the forest to the Germans, which were about one hundred fifty yards on the other side of this minefield. We all had to turn back to our foxholes again.

We had just got back to our foxholes when the artillery started again. Off on the left flank the Germans started to move in. You should have seen us stop them in their tracks. We fought them off for three days and three nights. After the three days and three nights without food or water and with ammunition running low, the fourth morning came with "relief" and got us out of the forest. It had snowed on the third night, and that was what we ate to keep alive. When we got down to the valley, we took off our helmets, dipped them in the creek, and drank our fill.

Most of us were wounded and when we got back off the lines, they set up a first aid station. They put us through the first aid station, and then we were sent to the rear in ambulances. I was wounded with shrapnel in my neck the first day. At the first aid stations, the doctors tried to remove the shrapnel from my neck without any anesthetic. It hurt so much that I told them to leave it alone. I went to the 189th General Hospital outside of Paris. There they were afraid to remove the shrapnel because it could paralyze me.

Most of us were shipped back to Germany in January of 1945, sent through replacement pool camps, and then shipped back to our outfits. When we got back to our outfits, they were across the Rhine River, and we had some hard fighting ahead.

Lloyd Crotteau, Wisconsin Rapids, WI
Company C, 1st Battalion, 22nd Infantry Regiment

Don't Bathe in the Woods

You want stories? As Jimmy Durante would say, "I got a million of them." I made the D-Day invasion. I was hit at Monteberg, St. Lô, and the Hürtgen Forest. In the Hürtgen Forest, on November 19, 1944, we were ordered to hold until afternoon. I was on C Company's right flank when I spotted three officers heading straight into the German lines. I tried to motion to them, but they were looking at a map and didn't see me. I jumped the road and a small creek, and ran along the edge of the creek until they saw me. They were trying to locate Company C. I showed them where we were and ran back to my foxhole. On the way back, I filled my helmet with water and when it looked safe, I took off my shirt and started to bathe. I heard the gun go off and the whine of the shell. I dove for my foxhole, but it was too late. It was a tree burst, and I got a piece of it through my left arm, paralyzing it. I had a young friend help me back to the jump-off spot where I ran into a medical jeep, and they took me back.

I've often wondered who those officers were and if they knew I was hit. Lesson learned—don't take baths in the woods.

Emanuel Goldstein MD, New York, NY
Battalion Surgeon, 22nd Infantry Regiment

Medical Proof of the Hürtgen Forest Hell

Emanuel Goldstein, MD, sent the following letter that he wrote to the VFW in 1994, referencing the Hürtgen Forest Campaign. The letter was never published by the VFW.

I served with the 3rd Battalion, 22nd Infantry, during the Hürtgen Forest Campaign and the Battle of the Bulge. I was a captain in the Medical Corps Reserve and Battalion Surgeon. My aid station was functioning from the beginning to the end of the Hürtgen Forest Campaign. According to my station log, we did not get into too much trouble until November 16, when we had twenty casualties. On the November 17, we had 36. Most were wounded by shell fragments or suffering from battle fatigue. Remember that we were fighting in a forest, so unless the wounded were somehow able to make it on their own or with the help of their buddies to a trail, they could not be picked up with our limited resources of two jeeps, each with two litter-bearers. The most severely wounded men probably were still there.

Remember that we were fighting in a forest, so unless the wounded were somehow able to make it on their own or with the help of their buddies to a trail, they could not be picked up.

After November 17 the fighting got worse, and casualties got worse. At about that time the 1st and 2nd Battalion aid stations became "out of action." My aid station began receiving wounded from the entire Regiment from about November 18. On that day, I treated 26. On November 18, my aid station consisted of one doctor (me), two jeeps, two drivers, four litter-bearers, one Technician 4th Class, four Technicians 5th Class, one Corporal, and three Privates First Class. On November 19, a contingent of twenty-five medics under the command of a MAC showed up to help in evacuating men to my aid station. They were volunteers who had been promised a week in Paris in return for taking on this hazardous assignment.

On November 19 I treated and processed 51 casualties. On November 20 I treated and processed 31 casualties. On November 21 the fight was less heavy; I treated and processed 12 casualties and even sent two back to duty. (The more casualties passing through the aid station, the less time I could spend with each. Therefore, on the heaviest days, I could only stabilize the men and transfer them back to the division-collecting companies for further evaluation and treatment.)

On November 22, I treated and processed 54 men. On November 23, I treated and processed 49 men. November 24, was the worst day so far; I treated and processed 99 men. On November 25, I treated and processed 108 men. I honestly don't remember those days very well. I worked as long as I could, ate something, went to sleep, woke up and went back to work. And it wasn't over yet. On November 26, I treated and processed

61 men. On November 27, it was 54 men, and on November 28, there were 52.

On November 29, Ernest Hemingway showed up. He was covering the 4th Infantry Division and said we would be relieved some time in December. That day I treated and processed eighty-three casualties. The next day, November 30, I treated and processed 104 casualties.

On December 1, I treated and processed 84 casualties. On December 2, fortynine. On December 3, the fighting let up somewhat and we had only 30 casualties; we were relieved and moved to Luxembourg to recuperate. There, we were on the extreme right shoulder that stopped the Germans in the Battle of the Bulge."

This totaled 919 casualties that were treated in this one aid station in an eighteenday period.—Bob Babcock

----

Fred Stromberg, Concord, CA
Company G, 2nd Battalion, 22nd Infantry Regiment

Dreamed of a Two-Day Pass

Once while I was a G Company radio operator, it was midnight when I crawled into my foxhole. We were now in the first week of the Hürtgen Forest Campaign in the worst weather in twenty years. Mud was all over my clothing, ankle deep over my shoes, and a heavy thickness of unshaven face caused my two buddies to moan and groan about my being so filthy and clumsy.

I was awakened at 0130 hours to report to Division HQ, who needed a radio operator. I eased out of the foxhole without the other two knowing it. While being driven back to division, I wondered why they would take a radioman off the line, especially when he was unable to clean up. Further, I did not know the division codes or call signs.

I was dropped off at the entrance to Division Communications. I opened the door, brushed back the blackout curtain and peeked in. "EEEK!" came a shriek from the far end of the room. I walked over to the sergeant sitting by the radio, tracking mud all the way.

"I'm your new radio operator," I said.

"My God, where did you come from?" the sergeant asked. He sat me down at his radio and told me to take over.

A flap dropped down. I inserted the cord, lifted the key up, and said, "World War Two," as I did not know their call signs.

A huge hand grabbed my shoulder, lifted me off the chair, and shook me hard—so hard that mud fell from my clothing onto the floor.

"Do you think this is funny? Don't you know there is a war going on?"

There stood an officer with one star on his collar. I was speechless.

"Sergeant, get this man a shave, shower, clean clothing, and get him the hell out of here!"

"Yes, Sir!" replied the sergeant.

This accomplished, I told the jeep driver on the way back that it sure was great to clean up. I arrived back at 0300 hours, crawled into our foxhole, and never awakened the others, who were still unaware of my absence.

Awakened at 0600 hours by my foxhole buddies to start the day, a long stare and silence greeted me; then, "What happened to you?"

"Nothing. Why?" I replied.

"How did you get all cleaned up?"

"Well, I'll be damned," I said as I looked down at myself.

Not wanting to reveal my episode, I answered, "My goodness, I dreamed I was on a two-day pass, got all cleaned up and went into town. I guess it was true." Bombarded all morning by questions on how I got so clean (even by the CO), I decided to stick to the two-day pass story. The true reason was never given until now.

Ken Kluger, Bellaire, TX
Company G, 2nd Battalion, 22nd Infantry Regiment

Outrunning the 88s

I was wounded late in July 1944 in France, and after being hospitalized in England, was en route to my unit through the pipeline in October or November 1944. I was leading about ten or fifteen rookies on the search for the 4th Infantry Division on the outskirts of the Hürtgen Forest.

We were following a trail marked by bandage gauze and started to descend into a steep ravine, only to be surprised by about twenty-five German soldiers who were whooping and hollering as they moved down the opposite side of the ravine. They were going to get water from a small creek at the bottom. We each took cover behind trees and waited until they had left; then we retraced our steps to find out where the wind had blown the markers away. Eventually, we found our units. A couple of days later a group of us were sent forward with five-gallon water cans on a backpack.

Engineers had built a small bridge, but the Germans kept blowing it up. I elected to go upstream and got across, with the intention of going up the steep hill, all the while dodging 88s that were trying to bracket my location. I succeeded in getting to the "military crest" and got behind a tree, only to find many smoking bits of shrapnel in the tree. I felt something running down my back. My first thought—that I had been wounded again—was erroneous, as it was only water leaking from the "jerry can" which had a few holes. Later, I really was wounded on about November 26, 1944. The Germans spent quite a bit of ammunition, but luckily, I zigzagged and outraced the 88s. It would be interesting if anyone out there remembers some of these events. I also recall that there was a dead SS officer in full dress uniform near where we lost the tape trail marker. We figured it was so obvious that he might be booby-trapped, so we did not check him out. Also, does anyone remember the surrender leaflets dropped on us by the Germans warning that Aachen was to be defended to the last man?

- - - - - - - - - - - - - - - - - - - -

Bob Frisby, York, PA
Company A, 1st Battalion, 22nd Infantry Regiment

Foxholes and Dead GIs

In the Hürtgen Forest, on November 26, near Grosshau, I took out a small patrol of about five men. Captain Surrat, Company A CO, sent a runner to tell me to hold up, that he was coming along. We moved out into an open area with a dirt crossroad where there was a small stone building and an M-8 Armored "greyhound" that had been knocked out. As we moved along, there were foxholes with dead GIs in each one. I seem to remember the 28th Infantry Division marks on the vehicles, so it's possible the dead were from the 28th Infantry Division. There were no covers over the holes, so they were probably hit by airbursts. Captain Surrat and I moved the patrol to where we thought there was cover to check a map. It soon became obvious that we had been observed because five or six airbursts exploded overhead. One man, Bob Gobelbecker, a replacement, was kneeling next to me and said, "Sergeant…" I glanced at him, saw blood, and knew immediately that he was hit in the head by a piece of shrapnel. He died instantly.

About this same time, some very large incoming shells were blowing huge holes in the ground—the largest I had ever seen. I realized then that some 88s were going over our heads and exploding along the tree line at the edge of the woods. Fortunately, the rest of the Company was far enough back in the woods and not under fire. (Does anyone in the Battalion know if the shells were from a railroad gun?)

Later Captain Surrat said, "If you are going to draw that much fire, remind me not to go along with you again." Captain Surrat was killed later (I can't remember the exact time) by a direct hit at his command post. He was one of the best company commanders…

I was hit on November 27, the next day.

David Roderick, Carlsbad, CA
Company H, 2nd Battalion, 22nd Infantry Regiment

Twenty-first Birthday

Back at my 81mm mortar section placement, I became aware of the usual "over and below" target landing of mortar shells near my position. What followed was the first barrage of firing for effect. I knew we were in trouble. I crawled from my hole next to the mortar placement into a ravine that ran in from my guns. Then, as shells burst around me, I scrambled along a ravine for seventy-five yards to our platoon CP, informed my platoon leader, and requested to move the men from the position. With permission, I hurried back up the ravine under fire and ordered all of the men out of their holes and into the ravine. I led them to safety and placed them into holes with our men from the other squads. A tremendous mortar barrage continued for some time.

Later, I went back to observe the situation and found direct hits on one gun emplacement and direct hits on two foxholes that would have been occupied by four men, including my own. Seven lives had been saved from serious injury or death.

I received my second bronze star medal for my efforts. That night while discussing it with my close friend Sergeant Bert Smith, I remembered that it was November 18, my 21st birthday.

From the March 1996 22nd Infantry Regiment Society Newsletter

Hürtgen Forest Monument

For the October 22, 1995 issue of The Arizona Republic newspaper, Steve Wilson wrote the following article.

One of the longest, bloodiest, and least publicized battles of World War II was fought in the dense fir trees along the German-Belgian border called the Hürtgen Forest.

Thirty-thousand Americans were killed or wounded in six months of fighting that began in September, 1944, and lasted far into the bitter winter. Thousands more were disabled by combat fatigue and exposure. An estimated 12,000 Germans were killed.

"Whoever survived Hürtgenwald must have had a guardian angel on each of his shoulders," wrote Ernest Hemingway, who covered the battle for Collier's magazine.

One soldier who got out alive was retired Major General John F. Ruggles of Phoenix, 86 years old. He was then a lieutenant colonel serving with the 22nd Infantry Regiment.

Last year, to mark the battle's 50th anniversary, Ruggles organized an effort among veterans of the Regiment to place a monument in the forest. It is a very different monument. Unlike other World War II tributes, this one doesn't honor our own soldiers. This one honors an unheralded act of humanity by a 23-year-old German infantry lieutenant.

Ruggles wasn't interested in media attention last year, and the monument's dedication received no news coverage in this country. But a friend recently convinced him that others would like to know the story, so last week we talked about it.

On November 12, 1944, Lieutenant Friedrich Lengfeld was commanding a beleaguered German rifle company. Like most units on both sides, his had suffered heavy casualties. Early that morning, a wounded American could be heard calling from the middle of a German minefield in a no man's land separating the combatants.

"Help me," the man cried.

His unit had withdrawn, however, and no U.S. troops were close enough to hear. Lengfeld ordered his men not to shoot if Americans came to rescue the man, but none came. The soldier's weakening voice was heard for hours.

"Help me," he called, again and again.

At about 1030 hours, Lengfeld could bear the cries no longer. He formed a rescue squad, complete with Red Cross vests and flags, and led his men toward the wounded American. He never made it. Approaching the soldier, he stepped on a land mine, and exploding metal fragments tore deeply into his body. Eight hours later, Lengfeld was dead. The fate of the American is unknown.

Much of this story, unpublished in any American books on the war, is based on the eyewitness account of Hubert Gees, who served as Lengfeld's communications runner. Speaking at the monument's dedication in Germany last October, Gees said:

"Lieutenant Lengfeld was one of the best soldiers of the Hürtgen Forest. He was an exemplary company commander who never asked us to do more than he himself was ready to give. He possessed the complete confidence of his soldiers."

Ruggles said Lengfeld's sense of duty went far beyond the call.

"You can't go to any greater extreme than to give your life trying to rescue someone you are fighting as your enemy in war," he said. "Compare that to the indifference most people feel about each other today."

The bronze and concrete monument is believed to be the only one placed by Americans in a German military cemetery. In both German and English, the plaque reads:

HERE IN HÜRTGEN FOREST, ON NOVEMBER 12, 1944, LIEUTENANT FRIEDRICH LENGFELD, A GERMAN OFFICER, GAVE HIS LIFE WHILE TRYING TO SAVE THE LIFE OF AN AMERICAN SOLDIER LYING SEVERELY WOUNDED IN THE 'WILDE SAU' MINEFIELD AND APPEALING FOR MEDICAL AID.

To the young lieutenant, the voice crying out that day did not come from an enemy, nor from an American, nor a stranger. It came from a human being in need. Something inside Lengfeld compelled him to act—a feeling so strong and enduring that not even the madness of war could block it.

In the heavy silence of a German forest, where thousands upon thousands met death, that glorious impulse for life is now honored. The 22nd Infantry Regiment did not enter the Hürtgen Forest until four days after this act of bravery. It was believed by the late General Ruggles that the American was a member of the 12th Infantry Regiment, which had entered the forest earlier in November.

General Ruggles died on January 15, 1999. Major General (Retired) John F. Ruggles' career and his contributions to the war, the 4th Infantry Division, and in particular, the 22nd Infantry Regiment, can hardly be characterized here; he was too much the soldier, too much a man. Suffice to say, he was loved and admired by the men. –Bob Babcock

----

Paul Brunelle, Avon, MA
Company G, 2nd Battalion, 8th Infantry Regiment

German Artillery All Around Us

From the book Company G, 2nd Battalion, 8th Infantry Regiment, 4th Infantry Division *by Shirley Devine. Reprinted with permission.*

Well, I guess we moved through the Siegfried Line, and then into the Hürtgen Forest. The Hürtgen Forest, as we all know, was a terrible slaughter. Wonderful men were killed all around us. It was an experience that nobody who was there could ever forget. I can remember hearing about the big breakthrough that was going to take place. They moved us into the edge of the forest, had us dig foxholes, and prepare a jumping off spot to push through the Hürtgen. Immediately upon the resumption of the attack, tremendous German artillery came in all around us. A great number of American casualties occurred in those very first couple of days. I remember Joe Regario received a battlefield commission and Lieutenant Bernard Ray (who earned the Medal of Honor) was killed during those first couple of days, as were many other people.

I dug in with a fellow from Oklahoma who was an Indian. I never really knew what his name was, but everybody called him Chief. I guess every Indian who served in the armed forces was assumed to be an Indian chief, so we always called him Chief. We had not only battlefield casualties there, but we had a number of people who went back because of battlefield fatigue, shock, and one thing or another. It was truly a terrible experience.

After a few days, we were moved out of that position and attempted a penetration at another point. I recall seeing the tanks they brought in to clear a minefield. We had a number of casualties when the minefield was penetrated. People didn't know it was mined, and by the time the first person hit a mine, the troops were killed at that point. I also remember seeing a stream of German prisoners coming out of the forest. One poor soul was bleeding from the mouth and pleading for help. There was nothing that a poor PFC could do to help him, but I did have a great deal of compassion for him. I heard later on that he had died. It didn't surprise me, because when I saw him he was losing a great deal of blood.

Well, they moved us back again to that operation. The battle went on for some time and the casualties were great. The surviving troops were very few. Just about every day a whole new group of replacements would be sent up, and by nightfall we would be calling for more. This happened day after day. The casualty rate was high—very high—and the situation was gloomy. Everyone was depressed and expecting that he would be the next one to go.

In the Hürtgen Forest, I do remember how our company cooks strived to bring us hot meals whenever they could. They were always encouraging and really did the best that they could do to try to build up our morale. I can remember being served Thanksgiving dinner and just not being able to believe that all the traditional things that we knew of at home were served to us on that occasion. It was quite an achievement for the cooks in our company to have been able to prepare a meal for us like that.

Some of us survived, and we were then moved down to Luxembourg to regroup. When we were in Luxembourg, we were billeted in small towns. I recall staying in a farmhouse. Being a PFC, I didn't have any special privileges. So, instead of being inside of a house, I slept in the hayloft of the barn. But even that was a luxury after having slept in the cold frigid woods of the forest, so I didn't object. I considered myself very fortunate.

One night in the Hürtgen Forest or the Siegfried Line, they brought us up some wet blankets. As I said, our cooks and our rear echelon staff did the very best they could to try to help us. The blankets weren't really wet, they were damp, and when you rolled up in them at least you were warm. It was a rainy, cold night, and there was no way of digging a foxhole. There was mortar fire in the vicinity, but we just stretched out under the pine trees. We said if the mortars come tonight, there is no way we can protect ourselves, we'll just have to take it as it comes. But fortunately, they didn't drop mortars in on us. The next day we moved out, and we all made it safely.

I remember the corrugated roads. The engineers would come up and chop down these small trees and create wooden corduroy roads in the places that were just about a quagmire. Nobody could have gotten through them unless the engineers had been there and done this. I can remember the big trees and how the shells would land in the trees and scatter the shrapnel around.

Donald Faulkner, Winter Park, FL
Company E, 2nd Battalion, 22nd Infantry Regiment

Easy Six

November 27, 1944-Hürtgen Forest before Grosshau: Company E was on attack at 1230 hours and stopped dead in its tracks about 1235 hours by all types of enemy fire. I tried to bring in artillery fire, but it was stopped by the high trees and we were too close to the edge of town. So, Lieutenant Colonel Kenan said, "Watch for the tanks… on the road."

I stepped alone into a small field from inside the woods. As two tanks came around a corner of the road, an M1 rifle was laid on my left shoulder by a young recruit who fired a round or two at the town. I ducked and saw seven riflemen at the first building gathered in a circle. I watched one pull the pin of his grenade, and throw it in a window. Bang! Hooray! All of them climbed into the window of that house.

Our first tank was on fire, its bedrolls burning. Lieutenant Yoeman jumped out, grabbed a ramrod to beat out the fire and said, "My Sarge will take you in!"

We were off down the main street—to victory. It was movie stuff: Rifle fire, grenades, and the movement to the end of town. It was ours by around 1800 hours. Question: Did that recruit who used me as a rifle rest and had only been on the continent for ten days make it? I pray he did. Easy Six.

Recollection #900—The Use of Combined Arms, Nov 29—Dec 1, 1944. Company E had established itself east of the large field near Grosshau. The CP was in a big shell hole on a mound just inside the tree line. In the morning sunlight I saw a momentary flash of light reflected from something on the hillside to the southeast at about two hundred-fifty yards. Nothing more. Later in the morning I registered protective barrages around our position. Barrage "Baker One" was registered near the spot where the flash of light was seen.

A day later we were being relieved by fresh troops. They came in under German artillery fire. I was watching from the top of our CP, heard mortar fire and jumped into our hole. Question: they had observation on us, but from where? It could have been an OP (Observation Post) where I saw a reflection of light the day before. Maybe.

It was now our turn to withdraw. I sent our first platoon with Sergeant Ivey back across the field to town, and also called artillery fire.

"Baker One, fire for effect!"

It worked. Not a round was fired on Company E as we withdrew to Grosshau. The command group was the last across the field, all safe. Thank the Lord for my year at Fort Sill with the Field Artillery FO team. We won! Easy Six.

One more memory of how our supporting arms really did support us with only one battery: They had four guns with worn-out tubes in the Battle of the Bulge. The date was about December 22, 1944. The place was in the woods opposite Rodenbaugh, Luxembourg, and the time was mid afternoon. The Krauts with four mortars started to work Company E over. We were getting some casualties while digging in. By sound, we located the ravine on our map. We gave the location to our Artillery and they fired for effect. That was the last we heard of those four mortars. Merry Christmas, 1944. Easy Six.

Riley Taylor, Aberdeen, NC.
Company I, 3rd Battalion, 22nd Infantry Regiment

Shrapnel Would Come Down on the Men Like Rain

As told to his wife, Dib Taylor, in her book Not a Hero, Just Lucky

We were sent to the Hürtgen Forest. We were supposed to clear the Hürtgen Forest of the enemy. We set up in a wooded area and waited for the big push to start. Part of our division, the 12th Infantry Regiment, was sent earlier to help another division that was having a rough time.

When the big push started, it was in the middle of November, and the weather was real bad. We had rain, snow, sleet, and freezing temperatures. We were wet and cold every day we were fighting in the Hürtgen Forest. Some nights we didn't have any blankets, and when we did get them, they were wet. We dug a lot of foxholes, and we cut down a lot of trees. We would put the logs on top of the foxholes, and this would give us some protection from the artillery that landed in the trees. If you were not in a foxhole when the artillery shells burst in the treetops, the shrapnel would come down on you like rain. This inflicted heavy casualties on the men. Moving forward in the Hürtgen Forest was slow.

I asked Riley if he could remember what the forest l0oked like. He said, "The trees, probably fir, had been set out in rows. They were close together—all sizes, tall and skinny. The forest looked like a jungle. Every so often there was a firebreak lane."

He said, "The enemy had their antitank guns set up to fire down the firebreaks. This made it very dangerous to operate. Our tanks would cross these firebreaks when they could. Their tracks would make deep ruts and blow up the mines. We would follow in the tank tracks because they were free of mines and because we would have some protection behind the tank from the incoming artillery shells. Some days we would only take one or two firebreaks.

"One day, as we were following in the deep tracks, an antitank gun fired at the tank in front of us. The shell went through the tank and came out the back. The cans on back of the tank were covered with mud, and when the red-hot shell came out, it caused the mud to fly off the cans. The mud was hot and when it sprayed on us, we got blisters on our faces from it. We also felt the heat from the shell, it came so close to us. We lost several tanks crossing the firebreaks, but we had enough and kept pushing them back."

I asked Riley if he knew how big the Hürtgen Forest was. He said, "From where we went through, it was probably eight to ten miles across. It took us about sixteen days to get through the Hürtgen Forest, and we suffered heavy casualties every day. We received new replacements nearly every day. The replacements came up at night, and sometimes we never saw their faces in the daytime. Some of the replacements would be killed before daylight. We broke out of the Hürtgen Forest and onto the Cologne Plains the last of November. At this time, we had a lot of replacements, but we only had about twenty-three men left in the line when we reached open country."

Robert S. Rush, Ph. D., Sebring, OH
Quotes from the Hürtgen Forest

From his book, Hell in Hürtgen Forest: The Ordeal and triumph of an American Infantry Regiment, *written about the 22nd Infantry Regiment*

Quote from Technician 5th Grade George Morgan. "The forest up there was a helluva eerie place to fight. Show me a man who went through the battle of the Hürtgen Forest and who says he never had a feeling of fear and I'll show you a liar....You can't get protection. You can't see. You can't get fields of fire. The trees are slashed like a scythe by artillery. Everything is tangled. You can scarcely walk. Everybody is cold and wet, and the mixture of cold rain and sleet keeps falling. They jump off again and there is only a handful of the old men left."

Quote from Colonel Buck Lanham, Regimental Commander, in a letter to Carlos Baker, Ernest Hemingway's biographer. "At this time my mental anguish was beyond description. My magnificent command had virtually ceased to exist...these men had accomplished miracles...my admiration and respect for them was...transcendental."

Chaplain Bill Boice wrote: "Perhaps in the final analysis, the sacrifice demanded in the Hürtgen will be deemed worthwhile; we wouldn't know that....We are only the men who fought the battles...who lay in the slime and mud night after night...who did not come out of a foxhole long enough to eat Thanksgiving dinner, for life was more precious than food….A part of us died in the forest, and there is a part of our mind and heart and soul left there."

Captain Donald Faulkner in his diary recorded: "Company E had 79 men and six officers before Grosshau (when he took command of the company.) …received about 160 new men and now only a little over 80 with three officers are going back. It had better be worth it."

George Wilson, last commander of Fox Company, wrote in his book, *If You Survive:* "The objective lay only four-and-a-half miles away, but it took eighteen terrible days to reach…. It was an awful beating—a terrible price for that damned patch of ground."

Ernest Hemingway, war correspondent with the 22nd throughout the battle, penned the following: "Well, anyway, this Regiment was rebuilt as American regiments always are by the replacement system…. It boils down, or distills, to the fact you stay in until you are hit badly or killed or go crazy and get section 'eighted…' We got a certain amount of replacements, but I can remember thinking that it would be simpler, and more effective, to shoot them in the area where they detrucked, than to have to try to bring them back from where they would be killed and bury them…"

These quotes are reprinted here with permission from Dr. Robert S. Rush, author of Paschendale with Tree Bursts, *re-titled as* Hell in Hürtgen Forest: The Ordeal and Triumph of an American Infantry Regiment.*—Bob Babcock*

Milt Bremer, (Deceased) Sherman Oaks, CA
Company K, 3rd Battalion, 22nd Infantry Regiment

Baptism Under Fire

My introduction to the 4th Infantry Division, to the 22nd Infantry Regiment, to combat, and to the Hürtgen Forest were simultaneous experiences. I was a Second Lieutenant who had spent much of October and November slogging through the mud of France and Belgium with other bedraggled replacements catching up with our assigned divisions. In looking through my old 201 file (Personnel Records), I found Special Order 150, HQ 92nd Replacement Battalion, 3rd Replacement Depot, APO 153, dated 23 Nov 1944, assigning men to the 4th Infantry Division. Among the names listed were 1st Lieutenant Morris Goldschlager, 2nd Lieutenant Kenneth Bigus, Captain Donald Faulkner, 1st Lieutenant Gordon Gullikson, 2nd Lieutenant David James, 2nd Lieutenant Edward Arthur, 2nd Lieutenant Francis Boyle, 2nd Lieutenant Milton Bremer, 1st Lieutenant Robert Repass.

As we passed through Division Quartermaster Supply, I heard my name called. Then I spotted Captain Milton Mossholder, a friend from my home town in Illinois. He was the Division's Quartermaster CO. We had only a few moments to talk and I was rushed on, newly provided with an M-1 carbine, two ammunition clips (empty) and a box of carbine ammo.

When we finally got to the 3rd Battalion CP, the Germans heard the activity and started dropping artillery on us. Those of us who had just arrived had no place to go but into a hole with one of the regular residents. The soldier who shared his hole with me was sick, and coughed and wheezed all night. In addition, the space was not long enough for me, and my feet hung out into the fire step, which was full of water, and the "ceiling" was so low it was impossible to turn over.

That was not a night for sleeping, and I was actually relieved when someone pulled me out into a pitch-dark morning. "You're going to K Company, and we have a guide to take you out. We're scheduled to attack just before daybreak, so you don't have much time."

As we stumbled through the tangled underbrush, I realized I didn't even have a loaded weapon. In the dark, I tried to load my two clips and discovered that the box had broken during the night. and most of the rounds were probably lying in the mud back at Battalion.

I was having a hard enough time following my guide, when there was a "pop" and the sizzling sound of a grenade fuse.

I yelled, "Down!"

The grenade exploded, followed by a voice calling out, "Who goes there?"

Somehow, we had gotten out in front of the platoon, and they were a bit jumpy.

I had time to meet my platoon sergeant and medic, and the attack started. Believe me, I let the sergeant run the show. The next entry in my file made me one of the numbers in Doc Goldstein's list of casualties on November 28, as reported in the December newsletter. The funny thing about those two days is that I have no recollection of eating the night before or having any kind of breakfast the next morning. I guess other more important events took my mind off such prosaic considerations.

As a small footnote to the above: While at Fort Meade waiting to ship over, I got into Washington, DC one day. On an impulse while in the post Officers Quartermaster Store, I bought a field coat—warm and very smart looking; my gold bars looked great on it. I took very good care of it.

When we were privileged to ride in trucks through France, I wore a raincoat over it to protect against the mud spray that was thrown up by the wheels. I was wearing it when I met up with my new platoon in the Hürtgen.

I was quickly told to, "get rid of it—you'll get hung up in the trees."

I folded it carefully and wrapped it in my raincoat. My medic, Technician 5th Class Peter Campo, was going back to get supplies from battalion. Unfortunately, we got the signal to attack at that moment. I put the coat down at the foot of a tree I hoped I would recognize again, and we moved out. I hope whoever found that coat got good use out of it. Peter Campo was killed the same day I was wounded.

Don Lee, St. Louis Park, MN
Company B, 1st Battalion, 22nd Infantry Regiment

Third Purple Heart

I returned to the 22nd Infantry Regiment, I believe, in October 1944. I was out of the hospital after my second Purple Heart. I was sent to Company D in the Hürtgen and was wounded for the third time by a tree burst. The only time I had as much pain was years later when I had back surgery. They took the fragment out in Liege, Belgium. The surgeon came in to see me after the operation. He apologized, as he really had to dig to get it out. Then I was sent to Paris and later to England. After I recovered, I was sent back to the 22nd in the spring of 1945. The action was light so I was not wounded a fourth time. But after I read more about the Hürtgen and the Battle of the Bulge, I realized that third Purple Heart saved my life due to much less exposure in heavy combat.

Russ Wise, Matthews, NC
Company F, 2nd Battalion, 22nd Infantry Regiment

A Lone Enemy on Vacation

While I was lying in an aid station waiting to be evacuated from the Hürtgen Forest, I heard two GIs talking about a German they had captured in Grosshau. The German was in a basement and would not come out so they threw a hand grenade into the basement. This German came out fussing with papers in one hand and a wine bottle in the other hand—pretty much drunk. Said he was on vacation and did not want to be bothered.

After being evacuated to a hospital in Liege, Belgium, a German V1 "buzz" bomb hit one wing of the hospital, shaking it up pretty bad. This one GI said, "They took me out of a body bag and brought me here, and if this keeps up, I suppose I will be going back to my old body bag."

Peter Triolo, Pueblo, CO
HQ, 1st Battalion, 12th Infantry Regiment

The Hürtgen's Bloody Forest

The Hürtgen's forest was huge. The trees were planted about twenty feet apart, and some went as high as one hundred feet. Just like a cornfield. The problem with fighting in a wooded area—the artillery shells would burst overhead and come down like a big umbrella. This made it very dangerous. We dug holes and covered them with logs to try to survive the three or four days while we were in the forest. I was lucky that Colonel Jackson found a pillbox that we could turn into our headquarters.

While in the forest we received a whole bunch of new replacements. Probably about one hundred to one hundred-fifty. Before the men could be settled, the Germans opened up with a large artillery bombardment. The young recruits were caught before they could get proper protection. We lost about twenty-five percent of our men before they could even get into the war.

We got a call over the radio that some of these men had panicked and were running back to the rear. Colonel Jackson called me, "Pete, go out and stop those guys before we lose them or they get killed."

Of course, I ran out down the trail and ran into about six or seven men running away from the front lines. I don't know what I said to them but I must have called them cowards because one of them stuck his rifle barrel into my stomach and asked what I had said. I thought the end was in sight. I very quietly talked to him and moved the barrel to the side. I talked them into joining me for coffee at the headquarters. I guess it wasn't my day to die, but from the looks in their eyes, I wasn't too sure.

After coffee, we talked for a few minutes, and I calmed them down. Then the sergeant from their company came to get them. Sometimes I used to say to myself, "Why me? I think the Colonel is trying to get me killed."

John Worthman, (Deceased)
Medic, 22nd Infantry Regiment

Battlefield Commission

The Hürtgen Forest is about fifty square miles of densely wooded hilly terrain just east of Malmedy and Spa, Belgium. The trees are fir, spruce, and cedar and cover it densely except for the firebreaks and occasional roads. It contains no villages. Just east of the forest is the small town of Grosshau, and well east of it over flat country is the Ruhr Valley industrial complex. The Hürtgen was our direct approach to the Ruhr. The Hürtgen contained some of the innermost elements of the Siegfried Line, primarily pillboxes with interlocking fields of fire placed on strategic high ground.

The soil is very shallow except in the valleys, and under it is a shale bed that accepts water poorly. During the autumn rains the topsoil is very wet, and if you dig down to the rock you seem to have gotten to the ground water table, and your hole will scarcely be fifteen inches deep! In the Hürtgen, you did not dig a hole; you tried a build a "log topped" lean-to over a shallow hole.

From November 16, 1944 to December 3, the 4th Infantry Division fought a battle of great intensity and with casualty numbers we had not before seen. The fighting was very elemental. Infantry units would try to move forward and artillery and mortar fire would try to move them back. All shells were fused to burst on contact and most would strike a tree and spray the ground beneath with shell fragments. It was difficult to hold newly taken land in such shelling and no one could fight from log-topped dugouts. If, as the infantry moved forward, your own mortars and artillery could directly engage the enemy, you could succeed. But that required excellent communications between the guns and the infantry, which were usually four hundred to eight hundred yards apart. The radios were unreliable due to water and to concussion. The Germans had zeroed in all firebreaks, roads and trail intersections. Tree bursts wounded more and killed less than ground bursts. The casualties bore this out. Tree bursts are hard on morale, and you feel that you have no available protection.

In the first six days the fighting elements of the 22nd Infantry sustained approximately fifty percent casualties. In seventeen days there, the regiment suffered extremely heavy casualties. We medics worked harder than we ever had before. Most wounded had to be carried back to the aid station on litters. Carrying litters is cruel work on good terrain and inhuman punishment on wet hillsides under tree bursts. We all took turns on the litters. From the aid stations to the collecting companies, the movement was by ambulance or ambulance jeeps, trying the roads and firebreaks when we assumed there would be no shelling. In the ravines, they would churn through one to two feet of muddy soup. Replacements for the companies would be walking in on those same routes and very often were wounded and evacuated before getting to the company.

The attrition was just as bad for the Germans as they slowly fell back, and some of those units were never brought back to strength but absorbed into other units. It was the bloodiest, most frightening, and most fatiguing time in the war for me. We were certain that we would soon be wounded or killed. It is not rare to feel this, but usually you can shake off the feeling with rest, food, or with hard work. After about a week of the Hürtgen, I could not shake it off, nor could most of those I knew.

The attrition was so great that many infantry platoons were commanded by privates for a day or more, as the lieutenant, the sergeant and three corporals were gone. Some of those were given battlefield commissions as second lieutenants. Battlefield commissions were new to us, but on about November 28, I was ordered back to Regimental Headquarters to be commissioned a second lieutenant in the Medical Administrative Corps. My relief was enormous. I thanked Captain Goldstein, for I was sure he had a hand in this. At the regiment, I thanked Major Kirtley and Chaplain Boice. I was so grateful to be out of the Hürtgen and so proud to be commissioned. I had been a technical sergeant for only two months.

Chaplain Boice was staying in Malmedy in the home of the best cook in Belgium. He took me there, and we dined. What we had I do not remember, but I have not forgotten the rediscovery of tastes in my mouth that were pleasant, not just cold and nourishing. Then I slept a long night through. The next day, I left by truck for Luxembourg to join the 83rd Infantry Division in one of the collecting companies as the Evacuation Officer. Battlefield commissions in the infantry stayed with their unit, but I was transferred, as there was no place for me in an aid station as a second lieutenant, MAC.

For about five days the fighting continued as viciously as ever. At last Grosshau was taken, and the firing stopped. I can't imagine the Hürtgen without gunfire, without terror, without fatigue. This was my personal valley of the shadow. I left it with incredible relief and with a sadness I had never so far known.

James D. Casey, Plymouth, MA
Company C, 1st Battalion, 12th Infantry Regiment

Bloody Hürtgen Forest Battle Rages on in Memory

Late in World War II, the Hürtgen Forest, a 50-mile area on the German Belgian border covered with rugged, hilly woods was the scene of fierce fighting that cost the U.S. Army 30,000 casualties.

"We called it the 'Death Factory,' and it was aptly named," said Jim Casey, a former squad leader with Company C, 12th Infantry Regiment, 4th Infantry Division.

The fighting raged from September 1944 through February 1945. During those six months of forest fighting, elements of eight infantry and two armored divisions—plus several smaller U.S. outfits—were fed into the battle.

"It was really an infantry battle, where the American superiority in armor and air power could not be effectively used," Casey said. "Most literary pundits have taken the view that it need never have been fought. But once committed, the high command kept pouring troops into that forest, with appalling results."

For Casey, every November since the war brings back the memory of those bloody days in the gloom and mist of that "Green Hell" of the Hürtgen, near the city of Aachen.

"As an example, my company went into battle with some two hundred men in its roster. Two weeks later we mustered only a skeleton force," he recalled. "This was typical of all the units which took part. We used to say, if you lasted two days in the fighting, you were a veteran."

As in any battle in a heavy woods, command and communication are difficult. "At times it was really chaotic; we often did not detect the well-camouflaged and dug-in Germans until we stumbled upon them," Casey recalled.

Rations were difficult to get up to the troops, because units were often scattered. Many replacement soldiers who came up during the night were killed by morning. Dead of both sides, including the 28th Infantry "Bloody Bucket" Division, which Casey's division relieved, were scattered among trees.

"But it was the raw, penetrating cold and the incessant rains which compounded the difficulties for the infantry," Casey said. "Added to these were the tree bursts from German artillery which, together with mines, caused a lot of casualties. We were taught to stand up against the trunk of the tree, thus presenting a lesser target than a man lying on the ground."

Division after division of infantry took its turn in the meat grinder—the 28th, 4th, 8th, 1st, 9th, and others—as well as tank outfits, which were of limited use (because of terrain), but welcomed assistance. The 9th Division, which drifted into the forest fighting, lost 450 men, and the 28th took 600 casualties before being relieved by Casey's 4th Infantry Division.

Casey considered himself very fortunate to have survived the carnage. Although his unit fought through the Battle of the Bulge, the Hürtgen Forest battle seems to be his most vivid experience in World War II.

Morris L. Harvey (Deceased), Benton, KY
Company M, 3rd Battalion, 22nd Infantry Regiment

I Don't Want You to Shoot Me
As told to his son, Kerry Harvey

Kerry: What was going on when you were hit?

Morris: I was firing the machine gun. We could see Germans in the tree-tops, and they were firing rifles at us. One hit me. Everybody was shooting at the gun—the riflemen and the machine gunners down the line. We were firing everything we had at them, and they were falling out of the treetops like pine needles. We were slaughtering them, but they weren't doing badly on us either. I told my squad leader I felt that thing hit me. It really didn't hurt. I always thought it would hurt if you were shot but it didn't. I thought maybe just an empty casing popped out of the gun and I kept shooting, and I felt something warm down my leg. I looked down and there was blood running down my leg. It had soaked through my pants. I told my squad leader, "I'm hit, I'm going back to the aid station," and I said, "which way is the aid station?"

He said, 'I don't have any idea. We have Germans all around us, and I don't know which way to go. I couldn't tell you if my life depended on it."

I said, "I'm going to start—it has to be better than where I am now," so I started back.

Kerry: Were you having trouble walking?

Morris: No, it wasn't hurting. I got back a ways and came to another clearing. I had no way of knowing which way to go. I didn't see anybody: Germans, Americans—nobody. I heard somebody talking and thought I would find out from those guys where I was going. I took a couple of steps forward and I thought, whoa! They are talking the wrong language. I started looking for a place to hide. There was a shell hole, and I rolled over into that hole. I saw them and was just hoping they hadn't seen me. It was a machine gun squad of six or seven men. One of them had a machine gun over his shoulder. I figured they were lost just like me. I had a .45 automatic pistol with me, and I just pulled that thing out and cocked it. I figured if they found me, they weren't going to take any prisoners because they didn't know where they were, and they weren't going to mess with a prisoner.

I thought, "Well, that first one sticks his head over that hole ain't going to live, and we'll just go from there and hope for the best." They were close enough as they walked by my hole that I could see the top of their heads. I wasn't really scared then. I hadn't had time to think about it. I heard some voices, some yelling and heard some shots. The Germans commenced to yell, and there were Americans hollering. I wouldn't repeat the language some of them were yelling at those Germans."

"The shooting stopped, and the Germans were yelling, "Komaraden"—meaning "Surrender." I yelled from my hole and said, "I am an American and I am hit and I'm in this hole and I'm going to get up. I don't want you to shoot me," and I got up.

The voice said, "Man, I'm glad you hollered 'cause if you had stuck your head up, I'd have blowed it off."

I said I kind of figured that. They had those Germans, I don't know what they did with them, but they had them rounded up. The Germans looked amazed when I came out of that hole. They didn't know I was in there. One of those riflemen told me to get back to the aid station, and he put me on the right route, so I walked back to the aid station."

Patrick L. O'Dea, Grapevine, TX
Company F, 2nd Battalion, 22nd Infantry Regiment

The Front Lines

In early November 1944, the ship arrived in Le Havre harbor at dusk, but it was hours later, almost midnight, when we finally debarked. I was with a packet of American soldiers on their way to the Western Front as replacements for casualties. In the glare of powerful electric lights we climbed over the side of the ship and down the ladder into the flat-bottomed landing craft. The night was cold, and all the men wore overcoats. When filled with men, the landing craft chugged its 300-yard journey to shore, beached itself, and opened its wide vertical doors to let the men ashore. Each man grabbed a duffel bag at random from a pile on the beach, and we moved up a debris-strewn path to a street.

I was tired and stiff from the voyage, the pack was heavy, the sea breeze was chilling, and I was in no mood to hike up the high hills that were dimly visible in the background. As a result, I was pleased when we were ordered to climb into a line of two-and-a-half-ton trucks that stood at the curb. I got in the truck with Mack and the other friends I made aboard the Queen Mary and, without delay, the convoy drove up the deserted streets of the seaport. I got only an occasional glimpse of the darkened houses from the covered truck as we sped up the steep hills to the outskirts.

The convoy halted in the midst of a group of pyramidal tents on a wide field. About eighteen men were assigned to each tent and told to get some sleep. The tents contained no cots or blankets. No one had a candle, and in the crowded tent, everyone seemed to be in each other's way. In the darkness I located Mack, and we tried to make a mattress out of our duffel bags in the tiny space that was ours. We each took a blanket from our packs, deciding that two blankets would be sufficient along with our overcoats. The ground was damp and soggy, and my feet were getting cold. I got into a half-sitting, half-reclining position and tried to go to sleep. I loosened my combat boots, but left them on as did all the others, and my feet remained cold.

I fell into a doze and sometime later was awakened by one of the men who jumped up and down, complaining that his feet were so cold that he couldn't sleep. I realized that my own feet were painfully cold, and some of the others admitted it, too. One man suggested that we make a fire out of our tent stakes, but no one took any action. I was too sleepy to look for tent pegs in my pack, and it seemed like a waste of tent stakes at the time. Again, I tried to go to sleep, but slept only in fitful snatches until morning.

Soon after daylight we were called to chow, which consisted of nothing more than hot coffee and a single slice of bread with jelly on it. The early morning mist that overhung the damp ground was beginning to lift, and I examined our surroundings. We were on a plateau that dropped sharply through Le Havre to the sea on one side and stretched unbroken for miles into the interior. Our camp consisted of perhaps a hundred tents and a tiny, hastily constructed wooden shack that served as the kitchen. Other camps, the nearest of which was about a half mile distant, dotted the plain. We were warned not to stray too far away since the area had not yet been thoroughly swept for mines. We walked around a little, examined a German anti-aircraft gun that was damaged beyond repair, and looked at an old weather-beaten church that stood alone and unused near the camp.

About noon we were ordered to pack and prepare to leave. Then each man was given a D-bar, and we started the downhill march into Le Havre. I think we were all glad to leave the camp, for it was dull, damp, cold, and barren. There was nothing exciting about Le Havre; the streets were dingy, the houses were dingy, even the bistros were dingy. Although the seaport was utterly demolished, the residential sections bore few marks of the war. The people eyed us indifferently; they had seen American soldiers before. Some of our intelligentsia tried out their high school French on the citizens and were rewarded with replies that few understood. In little more than an hour we reached the railroad station. An American transportation officer led us to a long line of ancient French freight cars, the "forty and eights" of World War I. I hadn't given much thought to transport, and I was amazed that the army should be forced to use these decrepit wooden cars to haul troops.

"You didn't believe these things still existed, did you?" the old transportation officer chuckled. "We're going to give you a break. Thirty-nine men instead of forty in each car—so you'll have plenty of room."

With our immense packs, we were awfully crowded in the freight car. Along with Mack I managed to get a seat against the side and used my pack as a big pillow. The train started as soon as loading was finished. We had an officer in charge of our car. He was a young, newly commissioned fellow who scrupulously followed all regulations to the letter. This was probably his first experience in dealing with men under adverse conditions. He failed to realize a fact that we seemed to know instinctively— that over here, the men were allowed more personal freedom of action, as long as they performed their duties as soldiers. Needless to say, he made a disagreeable leader in this situation.

Hour after hour, the train slowly squirmed its way through bombed out marshaling yards, over precarious, hastily reconstructed bridges, through desolate, battle-wrecked towns, moving generally in a northeasterly direction. Stops were frequent, and while men from other cars bounced out immediately to stretch stiff legs and build fires to warm their C-rations, we had to remain in the car until the train commander gave permission to get off. Thus, we were the last to heat our Crations, and hot food was one thing men craved after a ride in the cold boxcars whose many chinks and cracks admitted the freezing wind.

Sleep was painful. In the cramped quarters, each man, in turning or stretching his legs, invariably disturbed others who were trying to sleep, and there was much grumbling and arguing in the swaying blackness. In the morning it was raining when we awoke, and the ancient wooden ceiling dripped icy rain on the disgusted men below. The rain and the train both continued intermittently all day. The Crations were cold and unappetizing, the countryside was wet and dreary, and the noise of the wheels and the bumping and swaying of the cars made the day seem endless. Toward evening we stopped in a station, and a Frenchman approached with a bag filled with bottles. He said they contained cognac and sold them to eager soldiers. Our car bought two bottles before the train pulled out and the bottles were passed around to all who wanted a swig. It tasted more like Calvados than cognac, and after a good drink, I could feel the warmth spreading through my body. Our officer did not take a drink but said nothing when the bottles were passed around.

The second night was worse than the first, and the men were irritable and uncomfortable. Day finally came, the rain continued, and we inched our way across northern France. In the late afternoon, the train made a long stop, and we found out that we were on the Belgian border. While searching for drinking water, we discovered a cache of crab apples, and almost every soldier on the train was eating crab apples in a few minutes. The officers told us not to drink any water that was not approved, and we blandly assured our lieutenant that our canteens had been full every day since we had left Le Havre.

He made no argument; he was learning how to handle enlisted men. Some hours later the train pulled into the town of Givet on the Meuse River, and we were told that we had arrived at our destination. We were happy that the cramped ride had ended and made haste to get ready to march to our quarters.

Our bivouac area was said to be about five miles behind the front lines, and a strong guard was posted. Mack and I were put on guard the first night for a twohour stretch from midnight to 0200 hours. We were posted near the bottom of the hill about fifteen yards from a small brook, told to challenge anything that moved, and to shoot at our own discretion. Mack and I sat about ten feet apart staring at the hill that rose abruptly from across the brook. It was impossible to listen for anything since the babbling brook and the occasional roar of artillery both nearby and far away drowned out any sound. I had about fifty rounds of .30 caliber ammunition issued in Givet. Some of the bullets were faulty; they were mashed out of shape, and I was given only two clips. Our U.S. Army supply system was in bad shape. The two hours passed without incident except that it began raining, and it was uncomfortable to sit motionless in the drizzle.

The next day was foggy and wet, and we stayed in the tent most of the time. Some fellow in a nearby tent shot himself in the foot with a carbine, and I stuck my head out in time to see him jumping around on one foot yelling for aid. He claimed that it was an accident, and it might well have been, but some of the men openly wondered if it hadn't been done on purpose in order to escape combat. One of the officers hinted that the man would be court-martialed.

That afternoon, we left by truck for the second battalion headquarters. I abandoned a lot of stuff that I didn't think I would need and made a blanket roll. It was a short but slow ride to our destination, and it was getting dark when we finally piled out of the trucks at a muddy crossroads flanked by hills. Throwing the blanket roll over my shoulder, I fell in behind Mack, and a single file of men started along the road up a hill. Shells were overhead constantly, but none fell very close. Leaving the road, we passed stretcher bearers carrying a severely wounded man back to the aid station. This was the first actual casualty I had seen.

Slipping in the mud, we went over the crest and started down the other side of the hill. We followed no trail, and only our leader knew where we were going in the grim forest. We followed a small creek in a narrow ravine between two high wooded hills. It was extremely rough climbing, and before long the sweat poured off me in spite of the cold. Our path was blocked by fallen trees, boulders, and deep mud. Once Mack tripped while climbing over a blasted tree and fell headlong into the shallow creek. For a few seconds, he lay there cursing in helpless fury. When I reached him he was up, and I could only ask him if he was all right. We continued on, and daylight faded. I opened my coat and shirt to try to cool off, but it helped little. The blanket roll made an awkward bundle, and I was tempted to throw it away. The pack straps bit into my shoulders. Finally, we left the creek and in the gloom, we started to climb a steep hill. Men slipped in the treacherous mud, and some would begin to roll downhill until they crashed heavily into a tree trunk. I slipped several times and was saved from some nasty falls by using my rifle butt as an anchor. Struggling up the hill was a terrific ordeal for all of us, and I could feel my heart pounding inside me. At last, weak-kneed and exhausted, we reached the top.

A company of infantry was dug in at the top of the hill. They were probably in reserve, and they offered advice spiced with wisecracks about the quality of the new replacements. One of them advised me to throw away my pack immediately, assuring me that I would not need it any more. It took little urging and I took it off, put it against a tree, vaguely intending to return the next day to retrieve it. I never saw it again and never again needed it.

After a short rest at the hilltop, we started marching again. The only question on our minds was, "How much further?" It was now dark, and we stumbled onward, scratching our faces on hidden limbs, barking our shins on hidden obstacles, and stumbling over roots. Exhausted, we finally reached our destination and were assigned to already-dug foxholes. By chance, Mack and I were assigned to the same foxhole, a large one that already had two men in it. The ground was wet and muddy, but no one complained; we were content to sit and rest after the grueling hike.

The foxhole was large enough for four men, deep enough to sit in, and had a roof of stout logs, except for the entrance hole. In a short time, the sergeant came by to give us instructions for the night. We were to maintain fifty percent guard at all times, and he warned us not to get out of the foxhole until daybreak.

About 0800 hours we were ordered to pack up and move out. We marched to a nearby draw whose steep sides offered some protection against shells, and we spread out so that each man was at least five yards from his nearest neighbor. A roll was called and then an officer with a heavy beard, a stained uniform, and a deep voice called out about twenty names of men assigned to Company E and the same number from Company F. Then a tracked vehicle, a "weasel," rode up and dumped a load of ammo on the ground. The driver yelled to the officer in charge of us and asked him if he needed food or ammo on the next trip. The bearded officer yelled back, "@#&% the food, bring me the ammo!"

Then he ordered us to each to take three bandoleers of ammo with us when we headed for the front. The idea of another march like the last night was too much for some of us. We took off our overcoats and threw them into a pile. Then we started out with a warning from the officer not to fall back. I, for one, was determined not to fall back and get lost in this gloomy dangerous forest. We marched in single file. Mack was behind me.

The hike was short, less than half an hour. It was on the hike that I saw my first dead man. Three German soldiers lay to the side of the path. They had evidently been dead for a few days, for their skin had a purple tinge, and their swollen necks bulged out of their collars. They lay face down as they had fallen, and grenades and weapons were scattered near them. I saw all this in one quick glance, for I was in no mood to stare at them. Further on, we crossed a narrow, muddy road where another dead German lay sprawled on his back. This one had evidently been caught in a burst of machine gun fire while trying to cross the road.

He had been hit in the face and chest, and his face was nothing more than a sickening mass of dried blood.

We continued along the trackless terrain, following a course marked out by white tape. The day was cloudy with the promise of rain or even snow if the temperature fell much lower. We didn't talk much; there was nothing to say. Everything was so new to us that we walked along almost in awe as we headed for the front lines. After we had been marching for perhaps a half hour through the green dripping woods, a halt was called, and cigarettes were lit up. We were in a tiny clearing at whose farthest edge our guide was conferring with a group of men. I was sitting next to Mack, but we said little to each other. In the distance, we heard the heavy booming of artillery shells and occasionally the rapid chatter of a machine gun.

Our guide, the officer, came back and ordered us to move on. Then it happened. There was a sudden short high-pitched scream, and a shell exploded nearby with a deafening roar. I was taken completely by surprise, and I suspect that my companions were, too. Instinctively I hit the ground. The explosion blew my helmet off, and it landed about two yards ahead of me. I crawled toward it with desperate strength because I wanted to cover my head before the next shell arrived. As I grabbed my helmet, another explosion shook the earth, then another, and then another. I was lying flat on the ground holding my helmet to my head with both hands, my face pressed against the earth. Clods of dirt rained down on us. In a minute, it was over. Our officer jumped up and said, "Let's get out of here before they throw some more in on us."

I got up and looked around for Mack. He was unhurt, and so were the others except for one man who lay on the ground, a deep gash in his throat gushing blood. Already a medic was rushing up to aid him. The officer pointed to a mudstained man at the edge of the clearing.

"You Company F men report to the First Sergeant there and he'll assign you to your platoons."

With a start, I realized that we had reached our goal. Here was Company F. We were standing on the front lines....

Patrick L. O'Dea, Grapevine, TX
Company F, 2nd Battalion, 22nd Infantry Regiment

The Enemy Lashed Us Again and Again

W ord was passed around that we would move out at 0800 hours to attack. Dan had been made a squad leader the previous day, so he was called up to the CP with the other leaders. He came back with a grim look on his face and said tersely, "We're moving into attack at eight."

He always used the phrase, "Moving into attack," when he spoke of an attack. I had an idea that he was trying to dramatize the whole thing. Then the lieutenant came up with a box of Milky Way candy bars and gave a couple to each man. I was pleased at this because I like them a lot, and I stuffed them in my pocket. Then we broke open the K-rations, ate the breakfast ration, and I kept such parts of the dinner ration as I thought I might want. I threw away the crackers and canned meat because they were too bulky to carry in my pocket. I had no idea who the other men in Dan's squad would be and he didn't know either. Finally, a few minutes before 0800 hours, three other men, all of them recent replacements, were brought over to Dan as the rest of his squad. I didn't know any of them. Naturally, I was in Dan's squad.

There had been an extremely heavy artillery bombardment of the enemy earlier that morning, lasting about fifteen minutes. From the sound, I concluded that it was directed at the Germans in some nearby sector, but not so much at those who were facing us. Perhaps it was directed at the German artillery support that lay further back in the enemy area.

Our attack started at 0800 hours. It began simply enough. Our platoon merely walked out to the left on the clearing and then turned right and moved forward in the direction of the enemy. I had no clear idea where the enemy was suspected of being and I was a little confused about the whole thing. Other units were evidently taking part in this attack further up the line, for there was a sharp increase in the small arms fire. We had only moved about fifty yards from our starting point when some small arms fire was directed against us. The shots were high and wild, and I concluded that they were fired at random. This was a lot less dangerous than if the shots had been actually aimed at us.

Then artillery starting falling on us, and I could understand why Dan had been so jumpy about it. Our attack was just getting started; our officers were trying to form some kind of a line that would move forward in unison. Not even the officers seemed to have a clear idea of what was expected of them. The whole operation seemed to be confused. The sergeant picked two others and me and told us to go over to the right of the advancing line and serve as flank support. I got the idea that we were supposed to stay about ten yards to the rear of the advancing line and a little to the right of it. In that way, we would be in a position to reinforce the right end of the line in case it was attacked from the right. And, we were also to prevent the enemy from sneaking in from the right end of the line and attacking from the rear.

As the line began to move forward, mortar fire began to fall on us. The small arms fire increased as bullets slashed through the trees too high to be effective against us. The mortar shells were more of a problem, and we would hit the ground after a nearby blast even though the damage had already been done by that time. Artillery shells began to fall close by and the advance became more confusing. Men hugged the ground more and more. Two or three men would jump up, run about ten yards, hit the ground, and wait for the rest of the line to catch up. It was extremely hard to keep contact when your face was pressed against the ground and your eyes were closed a good portion of the time. One of my flank buddies was wearing an army overcoat, and this helped me to keep him in view since all the others had on field jackets.

It seemed to me that the clearing was receiving the brunt of German artillery, and I was all for advancing as quickly as possible to what looked like safer ground. I kept moving up a few steps at a time. I still caught glimpses of my overcoated friend a few yards away. A fallen tree blocked my path, and I decided it would be quicker to climb over it than make a wide detour around it. But as I was half climbing, half walking through it, a shell hit close by, and the blast knocked me off my feet. I fell in a tangle of branches and lay there for a few seconds to see if I had been hit. I was OK, but the back of my hand was bleeding from where a broken limb had gashed it. I got up again and ran forward. I didn't see my overcoated friend and I couldn't see much when I looked back because of the undergrowth. I saw a couple of men disappear into a thicket of young pine trees to the front, and I decided to move in their direction. I came to a road running perpendicular to our direction of attack and was surprised, because I had no inkling that it had been there so close to our foxholes. I couldn't see my GIs anywhere. The clearing seemed deserted, but I was sure that many men were still there hugging the ground because it was still under bombardment. Also, I had no intention of being left alone on the ground because it was still under bombardment. I had no intention of being abandoned on the battlefield, so I headed for the dense thicket that began twenty yards or so beyond the road. It was difficult moving through the thick growth of pines, and I knew I would quickly lose my sense of direction if the young trees didn't thin out very soon. I couldn't see ten feet in any direction, and I was fearful that I might stumble onto a German position. I kept moving as slowly and silently as possible. Suddenly I heard a noise to the front, and I stopped perfectly still and listened. It was a swishing sound as if a large group of men was moving through the branches slowly, from side to side. Soon I was separated from the column of men by a single dense line of trees. I strained my eyes but could not identify the men. I didn't want to move the branches of the tree that hid me because that might startle the men on the other side and I'd get a belly full of lead. By this time, I was pretty sure that the men were Americans, but I wanted a little more reassurance. While I stood there, I heard a few words whispered in English, and that convinced me. I stepped quickly through the tree cover and stood in full view of the moving line. I startled a couple of nearby men, but they quickly recognized me as a GI, and everything was OK. This area was comparatively free from enemy shells; the enemy probably did not know that anyone was in this sector. I asked one of the men what company this was and he said it was H Company. We kept moving forward a few steps at a time. The man in front of me was a noncom who carried a walkie-talkie into which he talked in a low voice. Then, in a few minutes, a message came through that all men of the second platoon of F Company were to move to the front of the column immediately. Apparently a lot of our men got lost in the forest. With some embarrassment, I started for the front of the column.

On the way up, I passed a couple of German machine gun and mortar emplacements around which were scattered a few dead Germans and a lot of German equipment. The front of the column was halted at a narrow muddy road that had deep ruts from heavy vehicle travel. I reported to an officer that I was from the second platoon of Fox Company, and he told me that the platoon was regrouping on the other side of the road for a further attack. He pointed to another GI who stood poised ready to dash across the road and told me to follow him after a few seconds if he got across the road OK. He said the road was covered by German small arms and we would have to move fast to get across. Taking a deep breath, the man dashed across the road in about two steps, and no small arms fire tried to stop him. I waited about five seconds, and then, in a burst of energy, raced across the road. I seemed to move with agonizing slowness as if everything was in slow motion. I had picked out what appeared to be the best and shortest path, and I kept my eyes on the spot across the road where I intended to hit the ground. No shots were fired at me, and I thanked heaven for the safe crossing. I also doubted that the Germans were watching the road as closely as I had been led to believe, but it seemed better to take no chances.

I met our platoon sergeant on the other side and fortunately was not criticized for losing contact with the platoon. There were four others from my platoon with the sergeant. Apparently all of the others in the platoon were still lost. The lieutenant showed up and told us we were to move out in a few minutes, and he warned us to stay together and be careful. He said another platoon had just started ahead of us, and we were to give them support. Just before we started, the lieutenant told me to go back to the edge of the road where a third line was forming and tell them to be sure to keep contact with us because the forest at this point was composed of short dense evergreens. I started back to deliver the message, but the sergeant grabbed me and told me not to go sneaking off. I told him in some anger that I was delivering a message for the lieutenant, and he seemed somewhat abashed and told me to hurry back. I gave the message to the noncom in charge of the third line and got back to our platoon as it was starting to move.

We had only taken a few steps when machine gun fire broke out about fifty feet to our front, but the bullets were not fired in our direction. I realized that if those Germans knew we were so close and if they turned their machine gun on us, we would be cut to pieces because the lieutenant wanted us to keep advancing. We got within about ten yards of the machine gun emplacement and stopped while the lieutenant figured out what to do. We could hear the Germans talking and cursing when all of a sudden there was a grenade explosion, followed immediately by carbine fire and by a confusion of screams, howls, and then silence. Then an American voice yelled in triumph, "Did you see the surprised look on that Kraut's face?"

We moved forward and joined the trio that had silenced the gun. The leader was not at all like the big clean-cut American soldiers that one sees on the posters. He was not young and not big. He walked with a stoop, his face was thin and gaunt, and his shoulders were narrow. Yet, it was he who attacked the machine gun emplacement and made it safe for the rest of us to continue. And, we went on. We passed another hastily abandoned German position, and further on we found ourselves at the edge of the forest. The second platoon was told to dig in immediately.

There were still only five men in the platoon, plus the sergeant and the lieutenant. As a result, the sergeant placed us about twenty feet apart and told each of us to dig in by ourselves, but to make the foxhole big enough for two men. He said the remainder of the platoon would soon join us. He showed each man where to dig in and told us to work fast because it was a German tactic to counterattack before the newly won ground could be consolidated. I wasn't happy to be digging in by myself if a counterattack was expected, but I assumed that since it was still before noon I would have a buddy before nightfall.

Again, the ground was hard and full of walnut-sized rocks, which made for hard digging. My shovel would strike a rock before it had gone an inch into the soil and then would go no further. Hardly a handful of dirt could be scooped up at a time and this resulted in a great loss of time and energy. I was tired before I had a hole big enough to put my head in, but I kept digging industriously because I felt sure the Germans would toss plenty of artillery at us when they found out that we held this position. Suddenly, to the rear, I heard the unmistakable chatter of a burp gun. I dropped the shovel and grabbed my rifle. A German voice cried in broken English, "Come out, @#$% Americans! Come out and fight!"

I stretched flat on the ground and pointed my rifle in the direction of the sound. The heavy growth of trees made it impossible to see farther than ten yards. I heard a rustle, and the sergeant was beside me. He warned me to do no more digging but to stay flat on the ground until the Germans were taken care of. He warned me not to fire until I actually saw the enemy soldiers. Then he left for the next foxholes. The sound of the enemy voices was coming nearer and the fire of the burp guns became louder. I guessed it was a German combat patrol or else a squad that had been cut off and was now working its way back to its own lines. I favored the first possibility because the Germans did not seem to be in any hurry to get to their lines. They were well armed and spoiling for a fight. At the close ranges necessary in the forest, their Schmiesser automatic pistols were much more effective than my rifle. They seemed to be firing at random and occasionally the bullets would rip through the trees above me. I hoped I would not be in their path as they headed back to their lines, but their voices grew louder, and I knew they would pass close to me.

I strained my eyes watching for any movement, because I believed that if they saw me first, their heavy firepower would put me at a big disadvantage. I also wished that I were not alone. Actually, there was a GI twenty feet on either side of me, but I could see neither of them, and I knew that they were as lonely as I was. To my relief, the squad of Germans, which I guessed numbered about four or five, seemed to be passing about one hundred feet to my left. I followed their voices with my rifle, and they gradually died out. In our immediate sector, no one had answered the fire of the Germans. I guess our men wanted to see the Germans clearly before opening fire on them. After a while, I returned to my digging.

The enemy lashed us again and again with artillery. There were not so many tree bursts in this area because the trees were young and short, only about ten or twelve feet high, and were probably too flexible at the top to trigger a shell explosion. Tree bursts were particularly bad in the area we had left that morning. When a shell would hit a tree, the shell fragments would pepper the ground with a lethal rain. Even foxholes were not good protection against tree bursts unless they had stout roofs. Our holes were unfinished, so we would lie on the ground shivering while the shells fell around us. One could tell by the scream of an 88mm shell how close it was going to be. A long, drawn-out scream meant that the shell would strike away off some place. The shorter and shriller the scream, the closer the impact. Sometimes the enemy would make a traverse with what seemed like a single gun, and a shell would fall far away. Then another would fall closer, and another still closer, until you felt that the next shell would fall right in the hole with you. It would fall close by, however, with a terrific explosion that would jar your whole body. Then gradually, the shelling would move to another sector.

Patrick L. O'Dea, Grapevine, TX
Company F, 2nd Battalion, 22nd Infantry Regiment

Attacking the Hürtgen

The afternoon was rather mild, and I took the opportunity to clean my rifle since it was getting downright rusty in lots of places, and I began to doubt if it would work when I needed it. After I got it a little cleaner and oiled it, I felt more like a soldier. I was making plans to get a good night's rest with the blankets when the word was passed down that we were going to attack that night. This was really bad news since I hated the thought of fighting in the dark of night. So, we ate our evening meal with a great deal of somber thoughts about what might come later.

At dusk, we gathered into squads and prepared for the advance to our objective. I was in the third squad, and I remember the company commander flying into a rage and whispering furious curses, calling for the third squad. Actually, we were in the right place all the time, but Dan, the squad leader, had not spoken up when the CO called for him. There were only six or seven of us in each squad so we looked more like a couple of squads than a platoon. No wonder the CO got confused. He was in a vile humor when we started out. Incidentally, that was the first time I ever saw him. I never did learn his name.

We started out walking in a single file, following the perimeter of the forest religiously. It was a grueling march. The ground was soft and thick with mud. I had a pair of galoshes on, and these made walking difficult, and with my bad feet I was in no shape for easy walking, much less this kind of hike. We were supposed to keep five yards distance between us, and this was not easy. When we walked through patches of the forest it was impossible to keep five yards and still maintain contact with the man in front of you. And, if there was one thing I didn't want to do, it was to lose contact with the man in front of me. I had horrible visions of doing this and thus leading the scores of troops who followed me into some kind of a terrible trap or ambush.

To say that this march was tiring would be a miracle of understatement. It was a march through forest and bush, up slimy hills where roots and low brush tripped your feet and sent you crashing to the ground. It meant walking through forests, straining your eyes to see the man you were following, only to have a pine bough set in motion by the man in front come springing back to lash you across the eyes or in the mouth. It meant having strong branches reach out and try to knock the rifle from your shoulders. It meant plodding along gullies and stream bottoms where the soft mud allowed your feet to sink six or eight inches, and then closed over them like an earthen vise from which you struggled, cursing, to release your foot with a squishing gurgle. Every now and then, we would come to a flat area where, to our right, a large plain lay quiet and foreboding in the soft light of the newly risen moon. Occasionally we would stumble over a body. I hoped they were all Germans.

At one time we were moving along the side of a hill with as much stealth as possible when a young, clear, American voice rang out from higher on the hill, "Who's that walking along there?"

We were startled to hear the voice from what I thought was a "no man's island." No one answered. The voice came again, more insistent.

"Are you guys GIs?"

Still no one answered him, and I glanced around impatiently to see if the sergeant was nearby and whether he was going to answer. I didn't want to answer myself, but I was scared that the young soldier might start firing at us. I told the man behind me what I thought, and I could hear whispers along the line. The boy's voice came again, and I could still hear whispers. The boy's voice called once more, this time almost pleading, "If you guys don't answer me, I'm going to open up with this machine gun."

That was the final straw. Since the sergeant didn't seem to know what to say, a whole chorus of voices went up telling him, "Shut up—we're GIs."

I don't know how long we walked, but it was something more than an hour, maybe an hour and a half. We stopped once for a rest and then moved out again.

The second time that we stopped, I sat on the muddy ground, pretty well exhausted. After a few minutes I revived a little and started looking around.

I was surprised to see a house about one hundred yards away, faintly outlined in the moonlight. A few seconds later I heard the sound of many approaching footsteps. A group of German prisoners appeared, being herded by some GIs on their way to the rear. I realized then that we must be near our objective. This was the first time all evening that I had any idea of what we were supposed to do that night. Since there were no sounds of a battle nearby, I guessed that there was a village close by that some other company had already taken and that we would be used as reinforcements to hold the village. Sure enough, the sergeant came back soon and told us we were lucky because the village had been taken, and we wouldn't have to do any fighting that night. This news made me a bit happier, for I was very tired and my feet pained me considerably.

At a signal from the sergeant we started out again, and in a short time we emerged from the forest into a small village that had been destroyed by the war. All the houses had been severely damaged: some were burned out shells; others had huge holes in them. It was a typical German village, the first I had ever seen. None of the houses was more than three stories, and most of them appeared to be well built. A couple of the houses were still burning, and we ran past them as fast as possible because our silhouettes made fine targets against a background of flame. I saw a number of GIs throughout the village, but not one German civilian. I assumed that they all had fled the area long before the battle started. Other groups of German soldiers were being returned to our rear. Most of them looked dirty and exhausted.

We continued through the village and were ordered to take up positions on the outskirts, at a point from which we had a clear view of several hundred yards of bare ground. It was a good place to set up a line against possible German counterattack. At this point, the sergeant learned that several of our platoon had become separated and he got mad and went back through the town yelling for them.

Having found most of them, he came back and started assigning us spots to dig in. We were still tired from our hike, and none of us wanted to spend three hours or so digging a foxhole. But the thought of a possible German attack in the morning made up my mind for me. Our platoon started digging in about fifteen yards from a road that separated us from the village, which was probably called Grosshau. After we had been digging about twenty minutes, I realized that a tree only a few feet away might be a source of danger, because a shell hitting it would send a deadly shower of shrapnel into our hole. I remarked about this to Steve, my 21-year-old foxhole buddy. We were halfheartedly considering digging in at some less dangerous place, but I hated to have all that work on the present hole go to waste. The dilemma was solved from an unexpected quarter when the sergeant came over and ordered the whole platoon to fall back about forty yards to the other side of the road and dig in there instead. There was the usual grumbling, but I was willing enough. The area was pockmarked with shell holes, and most pairs of men selected a shell hole for conversion to a foxhole because it meant less digging. The hole that my partner and I got was sort of deceiving because we had to do a lot more digging than I estimated. The ground was rocky and our entrenching tools would only go an inch before they hit a rock. We both dug silently for a while. It was only about 2030 hours, and we had been in Grosshau for less than an hour.

I suppose it took the enemy a little time to dispatch messages to his rear echelon informing them of his withdrawal from Grosshau. They, in turn, would instruct their artillery to blast the town before we had a chance to dig in. The German artillery did just that, and soon the first salvo of 88s came screaming in. We dived for our half-completed holes and huddled in terror as the great shells exploded near us. In a few minutes the barrage was over and we jumped up and resumed digging with increased fervor. I wondered anxiously when the next barrage would be hurled at us. The time between barrages would be a good index of how frequently we would be blasted for the rest of the night.

As daylight came, it was time for the attack. To my surprise about a dozen GIs lined up on the road and headed as a skirmish line toward the enemy. I supposed they were another platoon of our company. One fell wounded before they had advanced a dozen yards. Our sergeant gave the order to move out and we followed about fifty yards behind the other platoon. Enemy shells began to fall and small arms fire began. Two German soldiers jumped up and surrendered about forty yards in front of us; they were manning a machine gun. I was amazed that the enemy had been that close to us all night. In a few minutes the enemy shells had disrupted our formation so that we and the other platoon were all mixed up together. Our own heavy weapons platoon observers were with us, and they passed back orders to raise or lower our mortar fire. It seemed to me that their orders were being garbled, as they were being passed back orally, and I expected our own mortars to fall on us. I don't know whether they did, but we were brought to a halt just a few hundred yards from the town. The artillery shells and mortars fell on us in such numbers that the men hugged the ground for safety. Most of us were able to find shell holes that were shallow and dish like, but they did afford some protection. Small arms fire would frequently come our way, but it was not as dangerous as the shellfire.

At one point during a heavy shelling, I noticed large lumps of what I thought were clods of dirt falling around me. A few of them hit me although they did not hurt me. One that fell looked like a potato, but on closer inspection, it turned out to be a turnip. I must have been lying in somebody's turnip field. It occurred to me that the army might have to send my mother a telegram saying, "Your son was killed by a large turnip." I still had my sense of humor.

Our platoon became more and more scattered. We were mixed in with people from other platoons. It was hard for our sergeant to pass orders along to his platoon. During a short lull, after we had endured a long artillery bombardment, the sergeant crawled over to me and some of the other platoon members and said he wanted us to move forward about a hundred and fifty yards because the enemy seemed to have his guns zeroed in on this spot. A few minutes later the sergeant yelled out the command to get started. Several of us jumped up and followed him, dodging shell holes and changing direction every few steps to prevent a sniper from getting a bead on us. When artillery shells exploded near us, we would hit the ground. Some people say it's too late to hit the ground when you hear the shell explode, but that's what we did. I was able to keep the sergeant in view and tried to follow him closely. In a few more minutes, it seemed to me, the sergeant and I were the only men who were moving forward. The others seemed to be lost. Finally, the sergeant stopped running, hit the ground, and motioned me to join him.

"Stay here," he said, "I'm going back to get the other men. I'll be back in a few minutes." All I could say was "OK," but I wasn't happy about it because it seemed to me that the sergeant and I had made the deepest penetration of the German lines in that sector. I could imagine a squad of Germans rushing up to me, blasting away with their burp guns. I fired at where I thought the Germans were likely to be dug in, but I could see no action there.

Sure enough, the sergeant returned in a little while with other men from our platoon. My foxhole buddy from the night before, Steve, dropped into a shell hole not far from mine, close enough so that we could talk. After each nearby, heavy shelling, we would rise up to see if the other had been hit. The shelling continued to be heavy, and I was convinced that the Germans had us under direct observation. Surprisingly, I did not see any of our tanks. I thought that this terrain would be excellent for tank support of an infantry advance. The tanks could smash machine gun emplacements and even bunkers that were holding us up. Off in the distance, to the north, I thought I could see GIs from other companies also trying to advance in the face of withering artillery.

Finally, during a severe bombardment by 88mm shells, I felt a sharp blow on my arm as if someone had hit me with his fist. I was lying in a shallow shell hole holding my helmet on with my hands when it happened. As usual, I was praying for protection from the shells. I was pretty sure that a shell fragment had hit me. I could still wiggle my fingers and move my arm, so I thought I was not in immediate danger from the wound. After awhile, I could feel blood running down my arm and I stuck my other hand inside my shirt. I raised my head and asked my buddy if he had been hit. Sure enough, he had. The shelling continued, and I decided it was too dangerous to try to go back to the village and look for a medic. My buddy agreed, so we remained.

Our attack was probably part of a general advance by a battalion or two in our sector, but it seemed clear that our attack had stalled. None of the men near me were trying to advance. We were all pinned down by artillery. Small arms fire swept over us at times, but the artillery was causing the casualties. As far as I could see, no American units were making any progress as the afternoon dragged on. The last time I saw the sergeant, he was about twenty yards to my left in a shell hole. I debated whether to wait until dark and then try to return to the village or whether it would be smarter to start back right away. But the artillery shells bursting around us made me postpone any attempt to go back to the village.

The hours dragged by. I felt sure that the wound was not bad and that I would not bleed to death. As evening approached my buddy and I agreed that we should start back for the village and try to stick together. We waited for a lull in the shelling and then jumped up and headed for the village. It was a long run. We would hit the ground every hundred feet or so and sooner, if shells fell nearby. It was hard to maintain contact with each other. I left my rifle in a shell hole. While running, I noticed that my web belt with an entrenching tool hanging on it and a canteen and several clips of ammunition was slowing me down. I had already discarded my bandoleers of ammo. At one point, I jumped up and looked for my buddy to do the same, but I couldn't see him. I hesitated for a few seconds and resumed running toward the village. I met a GI who was lying on the ground, badly wounded and promised to get a medic for him. As I reached the village edge, a mortar shell seemed to explode a few yards away from me. I was running at the time and couldn't believe that I wasn't wounded. I saw a red cross and headed for it. The officer in charge, a doctor I suppose, made me take off my jacket and open my shirt so that he could see the wound. He then told me to wait for transportation back. I told him about the wounded man out on the field. Here in the village, there was a semblance of normality; jeeps and trucks came and went and men walked around…but carefully.

After a while, a jeep drove up to the aid station, and I was sent back to another aid station about a quarter mile back. The medic examined me, and since my wound was not life threatening he offered me a cup of coffee and told me to sit down and wait for the truck going back to the next aid station. The coffee was hot and revived my spirit. Eventually a truck drove up. By now it was dark, and several wounded men were helped into the truck. We drove in the darkness for what seemed to be a long time and were taken, finally, to a building where our names and other information was taken. We were given more coffee and some doughnuts, I think. Then we took another truck ride in the darkness and ended up in town, probably in Belgium, and were taken to a field hospital. About one hundred wounded men were there waiting for some kind of treatment. Most were American, but a few were German. One German soldier sat on a chair with his chest bare and a neat bullet hole where his heart was supposed to be. A lot of us wondered how he could still be alive. He sat up straight and never whimpered. Before long, he was taken by a medic to the operating room.

My feet were hurting, and I thought the warmth of the building had something to do with it. At least I knew that sooner or later somebody would treat my feet as well as my wound. Eventually my name was called, and I was led to an operating room. I got to see my wound in the bright light. A shell fragment had entered my right arm near the shoulder. It missed the bone and had partly exited on the other side of the arm. I could see the metal fragment sticking out of the arm. The doctor told me that he would put me to sleep and would remove the shell fragment and dress the wound. He and his helpers gave me sodium pentothal, and I drifted to sleep almost immediately.

I woke up the following morning in a ward with about two dozen other GI patients. Someone was shaking me and telling me to wake up. Someone else was handing me a cup of coffee telling me that it would wake me up. Someone was holding me in a sitting position, but I kept going back to sleep. They kept talking to me and asking me questions and trying to make me wake up. One nurse was being helped by the GI patients from nearby beds who were trying to awaken me. After I was wide awake, they asked me my name, where I was from, and what outfit I was with. One man, who I later found out was a sergeant from the 29th Division, asked me where I was when I was wounded. All I could say was that I was in "the woods."

He then told me that it was the Hürtgen Forest, and that it was a major German defensive point that protected Cologne.

So, for the first time, I learned where my adventure had taken place. I was very dirty, and a ward man brought me a towel, soap, and water. I cleaned myself as best I could and felt a lot better. Shaving was next, and that turned out to be a painful process. My face had been caked with mud for ten days, and it had been ground into the skin. The razor was army issue and not very sharp to begin with. The ward man helped me all he could, and after a painful hour, my face looked a lot better. That ten-day growth of beard was tougher than I had ever dreamed it could be.

Wesley Trindal, Edinburg, VA
Company F, 2nd Battalion, 22nd Infantry Regiment

On December 1, 1944, Wes Trindal was selected to accompany a ten-man recon patrol to find out why the Germans had suddenly become quiet in their sector of the Hürtgen Forest. Their mission was to find out what the Germans were up to and report the "5 Ws"—the who, what, where, when, and why information—back to the command post. They were not to engage the enemy, draw fire, or get killed. As they came out of the forest into a narrow, triangular-shaped, open glen, the Germans opened up on them with three machine gun nests in a deadly crossfire. Soon German and American artillery fire started raining down into the trees they had retreated to. The slit trench Wes had jumped into protected him from the machine gun fire but not from the deadly shrapnel of the artillery tree bursts. The following picks up with what happened next. —Bob Babcock

Stuck in No-Man's-Land
From Wes Trindal's book *And Then There Were None*

About six hours later, just as dusk was descending, I came back into the land of the living dead. (I have no recall of any of these following events. I recall some things that took place the next day. The doctors in the hospital told me about it all, afterwards. This was weeks later, after I had gone though the truth serum treatment.) Again, I had a close call with death, but at what price? I found that I could not move. I hurt all over. I had an awful headache—a throbbing pain that made me nauseated. All I could do was to lie still in my slit trench. It was colder and a freezing rain had begun. After a while, I was able to move enough to sit up. I pulled my rolled-up raincoat and overcoat to me. I needed the warmth. From the number of bullet holes through both of them, the Germans must have concentrated their collective firepower, aiming at my coats. In doing so, they had missed me in my slit trench. And again, I was alive, but not exactly well. Death had visited just inches away. And again,

God saved me from being killed. In combat, and in my condition, little irritants become major ones, all out of proportion. In shooting up my coats, the Germans and their bullets had disintegrated my special salt-shaker, the one I had carried with me from the States. Now it was glass, salt, metal top, and a shredded left-hand overcoat pocket. That seemed to make me very angry and flustered. I would be needing a salt shaker to flavor those U.S. Army KRations. I didn't reason that I would have to get out of this situation first. No KRations were in my immediate future.

Painfully, I put on my overcoat and raincoat to get protection from the cold and rain. Next, I was surprised to find my water canteen on my cartridge belt was completely empty. I had just filled it that morning and we had been too busy to drink much water. That was another major crises. I crawled around the trees and up the ridgeline to the right. There were four foxholes and three dead GIs. I discovered that their canteens were also empty. I crawled over to the left. I found five other foxholes, holes that held four more dead GIs. The recon patrol was wiped out.

Someone had collected all of the precious water from all of those dead corpses—including myself while I was knocked unconscious. Then it became obvious. It sunk in that I was the only living person up on this ridge on the American side. Also, no one was shooting at me from the German lines as I was crawling around. Was there no one on the German front lines, either? What was this sector I was alone in? I was all alone on top of this ridge of death in No-Man's-Land.

It was getting dark on the northeast side of the Hürtgenwald. Night would soon come. The German artillery lobbed an occasional shell onto the ridge and then, one would come in from the American lines. Tit for tat. The cold rain began to increase and then freeze. I continued to crawl toward the left. On beyond the last of our patrol's foxholes, I located the German machine gun bunker. It was dark by then. By feel, I found the entrance at the rear and crawled inside. It was empty. The bunker was a large hole in the ground covered with a layer of logs, topped with earth, and covered with sod. It gave a lot of protection, not only against shelling, but also against the cold German rain and the colder German winter. The darkness and fatigue nullified my pain and fear. That night passed in fitful spasms. Cycles first in peaceful sleep and then awake in terror plus raw pain. Each time I woke up, the painful hell of being alive became greater than the fatigue. But then, the fatigue and shock overcame the pain and I fell back into a fitful self-healing sleep. Mrs. Trindal's Soldier Boy had sure got himself into a mess he couldn't get out of this time. Praying helped, but this was more than my inexperienced prayers could change. Why didn't I pay more attention to Mom's advice when I was younger? Now, she knew how to pray and get God's attention. I needed something for the pain.

The morning of December 2, 1944 came with more things falling out of the sky. First there was rain, the natural German water-based type, and second, there were shells, both German and American high-explosive artillery types. The Wehrmacht didn't want the ridge any more, so they shelled it so that the Americans would not have access. The U.S. Army didn't want it, so they shelled it so that the Germans couldn't retake it. I wanted it to rest and gain my strength back, but then, I did not have any say in the matter. I was just a private. Meantime, I stayed right there in that German bunker. I was nauseated—having had nothing to eat, they were just the dry heaves. My head throbbed with intense pain. The exploding shells just made my head pain unbearable—but there was no relief. With no choices, I tolerated that unbearable pain! Again, I was finding out that in this life there are so many unacceptable things, which have to be accepted. My right knee was so swollen as to be useless, it refused to bend. The rest of my body just complained all over. This sure was No-Man's-Land, in the truest sense. How did I get into this mess? And, more to the point, how was I going to get out of it?

I knew that I had better start thinking of something else. This string of thoughts was no good. I was just making things worse in my own mind. In the shape I was in, I certainly was not able to crawl for any distance away from there. Besides, shells were going off outside. I had to get my mind off of the situation. I had to think positive! I remember pulling out my billfold and going through each item repeatedly, over and over. That eased the situation. I reminisced with the photograph of Dad, Mom, and our car. Dad was in his army Major's uniform, and Mom was in her pretty, gray stripe suit with the perky hat on the side of her head. In the photo, they were standing beside the Hudson automobile....

My Mom taught me that the mind and prayer can conquer pain by concentrating on other things. At least, my mind was still functioning and still under my control. Prayer led to daydreams. I was an expert at daydreaming in school. Daydreams about the past kept me occupied; the fun times, my parents, our travels as a family, schools and those school-girls, and dates in Blue Babe (our Hudson). This led to fantasies about the future; college, cars, girls, and jobs. My dream was for a job at the car factories in Detroit, Michigan, designing and engineering new cars. I knew I had to think myself into "my own little world." The situation in this bunker and this world outside was an experience over which I had no control. I learned I could, however, control my inner thoughts by concerted effort.

My mind slipped into the present. But the idea was to keep my mind off of my dead buddies and my desperate circumstances. Ignore the present. Let it disappear. I couldn't fix it, anyhow. During the loss of control, I remember asking myself a flurry of questions....

"Where are our front lines now? Should I stay here until the U.S. Army troops take the ridge? What if the German troops retake it? Shouldn't I try to crawl out? Would I get very far in the shelling? What if I got wounded out there and couldn't crawl any farther? NOW! Just cut that out!"

I had to bring a halt to this runaway, mental torment of war. I forced myself to restore mind control again. Positive thoughts were needed to bring a halt to the torment. And so, another day and another night passed by in the bunker with more of the same—pain and fitful sleep, raw fear conquered with positive mind control, shelling and pain alleviated by moments of quiet remembering. Since the nausea had subsided, hunger and thirst added to my problems.

German Soldiers

The third day in the bunker, December 3, 1944, I was partly asleep and partly awake. Just at dusk, two people suddenly sliding in through the entrance awakened me. They were escaping another one of the intensive shelling periods. They surprised me and I surprised them. In the pitch-black darkness inside the bunker, we had no way of knowing who was who. I pointed my rifle toward what I thought might be the bunker entrance and yelled at the intruders.

"Who goes there?"

"Two German soldiers." A voice answered in perfect English, and continued, "Are you an American soldier?"

"Yes," I responded. In the darkness, I fully expected to be shot. I moved my M1 rifle muzzle toward the sound of the voice, ready to empty the clip of ammo at the source.

"We want to surrender to the Americans," the German soldier continued. "Will you help us get to the American lines safely?"

"OK, I will. Come on in," I answered.

They had already entered because of the shelling. Obviously, we had two mutual goals in common, first that of staying alive during the shelling going on outside, and, then second, getting safely to the American lines. That was logical. They moved around in the bunker while I moved against the far wall. I wondered how all of this was going to turn out. Training for combat had taught us to look out for tricks—stay alive by shooting first. On the other hand, the Geneva Convention said to never shoot surrendering enemy soldiers. I had seen, first hand, never to scare them either. That's what started this mess. What was I to do? One of the German soldiers had a piece of a candle. He lit it and stuck it on an empty tin can. He set it in the middle of the floor. Then, he quickly closed the cloth draped over the entrance. We all saw each other. These super-soldiers looked just like the rest of us.

One of the German soldiers was an older man, probably in his forties or fifties. He spoke English fluently with a definite English accent. He said he had been on the Eastern Front during most of the war since 1939. He was a German Army translator, speaking Polish, Russian, and many Slav languages, in addition to English. When the German took off his helmet, I saw a round face that was topped with brown hair, having a lot of gray hair about the temples. He was stout and of medium stature: I'd guess he was about one hundred-eighty pounds and stood about five feet eight inches tall. Then, his young German friend was my age, about nineteen years old. With his helmet off, he was a typical blue-eyed, blond-haired German. His eyes transmitted fatigue and fear, the same as mine did. He was about a hundred thirty five pounds and stood about six feet tall, the same as I. He couldn't speak any more English than I could speak German. He and I were alike!

The translator told me that his companion had been a cadet-pilot in the German Air Force, the Luftwaffe, until a month ago. Then, he and some of his classmates had been transferred into the German Infantry. The blond German had taken the transfer very hard. He figured it was a reflection on his performance in school. The older German was trying to convince him that it stemmed from the downturn of the war. All the German Infantry needed was warm bodies to shoot at the attacking Allied troops, which were swarming into Germany on the wide, Western Front. War is sure ironic. That was exactly the same reason we replacements were up there on the U.S. Army side. They needed warm bodies in the 4th Infantry Division to shoot at the defending Germans. We were to replace casualties. We had a crusade, though. We were overseas here to stop the German Third Reich and the Axis Powers from conquering all of Europe—and tomorrow, the world. The older German soldier and I fraternized freely. At that time, there was a $65 fine imposed by the U.S. Army on any GIs caught fraternizing with the enemy.

There was no one else in this No-Man's-Land to report our fraternizing. So, in time we became friendly, not as soldiers on opposite sides, but as human beings, enduring a common danger of war. We got into quite a serious discussion of this particular war through which we were living. From what the older German had seen, he concluded that Fuhrer Hitler, the Nazi Party, and the Third German Reich were losing the war….

The young German opened the round food canister he was carrying. From its depths, he produced and unwrapped real Danish butter. Around the edges, he had placed a few pieces of hard candies. Then, he extracted another wrapper containing blue-Roquefort-type cheese. The older German opened his overcoat and produced over half a loaf of dense, black, German bread. I unsheathed my U.S. Army trench knife—the same one that had done such a good job making our forty-andeight boxcar stove. I suggested that cutting the bread into slices would be better than tearing it into hunks, as the German was going to do. With the knife, I sliced the loaf of bread into half-inch slices. I spread on a wipe of butter and crowned it with a crumble of that good cheese. We each had a slice and washed it down with the water they passed around from their canteens. That was surely, in-depth, German-American fraternization.

After being so long without food or water, I felt that this was a wonderful, delicious feast. The heavy, tough-textured bread provided the body for the sweet butter and the pungent, biting Roquefort cheese, all in perfect balance. This was a gastronomical delight, right in the middle of a full-blown war! Here we were. Enemies engaged in breaking—technically slicing—bread together on a ridge deep in No-Man's-Land that neither side wanted! With food in our stomachs, we went to sleep. Wasn't I afraid of getting my throat slit in the middle of the night? No! At that point, I just didn't care.

Dawn came. It was now December 4. At first, things were quiet on this ridge that was our Hell on Earth. All three of us stiffly crawled out of the bunker into the dark gray light of another overcast, winter's day. I was still in poor shape. Even with the two German soldiers helping, I was in poor condition to walk out of there. My head ached and pounded, my back was in agony, and my right knee was throbbing and would not bend. Moving around on my feet was painful! Just at that moment, our decisions, regarding local travel arrangement, were made for us. Heavy shelling started. Again, both the Germans and the Americans must have thought that the other side was attempting to occupy this ridge. Again, they collectively targeted it. Quickly, we headed back down into the bunker. For me, the feeling of fear rapidly overpowered those major ache and pain troubles of only a second before. It was another case of my mind over my matter. The concussions of exploding shells, followed by numerous shrapnel "thuds" and "plunks" into the sod and log cover on our bunker, said it all. This plainly told us we would have been killed out there had we remained. Now, we were imprisoned back in the bunker, listening to the dueling artillery shells bursting outside. It was quite an impressive orchestration being played. It was not music to our ears. The percussion instruments lacked rhythm. This was no 1812 Overture. It was way too loud. It was way too deadly, too.

Meanwhile, I told the older German my secret method of taking my mind off of the war by going through my billfold. So, we fraternized, in spite of U.S. Army orders. I showed the Germans the photographs of my Mom and Dad. I pulled out pictures of our 1941 Hudson car and went into detail on how I saved and scraped enough money for installing a hand-operated spotlight through the left front windshield A-post.....

We went very, very easy in consuming the Germans' supply of food and water. The older German considered going down from the ridge into a ravine and getting all the canteens filled with water from the creek. We determined that the risks of getting hit from the random shelling were not worth it. We'd just wait on drinking water until we got worse off. We'd wait for a longer lull in the shelling.

The sky got darker and it began to rain, again. The older German spread my raincoat across the back entrance and collected rainwater in a cup as it dripped and drizzled through the biggest of the bullet holes. The rest of the day, we shared a couple of cups of good rain water, even if it was more than a little salty and gritty. All day long, we also shared the barrages of German and American artillery. A siege of shelling takes a lot out of a person, no matter if German or American. By dusk, we were certainly beginning to feel the wear and tear of this day!

That night, we had company. Two other German soldiers stopped by our bunker for a visit. The older German went part way out of the entrance to talk with the newcomers. The older German soldier filled the entrance hole so these new arrivals would neither be able to see nor hear us from outside. For what seemed like a long, long time, we silently waited while the three outside talked in German. At times, the tones became excited. I worried that I might be turned in as a Prisoner of War (POW). Finally, the two Germans departed back into the night. The older German slid back in our bunker. He was scared! He passed that fear on to us. The two German soldiers outside had told him they were lost and they were trying to get back to the German front lines. He told them that this bunker was a secret, advanced listening post. They must not stay. He directed them down off of our ridge toward the east and the German lines, cautioning them neither to discuss nor to give this location away. To us, the older German added that the two, "lost," German soldiers were likely to be members of the dreaded SS Troops, the Schutzstaffeln. They could be merely acting as if they were lost. We had potential problems. If the SS Troopers discovered unauthorized German soldiers too far ahead of the German front lines, and especially, if Germans and Americans were together, no questions were asked, all were shot. The older German saved all of our lives by keeping the two Germans out of our bunker and sending them on their way down off the ridge. Any German-American fraternization could prove to be very costly. One side imposed a $65 fine. The other side just shot those involved. I was so glad that the older German knew the correct procedures of these situations. Very uneasily, we all went back to sleep.

We were out of food and we only had a small sip of water left in the collecting pan. Our troubles were mounting and our situation was desperate. We decided it was time to get the hell out of there.

On December 5, the dreary dawn divulged that a layer of wet snow had covered the ground that night. Soon, it turned to freezing rain. It was the bonechilling kind where you just can't get warm. After a meager breakfast of the last of the German bread, we were out of food and we only had a small sip of water left in the collecting pan. Our troubles were mounting and our situation was desperate. We mutually decided it was past time to get the hell out of there, brave the shelling, go through the dangerous forest, and travel in what we hoped was to the west. We knew that the westerly direction led towards the American front lines. Our contingency plans included that we all keep our rifles at the ready, not knowing what we might encounter. There was a good possibility, out there, that the two Germans from the night before would return. They would be likely to investigate after they found out that none of their troops had authorized any advanced listening posts.

Sooner or later, one of the hundreds of shells was bound to make a direct hit on our bunker. We were out of food and water. Also, we were running out of good luck. No deliveries of food, water, or luck could be expected from either the Germans or the Americans. There would be no friendly American platoon sergeant dropping by this bunker with "Breakfast" K-ration boxes in his hand and a "Good Morning" on his lips. I had to go, despite the physical ailments. The strong incentives to get the hell out of there greatly overwhelmed the self-preservation incentives to remain undercover in the bunker. More mind over matter.

In 1851, Mr. John Soule was a newspaperman who worked in Indiana. Mr. Soule's advice at that time to the unemployed people of New York City was, "Go West, young man." His phrase became popular after the prominent newspaper publisher, Horace Greeley, editor of The New Yorker, copied the phrase into his magazine. They both were referring to the Western Frontier of the United States. Now, we took their advice. We vacated the bunker premises, and headed west to our destiny.

Leaving No-Man's Land

It was about noon that the three of us left the safety of the German bunker, one American GI and two German soldiers. The older German supported me. I hobbled along on my one good leg. We all were carrying our weapons, depending on whom we encountered. We had no plans to engage in a firefight with either side. We were to solve that problem when and if it came up. The hardest part for me was when we passed the foxholes of my buddies, the dead GIs from the recon patrol. I couldn't look. We went past the "sleeping" GIs and got down off of that ridge pretty fast. We went through another ravine and climbed to the crest of the next ridge. With the incentive of random, tree-burst shelling going on behind us, I made pretty good time for a cripple. All of this just proves what a person can do when the chips are down. In this case, the chips were of wood, accompanied by deadly, steel shrapnel. All of this was caused from the tree-bursting American and German artillery and mortar shells.

When we got away from the shelling barrage, we slowed and worked our way carefully through the forest. We gingerly observed everything to our front. We stopped and stared intently for any sign of movement. We knew we had to see and recognize anyone else in the forest before they saw us or we would be fired upon. We were coming from No-Man's-Land. Training on both the American and the German sides taught soldiers that it's an area from where only the enemy would emerge. I recall the wonderful sight of American GI helmets poking out of foxholes. We stopped dead in our tracks. The two German soldiers dropped their weapons on the ground. I shouted out to the GIs, who by now spotted us and who immediately had us in their rifle sights. I yelled out!

"Hey! Don't shoot! I'm an American with two German prisoners."

My head exploded from the pain of yelling. Nevertheless, I kept repeating and repeating the yell, so there would be no doubt who we were. No errors, no misunderstandings, no mistakes. The three of us stood there very still, while I yelled my head off! In front line combat situations, it is normally prudent for Infantrymen to shoot first at anything that moves, and then ask identifying questions later. Soldiers tend to live much longer when there are no surprises. Fortunately, this time, no one squeezed off a shot. Soon, we were safe in the American front lines. A couple of GIs took charge of the two German soldiers, who were now POWs. For them, the fighting and killing was over. Two other GIs helped me back to the medic at the Company first aid station, located back from the front lines in an exGerman log bunker. The medic gave me a couple of APC tablets (the U.S. Army's do-it-all equal of aspirin) for the pain.

He dug up a canteen of water and something to eat. The food was a box of very welcome K-Rations. He told me that my outfit, the 22nd

Infantry Regiment, 4th Infantry Division, had been relieved on December 3. The 83rd Infantry Division had taken its place in the front lines. He added that they were expecting a heavily reinforced, counterattack at any time. The thinking was that the Wehrmacht must try to retake the terrain the Americans had gained so dearly since Grosshau. The medic highly recommended that, as soon as I felt able, I should head back to the battalion first aid station in Grosshau. When someone returned to Grosshau for supplies or went to take someone back—wounded GI or prisoner of war—they'd help me get back there too.

I went outside to wait. The medic was attending to other patients with serious wounds. I had spent enough time in another one of those ex-German bunkers. Besides, out in the light of the gray sky, I could see how to open the rations and see what I was eating. The medic's bunker was located just in from the edge of the beet field we had tried so hard to take on November 30. Outside, up the trail from the bunker, well hidden in the forest, was a burned-out, German Tiger tank and, farther on a ways was a log emplacement with a destroyed flak 88mm field artillery gun, that once was wheel mounted.

Now, it all became very clear what we had been up against in trying to cross the beet field. From the German position, I could see how vulnerable we were as we came out of the trenches after the Company Commander egged us forward on the attack. Damn! We were fodder for the German weapons. What targets we made! The German riflemen, machine gunners, tankers, and artillery crew had a clear field of fire on all of us as we advanced. No wonder we had such losses. These two 88mm heavy guns became close support, antipersonnel weapons because of their flat trajectory. The gunners' ability to aim and wipe out each individual GI was demoralizing as hell during our attack....

After a bit, the medic cleaned out his patients and came out of the bunker with hot coffee for both of us. We talked for about half an hour. Two GIs came, helping their buddy to the medic's bunker. The third GI was badly wounded in the thigh. It was a tree-burst shrapnel fragment that was causing a lot of bleeding. The medic went right to work, cleaned the area, treated the wound with sulfa powder, and applied a bandage to slow the bleeding. He asked the soldier's two buddies to get the patched-up GI and me back to the aid station in Grosshau.

So, we headed off, following the edge of the forest. We came to that same deadly beet field, stretched out on our left, where the 22nd Infantry Regiment had been mowed down a few days before. Horrible memories of my buddies being slaughtered were rekindled anew in my mind. I tried to look away from it all. That is a sight, an experience, which a person never forgets.

I was getting woozy, nausea returned with a vengeance, and my legs wouldn't move fast. I told the other three GIs to move on out. The wounded GI needed to get to Grosshau as fast as possible. The two GIs had their hands full aiding the wounded man. I was just slowing them down. I told them I knew the way, now, past the old stone farmhouse and down the road into town. I'd be along at my own, slow speed. A little farther on, I found a log bunker. I went around to the rear entrance and crawled inside. There, my world began spinning out of control and I passed out. I had no idea how long I was peacefully out of the war. On waking, it all came back. Both the Germans and the Americans were shelling each other again....

All I had to do was crawl out, put one foot in front of the other, and maintain a heading for the old stone farmhouse. The one, way off there in the distance. Again, I had very positive reasons and incentives. I needed to get my mind concentrating, my body working, and overcome the nausea and the pains. I had to get back to that aid station in Grosshau. There, I could get more APCs. I followed the edge of the forest and started out across the open beet field to the farmhouse. I had covered a little over one third of the distance to the farmhouse when a German soldier, somewhere over on my left, opened up with his burp gun. The German burp gun, with its high rate of fire, sprays a deadly swath of bullets in a short time.

Despite the urgency of this situation, my body and my legs just would not respond to my mind's very excited commands. It was like a movie in slow motion. I placed one foot in front of the other, made it to a shell crater, and dived in. On the way to the hole, I remember seeing the burp gun's bullets kick up the dirt. The German gunner sprayed past me once. With another burst, the burp-gun bullets returned past me a second time, and even another burst returned a third time. It was a Divine Miracle that none of those many bullets touched me. It was as if I had the protection of an invisible shield, unmistakably the hand of God. Another time, my candidacy for certain death had come and gone. I felt like a fugitive from the law of averages.

It was getting dark in the shell-crater when I regained consciousness the second time and returned into this living hell. It took a good while for me to figure out where I was, what had happened, and why. Finally, it all came back. I was on my way to the rear, away from all this. I clawed my way out of the shell hole and got to my feet. No burp gun fire. It was hard going, stumbling across that beet field at dusk. I could barely make out the shadow of the old stone farmhouse. It was just my luck to become tangled in barb wire before I got to the corner of the house. With the pitch-blackness of the cloudy night and my state of exhaustion and pain, this was too much. I sat down and cried.

In my imagination, I just "knew" that the Germans had booby-trapped the barb wire entanglement before they retreated. In my efforts to pull loose, I was certain to actuate the trip wire and a "Bouncing Betty" antipersonnel mine would ignite. These mines popped up off the ground to about chest high. They exploded into a spray of shrapnel, killing all within range. Here I was. I had almost reached Grosshau before I met my death. So close, but yet so far. Finally, I collected my wits about me. Only I could get myself out of this situation. In the darkness, I felt out each barb and unhooked it from my clothes. In time, I had freed myself. I was still alive. No mines exploded. Free at last, I moved around the side of the house and headed off in what I remembered was the direction of Grosshau.

Out of the night, two medics came upon me. They were on their way to the front lines to get more wounded out under the cover of darkness. They had heard I was out there, but it was likely that I had been killed in that burp-gun fire. When no movement had come from the shell crater, they knew that I was another goner. Those two wonderful medics assisted me down the drive into Grosshau and to the battalion first aid station. It was located in a partly destroyed building on the northwest side of the main street, down in the basement. The place was jam-packed with wounded GIs. The medics led me to a stretcher and had me lie down. Other medics gave me painkilling APCs again. Someone brought me a cup of hot soup and a cup of hot coffee, both delicious. However, the icing on the cake (pun fully and literally intended) was to come. Someone was handing out slices of the best chocolate cake I have ever eaten, before or since. That hunk of cake had about three-fourths of an inch of chocolate icing on the top. It was that delicious, sweet, chocolate icing that every child loves. It seems a thoughtful cook in the rear echelon area, had baked this cake just for this first aid station in the Hürtgen Forest. Then, an equally thoughtful ambulance driver had just as carefully delivered the cake, over almost impassible roads, that night to Grosshau. And just by coincidence, I had made it to the battalion first aid station on this very night, at the same time as the cake.

Finally, a medic questioned me and filled out a medical diagnosis tag. Then, a doctor looked me over. He found and entered on the tag that I had a possible concussion, combat fatigue, a swollen knee, and two bad cases of trench foot. With all of that wrong, I dropped off to sleep. I was awakened in the early hours of the next morning. All night long, ambulances had gathered up the more seriously wounded from the first aid station and had taken them to the nearby U.S. Army 130th General Hospital in Ciney, Belgium. I was included in this next load. The medics strapped another GI and me onto our stretchers and loaded us, one over the other, on the roadside of a three-quarter-ton, 4x4, Dodge WC-54, Ambulance Truck. About four or five walking-wounded GIs were loaded next. They were seated sideways on the curbside bench seat. Despite the expert driving ability of our ambulance driver, the ride out of the Hürtgen Forest to Ciney was rough. The other GIs and I winced with pain as the truck eased through potholes and slid and lurched in the ruts. One of the seated GIs had to stretch out his leg to ease his pain. He laid his leg across my legs. But there was nothing either one of us could do about it. We were on our way to the hospital. Soon, this ordeal would be over. We were just glad to be alive. Of an Infantryman's' choices, we all face Heaven, Hell, or the Hospital, the three Hs! For us, thank God, it was the third H, the Hospital. With all of the suffering and the pain, most of us in the ambulance had drawn faces. Faces that one sees only on old, combat infantrymen. We were all survivors. We were still alive, and we appreciated it very much. Thanks, God!

John K. Lester, Stone Ridge, NY
Battery B, 29th Field Artillery Battalion

No Regrets—Just Memories

As a member of Battery B, 29th Field Artillery (part of a forward observer party), I sometimes think about the mud and cold of the Hürtgen Forest. I remember at times having chains on all four wheels of my jeep and worrying about whether the enemy would hear the clink of them when I was driving from point to point. I didn't have them on any longer than was necessary. When I did have them on, Technician 4th Class George Doolittle, our motor mechanic, adjusted them so they would be as noiseless as possible. I owe a lot to George. He installed a vertical bar on the front of my jeep to protect me from cables strung across roads. He put extensions on the pedals so he could put sandbags on the front floor, hoping they would protect me if I happened to run on to a mine. If there was anything he could do to my vehicle to make my job safer, he did it.

I remember the crossroads that were zeroed in by the enemy artillery, the dreadful tree bursts from which there was little protection, and the mines, both antitank and antipersonnel. When the infantry was in a holding position, between attacks, the trip between their position and the artillery battery of 105s, was always a nerve-wracking experience. We used the jeep to run communication wire between the positions. We had a reel of wire mounted on the rear of the vehicle for this operation. Sometimes the enemy would infiltrate and plant mines in the so-called roads we used that had previously been cleared by the engineers. I remember one time when the radio operator and I were bracketed by German artillery while we were returning to our unit. We were caught in the open. We had been through that area four or five times before without any problems at all. It was a miracle that we got to cover. That's just an example of how fast situations could change.

A number of the casualties I saw in the Hürtgen Forest were the result of antipersonnel mines. One incident I'll never forget was when a GI stepped on a mine, lost or mangled his foot—and two other GIs trying to help him were injured by the same mine. I sure am glad I wasn't a medic. They had a real rough job. I can't imagine what must have gone through their minds at a time like that. It must have been awful.

One thing that has, and still does, haunt me is wondering how many enemy soldiers and civilians were killed or crippled for life due to the artillery fire that my observers directed on enemy positions. I have had mixed feelings about that over the years. The only consoling thought is that, at the time, it had to be done. It was our job and we did it well. I have no regrets—just memories.

Bill Parfitt, Elmira, NY
Company G, 22nd Infantry Regiment and HQ,
4th Infantry Division

Little Laughter in Those Terrible Days

During the Hürtgen Forest battle, I was in Zweifall, Germany, with the 4th Infantry Division HQ. During one of those terrible seventeen or eighteen days, we had a call from a guard outpost that needed a medic and a jeep to evacuate a wounded man. I was the only one available, so I grabbed the jeep and headed to the bridge on the edge of town where these guys were.

Arriving there, I could hear the guy hollering and found him in a hurry. He was lying face down and refused to roll over. After some minutes of persuasion, we got him turned over, and then he wanted us to check him out as he thought he had lost his "manhood," shall we say. It turned out he had climbed out of his hole to relieve himself and just then a shell dropped near him, and a fragment hit him. He was sure he was a loser! When I informed him this was not so, that he had just lost part of his thumb and a cut in a finger, he jumped to his feet and laughed and laughed as if he was nuts. We got him into the jeep and I took him to a hospital a mile or so from Zweifall. The last I heard was something about a million-dollar wound and his continuing to laugh like he had really gone nuts. There was little laughter in those terrible days, but this was the one that really took the cake.

I had another strange one there in Zweifall as well. The cooks had set up to do business in an old barroom. Someone had been able to get one of those gray-looking rolls of meat that came in one of those cold storage packs. It didn't look like hamburger, but we were looking forward to having it hot. Suddenly, there were shells coming in. One or two came through the roof and filled the room with shrapnel. The loaves of meat lying on the bar were shredded. After the shelling was over, the cooks went at it and desperately tried to find the bits of steel, wood, and such but had to toss the stuff out. We ended up eating either K or C rations that night. The only ones getting hot food that night were the General Staff.

Billy Cater, Cambridge, OH
Service Company, 22nd Infantry Regiment

Thanksgiving in the Hürtgen Forest

During the Hürtgen Forest campaign, I was Services Company commander. The HQ company commander was killed, and I was assigned as Headquarters CO. The personnel wanted to take a patrol to recover his body. I did not approve it and so was not in very good with the troops.

The cooks were trying to prepare turkeys for Thanksgiving dinner. We were under artillery fire from the Krauts—they carved our turkey.

The last available men from our Regiment (I think about 135 cooks, clerks, and truck drivers) were assembled, and we were assigned a sector of the front line with me in charge. We established a line of defense in previously dug foxholes. I was checking positions toward a concrete pillbox with a door, where my company clerk (probably seventeen years old) and a recently decorated truck driver (who was still badly shook up from moving a truck load of ammo that was on fire from a congested area) were standing. The pillbox and our sector came under a heavy shelling with a direct hit. Both men were standing in the door; the company clerk in front was critically wounded and died in the hospital.

From Medal of Honor Citations

Medal of Honor Recipients— Hürtgen Forest

Four of the five Medals of Honor earned by 4th Infantry Division soldiers were earned in the Hürtgen Forest. Following are the citations:

Ray, Bernard J. (Posthumously)

RANK AND ORGANIZATION: First Lieutenant, US Army, Company F, 8th Infantry, 4th Infantry Division.

PLACE AND DATE: Hürtgen Forest near Schevenhutte, Germany, 17 November 1944.

ENTERED SERVICE AT: Baldwin, New York

BORN: Brooklyn, New York

G.O. # 115, 8 December 1945

CITATION: He was platoon leader with Company F, 8th Infantry, on 17 November 1944, during the drive through the Hürtgen Forest near Schevenhutte, Germany. The American forces attacked in wet, bitterly cold weather, over rough, wooded terrain, meeting brutal resistance from positions spaced throughout the forest behind mine fields and wire obstacles. Small arms, machine gun, mortar, and artillery fire caused heavy casualties in the ranks when Company F was halted by a concertina type wire barrier. Under heavy fire, 1st Lieutenant Ray reorganized his men and prepared to blow a path through the entanglement, a task that appeared impossible of accomplishment and from which others tried to dissuade him. With implacable determination to clear the way, he placed explosive caps in his pockets, obtained several bangalore torpedoes, and then wrapped a length of highly explosive primer cord about his body. He dashed forward under direct fire, reached the barbed wire, and prepared his demolition charge as mortar shells, which were being aimed at him alone, came steadily nearer his completelyexposed position. He had placed a torpedo under the wire and was connecting it to a charge he carried when he was severely wounded by a bursting mortar shell.

Apparently realizing that he would fail in his self-imposed mission unless he completed it in a few moments, he made a supremely gallant decision. With the primer cord still wound about his body and the explosive caps in his pocket, he completed a hasty wiring system and unhesitatingly thrust down on the handle of the charger, destroying himself with the wire barricade in the resulting blast. By the deliberate sacrifice of his life, 1st Lieutenant Ray enabled his company to continue its attack, resumption of which was of positive significance in gaining the approaches to the Cologne Plain.

Mabry, George L., Jr.

RANK AND ORGANIZATION: Lieutenant Colonel, US Army, 2nd Battalion, 8th Infantry, 4th Infantry Division.

PLACE AND DATE: Hürtgen Forest near Schevenhutte, Germany, 20 November 1944.

ENTERED SERVICE AT: Sumter, South Carolina

BORN: Sumter, South Carolina

G.O. # 77 September 1945

CITATION: He was commanding the 2nd Battalion, 8th Infantry, in an attack through the Hürtgen Forest near Schevenhutte, Germany, on 20 November 1944. During the early phases of the assault, the leading elements of his battalion were halted by a minefield and immobilized by heavy hostile fire. Advancing alone into the mined area, Lieutenant Colonel Mabry established a safe route of passage. He then moved ahead of the foremost scouts, personally leading the attack, until confronted by a booby-trapped double concertina obstacle. With the assistance of the scouts, he disconnected the explosives and cut a path through the wire. Upon moving through the opening, he observed three enemy in foxholes, whom he captured at bayonet point. Driving steadily forward, he paced the assault against three log bunkers, which housed mutually-supported automatic weapons. Racing up a slope ahead of his men, he found the initial bunker deserted, then pushed on to the second where he was suddenly confronted by nine onrushing enemy. Using the butt of his rifle, he felled one adversary and bayoneted a second, before his scouts came to his aid and assisted him in overcoming the others in hand-to-hand combat. Accompanied by the riflemen, he charged the third bunker under point blank small-arms fire and led the way into the fortification from which he prodded six enemy at bayonet point. Following the consolidation of this area, he led his battalion across three hundred yards of fire-swept terrain to seize elevated ground upon which he established a defensive position which menaced the enemy on both flanks, and provided his regiment a firm foothold on the approach to the Cologne Plain. Lieutenant Colonel Mabry's superlative courage, daring, and leadership in an operation of major importance, exemplify the finest characteristics of the military service.

Garcia, Marcario

RANK AND ORGANIZATION: Staff Sergeant, US Army, Company C, 22nd Infantry, 4th Infantry Division.

PLACE AND DATE: Near Grosshau, Germany, 27 November 1944.

ENTERED SERVICE AT: Sugarland, Texas

BORN: 20 January 1920, Villa de Castano, Mexico

G.O. # 74, 1 September 1954

CITATION: While an acting squad leader of Company B, 22nd Infantry, on 27 November 1944, near Grosshau, Germany, he single-handedly assaulted two enemy machine gun emplacements. Attacking prepared positions on a wooded hill, which could be approached only through meager cover, his company was pinned down by intense machine gun fire and subjected to a concentrated artillery and mortar barrage. Although painfully wounded, he refused to be evacuated and, on his own initiative, crawled forward alone until he reached a position near an enemy emplacement. Hurling grenades, he boldly assaulted the position, destroyed the gun, and with his rifle killed three of the enemy who attempted to escape. When he rejoined his company, a second machine gun opened fire and again the intrepid soldier went forward, utterly disregarding his own safety. He stormed the position and destroyed the gun, killed three more Germans, and captured four prisoners. He fought on with his unit until the objective was taken and only then did he permit himself to be removed for medical care. Staff Sergeant (then private) Garcia's conspicuous heroism, his inspiring, courageous conduct, and his complete disregard for his personal safety wiped out two enemy emplacements and enabled his company to advance and secure its objective. (It is said by those who were there that when President Truman put the Medal of

Honor around Marcario Garcia's neck during a White House ceremony after the war, he said, "I'd rather have earned this Medal than be President of the United States.")

Cano, Pedro

RANK AND ORGANIZATION: Private, US Army, Company C, 8th Infantry, 4th Infantry Division.

PLACE AND DATE: Near Schevenhutte, Germany, 2-3 December 1944.

ENTERED SERVICE DATE: 1944

BORN: 19 June 1920, La Morita, Mexico

(Initially awarded as a Distinguished Service Cross in 1945, PVT Cano's award was elevated to the Medal of Honor in a ceremony at the White House on 18 March 2014)

CITATION: For conspicuous gallantry and intrepidity at the risk of his life above and beyond the call of duty:

Private Pedro Cano distinguished himself by acts of gallantry and intrepidity above and beyond the call of duty while serving with Company C, 8th Infantry Regiment, 4th Infantry Division during combat operations against an armed enemy in Schevenhutte, Germany on December 2 and 3, 1944. On the afternoon of the 2nd, American infantrymen launched an attack against German emplacements but were repulsed by enemy machinegun fire. Armed with a rocket launcher, Private Cano crawled through a densely mined area under heavy enemy fire and successfully reached a point within ten yards of the nearest emplacement. He quickly fired a rocket into the position, killing the two gunners and five supporting riflemen. Without hesitating, he fired into a second position, killing two more gunners, and proceeded to assault the position with hand grenades, killing several others and dispersing the rest. Then, when an adjacent company encountered heavy fire, Private Cano crossed his company front, crept to within fifteen yards of the nearest enemy emplacement and killed the two machine gunners with a rocket. With another round he killed two more gunners and destroyed a second gun. On the following day, his company renewed the attack and again encountered heavy machine gun fire. Private Cano, armed with his rocket launcher, again moved across fire-swept terrain and destroyed three enemy machine guns in succession, killing the six gunners. Private Cano's extraordinary heroism and selflessness above and beyond the call of duty are in keeping with the highest traditions of military service and reflect great credit upon himself, his unit and the United States Army.

From the Booklet Produced by the 4th Infantry Division in Europe during WWII:
Famous Fourth, The Story of the 4th Infantry Division

Death Factory

Hürtgen was a cold, jungle hell—a death factory. Blocking approaches to Cologne and the Ruhr, Hürtgen was a "must" objective. The terrain was difficult enough with steep hills, thick woods, numerous creeks, and poor roads. Across the front, stretched belts of mines and barbed wire rigged with booby traps. Dug-in machine guns were set up to spray the entire area with interlocking fire.

Artillery, doubly dangerous in the woods because of tree bursts, was zeroed in on every conceivable objective. Weather was pure misery—constant rain, snow, near freezing temperatures. Living for days in water-filled holes, usually without blankets, our troops had no escape from cold and wet.

Before the main offensive got underway, the 12th Infantry Regiment rushed south to aid a division under heavy enemy pressure. The regiment fought bitterly for eight days, attacking and counter-attacking without flank support. Although it suffered heavy casualties, the 12th returned to join the division's assault on November 16.

On the south flank of the offensive, the 4th attacked through the forest toward Düren. Again, its front was extended. To the left of the 12th were the 22nd and 8th Infantry Regiments. For three days, the regiments struggled to crack the first enemy line.

Every yard was difficult, dangerous; firebreaks and clearings were mined. In the thick woods, German positions couldn't be detected more than five yards away. Yet, Nazi outposts could observe the 4th's approach. Every move brought instant artillery and mortar fire.

The line of wire and mines seemed impossible to crack. Machine guns and artillery blunted every attack. Reaching a firebreak, which crossed the front, the 70th Tank Battalion finally broke the wire and rolled beyond. Infantry followed in the tracks made by tanks after armor had detonated anti-personnel mines.

In pushing the front forward one thousand yards, the division suffered heavy casualties the first five days. The next enemy line was as tough as the first. The identical procedure had to be repeated.

Another five days produced another destroyed line. Another mile gained. Germans brought up fresh regiments, counter-attacking daily. Often, companies were caught before they had a chance to get set. It took another battle to throw back the stubborn Germans. After every advance, men spent hours digging holes and cutting logs to cover them. Artillery often whined, bursting in the trees before shelters could be finished.

After a day and night of vicious fighting, the 22nd reached Grosshau, November 27, wiping out German defenses before going on to the last strip of the forest beyond the town. Still in the woods, the 8th and 12th crashed the third MLA, which was as rough as the others were. The Nazis had overlooked no bet. Every approach was covered with every device of defensive warfare. Neither skill nor genius could find an easy way. It took sheer guts to win.

After three days, both regiments shattered the last line and broke through near the east edge of the forest. Then came welcome news. Relief! The 22nd moved to Luxembourg on December 3, followed by the 12th four days later and the 8th on December 13.

The drive required a continuous display of top-notch leadership and the highest order of individual courage under the most adverse conditions. The fact that the 4th Infantry Division overcame these many difficulties and drove the enemy from the dominating hills overlooking the Roer River is a tribute to the skill, determination and aggressiveness of all ranks.

Luxembourg and the Battle of the Bulge
December 1944

After leaving the hell of the Hürtgen Forest, the 4th Infantry Division moved to the relative safety of Luxembourg for rest, refitting, and bringing replacements into their decimated ranks. The plan was great, but the Germans had a different idea. After less than two weeks of rest and refitting in Luxembourg, the most famous battle of WWII began—the Battle of the Bulge. Immediately, the 4th Infantry Division was thrust back into combat with the responsibility to hold the southern edge of the Bulge. Following are stories from that period.

Chronology of the 4th Infantry Division, 7 December 1944 – 27 December 1944

Courtesy of Robert S. Rush, Ph.D.

7 December. Luxembourg: 83d Div, less 329th Inf, takes over zone of 4th Div on S flank of corps, with 8th Inf of 4th Div under its command. 4th Div (-8th Inf) passes to VIII Corps control.

16 December. Luxembourg: VIII Corps' 106th Div (reinf by 14th Cav Gp) 28th Div, 9th Armd Div, and N flank elements of 4th Div all fall back under enemy onslaught.

17 December. Luxembourg: 4th Div halts enemy S of Osweiler and Dickweiler, but units are isolated at a number of points.

18 December. Luxembourg: Troops of 4th Div and 10th Armd Div remaining S of the breakthrough are placed under 3rd Army command. CCA attacks N and E through the 4th Div to Berdorf and Echternach areas. 4th Div mops up infiltrators beyond Osweiler and Dickweiler and repels thrust from Dickweiler.

19 December Luxembourg: US 3rd Army forms provisional corps from former First Army units S of the Ardennes salient, 4th Div and 10th Armd Div (- CCB); the corps is to hold enemy on S flank of the penetration and plug gap existing between it and elements of 9th Armd Div and 28th Div near Ettelbruck.

20 December. Luxembourg: CCA, 110th Armd Div, withdraws to assembly areas as 4th Div moves up to take over its positions near Echternach. Tanks assist 12th Inf of 4th Div in futile effort to relieve isolated infantry in Echternach.

21 December. Luxembourg: 4th Div repels attacks toward Consdorf and Osweiler; is out of communication with troops in Echternach. RCT 10 5th Div, is attached to 4th Div.

22 December. Luxemboug: XII Corps, in new zone along E border of Luxembourg, attacks with 4th Div SW of Echternach but is held to small gains.

24 December. Luxembourg: In XXIII Corps area, 5th Div, to which RCT 10 has reverted, relieves left flank elements of 4th Div and attacks toward Haller and Waldbillig, making slow progress.

27 December. Luxembourg: 4th Div patrols find Echternach deserted.

John E. Kunkel, Springfield, OH
Company L, 3rd Battalion, 22nd Infantry Regiment

Smelled Like Billy Goats

I would like to relate something that took place a day or two after we were relieved in the Hürtgen and pulled back to what I recall was an old German training camp. A short time after we got there, we were all given a bunk and a gray German army blanket. Well, about midnight it happened—we all started to itch all over. My buddy said he felt something crawling on his neck. I took my pen flashlight out and, sure enough, there they were—body lice. Now the problem was getting rid of the lice. About daylight we found an old kerosene lantern. We poured the kerosene into a steel helmet and with an old dirty sock, we all took a sponge bath. It was hard on the skin, but we got rid of the lice. It was some time until we could take a real bath with good old water. We started to smell to the point we all smelled like Billy goats—it got to where we could not live with one another.

I am now 75 and still love to hear stories about the 22nd Infantry Regiment and the 4th Infantry Division.

Donald Faulkner, Winter Park, FL
Company E, 2nd Battalion, 22nd Infantry Regiment

Excerpts from his diary

First Bath

When Company E pulled into Manternach, Luxembourg, from the Hürtgen Forest, we were dirty, muddy, pooped, bashed, and dead tired. It was December 8, 1944. The next morning, two or three of my men arrived at our CP and shouted, "Come with us for a bath!"

So, down the street we went to a bombed-out house and up to the second floor. It was all shelled out, but visible to us all was a tub and a small wood stove above it, filled with burning kindling, making hot water. I took off my boots and jumped into the tub, muddy clothes and all.

As my men applauded, I disrobed and had the first bath since leaving the USA on September 15, 1944. Wow!

Talking in Tongues

December 9, 1944: Company E sent its first platoon, eighteen men, from Manternach, Luxembourg, up to the Moselle River to guard and observe from a wine distillery. Next morning, the phone check sounded like blabbering idiots. Someone was "talking in tongues!" A relieving squad revealed the mystery when they found they had all drunk the green wine from the fall crop of grapes and were simply "stewed."

Two Grenades

December 22, 1944: On the ridge in woods west of Rodenbaugh, Luxembourg, at 0900 hours, Sergeant Hughes and Captain Faulkner, leading the first platoon ran head on into a Kraut company. They took shelter in a ten-foot draw. Faulkner tossed one of his two grenades to Hughes. They pulled the pins and tossed…boom! Krauts retreated! Thank God. We had no more grenades.

- -

Tom Reid, Marietta, GA
Cannon Company, 22nd Infantry Regiment and Company I,
3rd Battalion, 22nd Infantry Regiment

Battle of the Bulge Begins

Early in December 1944, the 22nd Infantry Regiment moved to Luxembourg after a bitter three weeks of fighting in the Hürtgen Forest.

It was supposed to be a quiet area and a much-needed time to rest, receive replacements, and refit. However, such would not be the case. In the redisposition of the troops in Luxembourg, Service Company of the Regiment, commanded by Captain Billy Cater and Captain Clarence Hawkins (known as "Big Hawk"), the regimental motor officer, managed to set up shop at the Luxembourg Country Club. This was an elaborate facility complete with hot water, showers, real beds and the comforts of home.

Captain Cater and Big Hawk invited anyone in the regiment to come by and take a hot shower, and many availed themselves of that privilege. I just didn't have the opportunity until that fateful Saturday, December 16. I say fateful, because just as I finished the first hot shower I had enjoyed in over a month, I received word that my company had been alerted to move to northern Luxembourg immediately. The Battle of the Bulge had begun, and the 22nd Infantry would help stop the advance of the Germans on the southern shoulder of this penetration.

I got in my jeep, hurried back to my company, and by dark we were in position north of Luxembourg City.

Nothing was unusual about the alerting of the Regiment and its hurried move that day but after the first hot shower in weeks, I was a prime candidate on that cold move to catch pneumonia.

Luckily, I did not get sick. The Regiment performed at its usual peak efficiency; eventually the Germans were driven back, and the war was ultimately shortened by the last great fling of the Germans that December. I will always remember my only December 1944 bath.

Although Billy Cater is still with us, Big Hawk has gone on to that great motor pool in the sky. Deeds not words!

William G. Cole, Tacoma, WA
Battery C, 29th Field Artillery Battalion

Glenn Warren's Memories and Mine

I recently found a map which I had used during the winter in Luxembourg during the "Bulge." It is very detailed and may be akin to Michelin road maps. Certainly, as John Ausland points out, they have been mapping that area for military purposes for centuries. The good detail of that map helped me determine the approximate location of the observation post shown on the situation maps from John Eisenhower's book, *The Bitter Woods*.

Before and during the Battle of the Bulge, Jack Cunningham and I alternated at an observation post at an infantry outpost overlooking the pillboxes of the main German defense line. When I think about it, I see snow covering everything and can't visualize it otherwise. We walked half a mile or so from the nearest road, partially through woods and partially in the open, to get to the OP. I felt vulnerable making that walk because the area was very lightly held by our outpost. We spent the night in a small crossroad village, perhaps two miles behind the outpost.

Glenn Warren, a bright young noncom who had been recommended for consideration for a direct commission, was wounded while he was with me at that OP. There was a hedgerow across the front of the OP. In about the center of the position there was a dry-masonry stone enclosure without a roof, which afforded some cover. I was at the hedgerow in a place that gave me the best visibility when German mortar fire began to fall on us. I stayed where I was, trying to see something, and sent the radio crew to the stone enclosure. A mortar shell hit the wall or the ground inside the enclosure and wounded Glenn. He got many fragments in his leg and one in an eye. He absorbed all of a 60mm mortar shell. He lost sight in the eye and spent months in the hospital.

From the Booklet Produced by the 4th Infantry Division in Europe during WW II: *Famous Fourth, the Story of the 4th Infantry Division*

Stopping the Germans in Luxembourg

After Hürtgen, Luxembourg was heaven. Dry, warm, houses were a welcomed change from holes full of icy water—from incessant shelling. Since the division's sector extended thirty-five miles, each platoon covered about a mile. Although there was snow, rain, and cold for men on post, it was a comparative rest.

But it didn't last. Germans crossed the river at dawn December 16, attacking the 12th and hitting division outposts from all directions. American platoons battled German battalions. Some platoons, struck from the rear, were overcome. Others withdrew, fighting their way to company areas.

That morning, General Barton issued an order: "There will be no retrograde movement in this sector."

When a German battalion swooped down on Berdorf, lone defenders comprised a company headquarters, one rifle squad, two anti-tank squads and a four-man mortar squad. The makeshift defense took refuge in the Parc Hotel, a rifle in every other window, and withstood repeated attacks. Pulverizing German artillery blasted off the roof and part of the hotel's third floor. "Doughs" moved to other windows and kept firing.

Two platoons were at Dickweiler, three at Osweiler. Units in both towns were surrounded by full strength battalions. Every time Germans attacked, "Joes" waited until they closed in, and then sprayed the Nazis with a withering fire that stopped succeeding assaults with heavy losses.

Other German units, bypassing the two towns, ran into the 12th's reserves.

Companies, with a few tanks for support, boldly moved forward to take on a complete battalion. The Americans disregard for the odds confused and worried the Germans. This thinly spread outfit was supposed to be easy pickings. Instead, it was giving the Nazis a terrific headache.

Transferred from their own thinly defended sectors, battalions of the 8th and 22nd came up the next morning to plunge into action. A fresh German regiment attempted a flanking move through a valley at the sector's edge, but the 4th Engineer Battalion and the 4th Recon Troop repulsed the attack.

Moving through the undefended woods at the center of the division's lines, the Germans 316th Regiment shoved all the way to the rear areas, surrounding a battalion CP. Although the 12th's Cannon Company was caught with its guns coupled up, the Krauts got the bigger surprise. Cannoneers loaded guns and fired point blank while the remainder of the company blazed away with carbines.

A second CP was surrounded when the Nazis attacked the 2nd Battalion, 22nd Infantry. Grabbing artillerymen to serve as infantry, Company C, 70th Tank Battalion, relieved the handful of Joes, staving off the assault. This was the straw that broke the German breakthrough attempts, but still the enemy wasn't finished.

Withdrawing to their original starting positions, Nazis stormed Berdorf and Echternach. After completely encircling Echternach, the enemy recaptured the town. By now, the 4th had no reserves to call upon. Cooks, quartermasters, MPs—every possible man in the division—was in the line.

General Barton decided to pull out of Berdorf and Lauterborn and withdraw to a solid MLA. Garrisons that had held against all odds fell back to the next line. Germans followed. But they were too late. After attacking monotonously for three days, three battalions of the German 212th Division, already badly mauled, were wiped out. Only one German of the 2nd Battalion, 316th Regiment survived the battle at Michelshof. He surrendered.

Transferred from the division on December 27, General Barton had commanded the Famous Fourth for two and a half years, leading it with brilliant success through nine operations. Succeeding him was Brigadier General Harold W. Blakeley, artillery commander. Taking over General Blakeley's post was Colonel R. T. Guthrie.

Under General Blakeley, the battle of Luxembourg was pushed to complete victory. Along with the 5th Infantry Division, which took over a portion of the front, "Ivy" soldiers seized the offensive. The Germans failed to hold the little territory they had recaptured. By January 1, remnants of the 212th Division reeled backward.

Edwin D. Williams, Champaign, IL
Company F, 2nd Battalion, 22nd Infantry Regiment

Short Round

I was one of a group of six hundred replacements shuttled from Marseille, France, north to Nancy, on Christmas Eve Day, 1944 by the Army Air Corps. Thirty C-47 planes were involved. There was no daylight left when the last planes unloaded. We boarded army 6x6s and traveled through the country and city of Luxembourg and farther east. I had the good fortune to be assigned to Company F. Two buddies and I from basic training were still together and as we approached the Executive Officer (Lieutenant Lee Lloyd), we heard him asking for volunteers for the mortar section of the weapons platoon. The three of us decided to volunteer.

As you know, the 4th Infantry Division had many casualties in the Hürtgen Forest and was trying to build back up to strength. The Division was holding the southern shoulder of the Bulge. Company F's CP was in a little town near what I think was the Moselle River. The mortars had been dug into a fair-sized hole, and we were putting harassing fire on the Germans across the river. The men in the observation post near the river had given me the targets, and we had aiming stakes around the perimeter of the hole, so it was no problem putting the rounds where they wanted them. Then it happened.

I dropped a round into the barrel and as it fired, it made a "clang" sound, and I could hear the round itself making a fading "loop-loop-loop" sound as it went into its trajectory. I visualized that round tumbling end over end and falling way short of the target. I grabbed the field telephone to the OP and shouted, "Tell your men to take cover! There's a short round coming in!"

A few seconds later I heard the round hit. I was advised that the round had not hit close enough to cause any casualties, but it had shaken the hell out of them.

It didn't take long for one of the sergeants from the OP to make it back to where we were, demanding to know what in the hell was going on. Luckily, I had found the cause of the problem and was holding it in my gloved hand when he arrived. The fire in his eyes faded and his demeanor changed when I showed him the metal fin from the mortar round which had broken off the tail piece of the round. This story could have ended in a different way. I feel fortunate it ended the way it did.

Warren King, Nashville, TN
Medic, Company B, 1st Battalion, 22nd Infantry Regiment

POW Christmas, 1944

This is my favorite war story (while in a POW camp). I stole one of the guard's ducks and ate it for Christmas 1944. The guards had a white duck that bedded down every night about the same place along the fence. They also had red cabbage planted along the fence. For a POW, food was scarce. I cased the duck and cabbage for several days. One day I asked my roommates if they would like to have duck for Christmas. They looked at each other in wonderment as if to say, "Where can you get a duck?" At the time we could cook on a small stove we had. I told them if they would cook the duck, I would get one. They agreed. So in total darkness, I went out to the fence, reached through, placed the duck's head under its wing, and brought it through the fence with never a sound being made. I also got some cabbage. I carried the meat and vegetables inside, killed the duck, plucked the feathers, and hid them under the floor. We ate the duck and cabbage for Christmas. A few nights later, an RAF bomber came over and dropped incendiary bombs on our building, burning it, and destroying all evidence. A true story (I would not lie.)

Donald Faulkner, Winter Park, FL
Company E, 2nd Battalion, 22nd Infantry Regiment

Battle of Bulge—Diary Entries

Donald Faulkner, CO of Easy Company, 2nd Battalion, 22nd Infantry Regiment kept a diary during WWII. Following are his entries from December 22-25, 1944.

12/22/44 - Our "Able Peter" patrol was halfway to Echternach. Battalion said, "Link up with Peter." I dared not divulge their position, so I replied to battalion on our radio: "My Peter will not stretch that far. Sorry."

12/23/44 - Company E was digging in at a point in the woods opposite the village of Rodenhauf, Luxembourg. We were heard; the Krauts started by dropping in heavy mortar shells—one, two, three, four—on us. It was a battery. By timing the sound, we were able to pinpoint the map coordinates of their battery. We called fire from our one battery of worn-out 105mm howitzers.

"On the way," came the reply.

We listened to them as they swished through the air over our heads and landed one, two, three, four—on target! We called for, "Fire for effect." Great! That did it—no more Kraut mortar fire at all. Thank you, Lord.

12/24/44 - On Christmas Eve, Company E was dug in a ravine in the woods opposite Rodenhauf. The weather was freezing cold. A visitor walking across the snowy frozen fields in the dark from Osweiler, Luxembourg, found his way to the Company E CP located in a "super hole," fashioned by a GI from a grave digger's family in Brooklyn, New York, and covered with logs and much snow. It was Lieutenant Stephen Sanders who made a presentation:

"From Colonel Kenan to Captain Faulkner— a half bottle of Red Label Scotch."

Wow! Seven GIs and the Captain pooled their orange powder from K-rations and one canteen of water drained from frozen canteens, and it was heated over a pile of K-ration boxes. Drink was shared by passing it around from man to man. Delish! Merry Christmas, '44.

12/25/44 - Christmas morning, Lieutenant Aldoerfer and one of his men crept through the woods to the nearest Kraut hole, killed two Germans in it, took their light machine gun, made their way safely back to the Company E CP and presented it as a gift to Captain Faulkner. Merry Christmas!

Jack Capell, Portland, OR
HQ, 8th Infantry Regiment

From Paradise Back Into Hell

The date is March 7, 1997. This is an oral history contribution on the Battle of the Bulge to the Eisenhower Center, New Orleans, Louisiana, attention Dr. Stephen Ambrose. This is from John C. Capell. I am known as Jack Capell.

I was a member of the 4th Infantry Division, 8th Infantry Regiment, Headquarters Company from D-Day until the end of the war, including the Battle of the Bulge. I was a combat infantryman. I am arranging these recollections in a series, rather than giving continuous narration, because I think it is a matter of record as to what the 4th Infantry Division did during the Battle of the Bulge, and I see no reason I should go over that or include many numerous details. I will give you some of the memories that I have of that period.

The first recollection begins just prior to the outbreak of the battle. When we arrived in Luxembourg on December 12, 1944 we had been fighting in the Hürtgen Forest and had been severely battered, were battle weary, exhausted, had suffered terrible casualties, and were seriously depleted in manpower and much in need of replacements. We were removed from the Hürtgen Forest and sent to the Luxembourg front in the Ardennes Forest.

The 28th Infantry Division had a similar experience. They also were among those divisions that were spread out alongside of us. We were, at the time, near the town of Senningen, Luxembourg, just to the west of the Moselle River near the Luxembourg/German border. Supposedly, we were facing a rather weak German unit and it was considered to be a quiet front. Some of the veterans of the Hürtgen Forest, especially those who had been in for the full time, were allowed forty-eight hours at a hospital rest camp in Arlon, Belgium. I was one of the first to be able to go and was to leave on December 15. There were about ten of us loaded on a two-and-a-half ton truck early in the morning to head back to Arlon.

The camp was in a large stone building, and there were cots complete with sheets, blankets and mattresses; hot water showers; and a supply of clean-laundered clothing. Good hot food was served in a mess hall, and it was pure luxury.

We spent December 15 with great pleasure and looked forward to a full night's sleep. We expected to have another enjoyable day on the 16th. However, early in the morning on the 16th we were ordered to get ready to go back. We were shocked and thought there must be a mistake. We loudly proclaimed that we had one more day to stay in Arlon. The officer who gave the order insisted there was no mistake and we were to go back. We protested loudly, and a major then came on the scene and ordered us to get ready to go out and to be ready to leave in a very short while. He said there was a problem at the front, and if we didn't go and follow orders we would be charged with refusing duty, so we reluctantly complied but complained bitterly.

We were loaded onto a two-and-a-half ton truck and headed back. The weather had turned cold that day, and there was a biting wind that blew through the back of the truck. We were not only extremely angry, but miserable from the cold. After a time we stopped to refuel. While waiting, we went inside the fuel dump shack to get warm for a few minutes and heard an English language broadcast on a radio the men had there. Suddenly, we forgot how cold we were when we heard about a German counter-attack and specific mention of the fact that the 4th Infantry Division had been annihilated in the fighting. We were stunned, since we were all from the Headquarters Company of the 8th Infantry Regiment, 4th Infantry Division. We frantically interrogated the driver, who was from division headquarters, and asked him where he was taking us. He said he knew nothing about it except that he was to take us to division headquarters for instructions. From then on, there was no further concern about the cold, but there was great anxiety.

At division headquarters, the driver was instructed to take us to the town of Senningen. Then we left. My foxhole, or shelter trench, had been half a mile forward from Senningen. When we returned, we came right back to the town and found that members of our company were in the cellar of a stone building in the center of Senningen. Immediately upon arriving, we were issued TNT and dynamite caps, or blasting caps, to set off the TNT in order to blast foxholes in frozen ground. We were also issued more grenades that we strapped around our belts and were ordered to check our M-1 rifles. If there were any malfunctions, there were a few replacement rifles for which we could exchange them. Immediately we were marched to a position near Senningen on the front and ordered to hold the position. By this time we had learned about the German counter-attack and about how our division had survived. We found there were few, if any, casualties in our company, but those who were around the town of Echternach, Luxembourg, were in serious trouble and probably were all killed or captured. That seemed to be the area where the 4th Infantry Division had suffered the worst losses. Otherwise, except for some minor withdrawals, the line was being held.

Artillery, mortar, and small arms fire were intense. We had begun hearing heavy artillery fire even before we reached Division Headquarters when we were coming back. The Germans had broken through just to the north of us, but had failed to penetrate very far into the 4th Infantry Division sector and the 4th Infantry

Division was now forming the southern border of the new front. Our division had lost Echternach and the area around it, but we fought very hard to keep from yielding any more ground and we apparently did prevent the Germans from breaking through to Luxembourg City. In just a twenty-four hour period, we had gone from paradise back into hell again. This concludes my recollection of how I first learned about the Battle of the Bulge.

My second recollection concerns Christmas Day, 1944.

The weather had cleared somewhat, but it was still very cold with snow having come on or about December 20. I recollect the Christmas Day situation because of its irony. We were promised we would have hot Christmas dinners on Christmas Day even though we were still holding the line at the front. I didn't know how this would be possible. On that day our kitchen truck came up to regimental headquarters about a quarter of a mile back from where I had chiseled a shelter trench out of the snow and ice. One by one we were allowed to go back to the kitchen truck and get our Christmas dinners. I had the mess kit lid (I had discarded the rest of it) and my canteen cup. I walked back through the ice and snow and was given servings of turkey, reconstituted dehydrated potatoes, some cranberry sauce and a cup of coffee. I was ordered to return to my hole and not to stay by the same truck and eat it there. So with my rifle over my shoulder, I precariously made my way back through the snow and ice, trying to keep from spilling my coffee and dinner until I finally arrived at my hole. When I sat down to eat it, I found the cranberry sauce had frozen to the mess kit and everything was ice cold, including the coffee. I chiseled out the cranberry sauce and had my Christmas dinner. It was the most unusual Christmas dinner I had ever had.

Another recollection occurred sometime during that period, but I am not quite sure what date. We had been warned about English-speaking Germans in American uniforms infiltrating our units. A rumor was circulating that our command post had been visited by mysterious strangers who left unidentified. My good friend, Horace Sisk, from Illinois, was the regimental clerk. I knew he could tell me what had happened, if anything.

He told me that a jeep driven by one enlisted man and two men wearing uniforms of high-ranking American officers as passengers arrived at regimental headquarters. The party passed the guard without being questioned after stating they were from corps headquarters. While the driver stayed in the jeep, the two officers walked into the regimental headquarters building and immediately asked for Colonel McKee, who was the 8th Infantry Regiment Commander. They were told he was not there but was expected back soon. They expressed anger and said that he had told them he would be there to meet with them, and they demanded to see the next in command. They were quite irate. They were directed to Lieutenant Colonel Strickland, with whom they spoke briefly. They then preceded to lower ranking officers, particularly a captain who apologized for the fact that McKee was not there. The officers continued to express their anger, and to appease them, he answered their questions about 8th Infantry positions and strategy, as well as detailed information about the deployment of our troops. The officers quickly left.

Colonel Strickland finally became suspicious and went to the captain. The captain said that since the officers had already talked to Strickland, he assumed that Strickland had identified them.

Strickland realized they had been duped. The officers were imposters. When Colonel McKee returned to the Regimental Headquarters, he became extremely upset and terrified because he had made no appointment. The imposters must have known that Colonel McKee was not at regimental headquarters. Possibly they had monitored radio transmissions from Division HQ and knew he was there.

The fourth recollection I have took place on December 31. By that time, we had moved to the town of Wecker, Luxembourg. The civilians had been evacuated. The German guns were quieter than usual. It was still cold, but it was a bright day, and I had gone into the lower floor of an evacuated two-story frame house to relax and get a bit warmer. Soon I heard bombs whistling, then suddenly a jarring explosion followed by one after another. I was struck with a terrible shock and deafening noise very close to the house. The air was filled with dust and debris, and I was aware of things falling on me. I quickly exited the house and returned to my foxhole. The bombing continued a while longer. Medics were coming to treat our wounded. I soon learned that one of my very good friends, a man from Pennsylvania by the name of Sepik, had been killed. Some of the men said they had seen the aircraft through some high clouds and they identified them definitely as American heavy bombers—B-17s, as I recollect. We were completely puzzled because we were not on the front at the time. We were back in reserve and wondered why they would bomb so short. We concluded that somehow or another there had been some American heavy bombers captured by Germans, and these were actually being flown by Germans. We could not believe that American pilots could be that far off target. However, it had happened once before. Prior to the St. Lô breakthrough on July 25, it happened when the smoke line marking to the target on the German side drifted over us. We lost many men in that bombing.

On the following day, January 1, 1945, the weather was even brighter. We were still in and around the town of Wecker, and we were astounded to see American P-38 fighter planes swoop down over our area and begin strafing us. This was the second day in a row we were hit by American planes. We immediately laid out cloth panels showing the American insignia. They had to be visible to the aircraft, but the strafing continued. Our regimental history indicates that there were twelve P-38's involved in this raid. After the raid, according to my friend in Regimental HQ, Horace Sisk, a command car came up to visit. It was carrying American officers with no identifying insignia. We learned that they were American air corps officers investigating what had gone wrong. Their identification was kept secret because of concern over what some of our men might have done had they learned who they were. That concludes the fourth memorable recollection.

The fifth recollection is probably the most memorable of all. It took place during the cold, snowy, winter weather during the latter part of December and January. Some of us still had no overcoats, and although we had the new longer and heavier field jackets, they were not sufficient protection against the cold. We had wool gloves and the new combat boots. They had leather tops, which replaced the old leggings, but they were not any more protection against severe cold. We wore rubber overshoes to help insulate, but had a deadly fear that we might rip an overshoe such that snow could work its way in.

Once the snow melted from the body heat, and then one stopped to rest, the foot would quickly freeze. Trench foot was a serious problem. It may have caused more casualties than actual battle wounds during that particular period. We supplemented our clothing by cutting up burlap sacks found in farmhouses. We wrapped those around our heads, necks, and legs. The Germans did the same thing, and some of the prisoners we took were so wrapped up they looked like mummies.

At night many of the men, in groups of two or three, would make a shelter from trunks of trees. I carried a crosscut saw in one of our company vehicles for this purpose. We would huddle together and use body heat to help keep us warm. Sometimes we half-filled a C-Ration can with gasoline and lit it. It would burn slowly, giving off enough heat to help considerably. This, of course, could only be done if the low, steady flame could be obscured somehow by having it in a shelter, or at least in a pup tent with snow heaped around so that the enemy could not see the light.

Sometimes I would be sent on a mission and return after dark. Being unable to take adequate protection against the cold, I would find myself unprotected from the cold for the night. I would sometimes seek a manure pile. There were huge manure piles in front of the peasant houses.

They were flattened on top, and by throwing some boards on top of the manure, one could crawl on top and keep warm as the manure fermented. It was so warm that the snow would melt off, and steam rose. There was strong methane gas being given off, and the pungent odor meant that one could survive only a short time without getting away for some fresh air. Then I would have to spend the rest of the night in the cold.

One cold and dark night, I was alone without protection. Searching for a building to get into, I found in the darkness a shed or a barn of some sort with an open door, and I sensed the feeling of warmth. I reached down to find a floor of concrete, which was warmer than would be expected. I felt around on the floor until it felt even warmer. At that spot, I lay down and immediately went to sleep.

Shortly afterward, I was awakened by something nudging me in the back. I reached over and felt a furry leg and a hoof. I realized I was sleeping by a cow that was resting on its side. I went back to sleep. When daylight came, I found I had spent the night sleeping between the cow's legs and considered that to be an excellent way to beat the cold.

The worst times in the cold were when we did sentry duty. There was little one could do to protect from the biting wind. More than once, after a seemingly endless session on sentry duty, I returned to my hole for shelter so cold and thoroughly fatigued that I was afraid to fall asleep for fear of freezing.

I was often assigned to take the weapons carrier to get back to division headquarters and pick up supplies and ammunition as well as a number of other miscellaneous missions. I often accidentally got into enemy territory. Sergeant Mike Camarote, who was wounded and being returned to the regiment, noticed what I was doing and volunteered to accompany me for some extra protection.

One time when Mike and I were together we were carrying a supply of TNT and dynamite caps for blowing foxholes. The explosives compartment was directly behind the driver's seat in the weapons carrier. As Mike and I were driving back on a narrow icy road, on top of a dike, we encountered a two-and-a-half ton GMC truck approaching from the other direction. It was impossible for both vehicles to come to a stop, and there was not room for both of us on top of the dike. We collided, and the weapons carrier went into a spin as the heavier GMC truck went on without stopping to see what happened.

We spun and slid off the edge of the dike, then dropped eight to ten feet. The vehicle was lying on the driver's side where the TNT was stored. When we hit, Mike bounced on top of me. I was not injured, and I asked Mike if he was OK. He was just shaken up a little bit.

Then I said, "What do you think, Mike? Are we in another world now, or, if by some miracle that TNT and dynamite did not explode when we hit?"

Mike gasped. "My God, I had forgotten about that!" Then he laughed and said, "Well, must be the same old world. I'm just as cold as ever."

Another major recollection also has to do with events that occurred during the extremely cold weather. We were on a ridge with a valley going down to a creek bed. An American tank column was attempting to move along the steep slope on the other side of the draw. An infantry column was also moving up about the same time. The lead tank began to attempt to traverse the side of the hill. The commander was standing with his upper body extending out of the hatch. The tank slid sideways and rolled over. The tank commander was crushed. The other tanks following stopped before attempting to traverse the slope. I looked back to see a most entertaining sight. The next tank was traversing the slope with ropes extended out from the front and rear of the tank and at least fifty infantrymen holding on to ropes to keep the tank from sliding sideways.

It was like a tug of war with the tank in the middle. Suddenly, one infantryman lost his footing and slid downhill toppling a dozen or so men. The same thing happened on the other rope, and this happened time and time again—the tank sliding sideways a few feet each time, but still making some progress forward. Eventually, all the tanks went across the slope. That would have been a great scene to capture on film as an example of sheer ingenuity and perseverance. There was an element of comedy as one man would lose his footing and topple a dozen or so, or more like dominoes. All of them would scramble to regain their feet and get going once more. Again, the foot soldier proved his worth.

During January, the 4th Infantry Division made a thrust into the territory the Germans had captured during the Bulge. We were transferred to General George Patton's 3rd Army on December 20, 1944, because we were closer to them than the 1st Army. Until then, we had been members of the 1st Army. At one time, we were apparently cut off because we received supplies by parachute. Our thrust was across the Saar River on January 18. When we reached Vianden, Germany, we captured many prisoners. We then withdrew to a more defensive location.

During January snow was on the ground and many of the dead were hidden in snowdrifts and not picked up by the graves registration men. Besides many corpses of men and animals, there was much human waste on the frozen ground. Our normal procedure to dispose of waste was to dig a small hole and cover it up. But with frozen ground and snow, this was not done, and all waste was simply deposited in the snow. When a thaw came, all the filth from human waste and corpses of men and animals ran off into the streams. It was from these streams that we obtained our drinking water.

I was often assigned to get water for the company. The equipment used was a pump on a trailer towed by a two-and-a-half truck. The water was taken directly from the stream, pumped through filters, and chlorinated tablets were added to help purify it. I noticed the water was coming out as dirty brown as it was when it was in the stream. I couldn't believe it was being filtered. I asked one of the water pump men and he said, "Every time we put a filter in it clogs up so fast we can't get water. So, we just have to leave the filters out—that's all right, we're putting in plenty of chlorine, enough to kill any germs."

Unfortunately, it was not. I brought the water back and warned everyone what the situation was. I was one of the few men who stupidly attempted to drink the water, and I suffered for it. I got a severe case of dysentery. The weather turned cold, it began to snow, and we were once again in blizzard conditions. I could not possibly have been more miserable—with dysentery, in a blizzard and with no place to get shelter.

There was no medical aid for dysentery. I was unable to eat, was completely dehydrated, and so weak I could hardly stand. After a couple of days, I began to recover, and I was soon healthy again. Because of the water problem, the men in the company insisted that something be done to get them good water. The company mess sergeant conceived the idea of filling all the water cans with wine. He found a supply of wine somewhere in the rear and the mess truck brought up a full truckload of water cans filled with wine, which men used in place of water.

John C. Clark, Spring Hope, NC
HQ, 29th Field Artillery Battalion

Milking the Farmer's Cow

I was recovered enough from my war wounds by Thanksgiving that the doctors thought I could return to my unit. We traveled by boxcars and by trucks. By December 17 I was near Malmedy, where we were supposed to stay all night. We began hearing reports of a breakthrough, and our officers told us to go to the supply depot and take anything we needed and could carry, for they were going to destroy the rest of it. I remember I got a map, an extra blanket, a .45 caliber pistol, and ammunition for it. I hung 24 grenades from my suspenders and belt. My knapsack was full of food—mostly K-rations, and extra socks. I had on two uniforms, a field jacket, an overcoat, a stocking knit cap, a helmet, a scarf, and gloves.

They started marching us south toward Malmedy and Stavelot. Just out of Malmedy, we met GIs coming in from the east. They told us that a German tank column was coming in behind them and that they weren't able to hold them. There was already some shelling on the road from the German tanks, still quite a distance away.

Some of us were concerned about the fact that we hadn't seen any sign of our supply depots having been blown up. We certainly didn't want the German tank force to have access to all that fuel and ammunition there.

Four of the infantry guys and I headed back to blow the dump. I had known several of the fellows for quite a while. They had also been wounded and were on the way back to their group, just as I was.

We ran most of the couple of miles back to the dump. Most of the gas was in 55-gallon drums. We pulled the plugs, then shot into them and watched them blow.

We five guys were just as glad to have left the soldiers who had been marching down the road. Some lieutenant just didn't realize that this was an unwise thing to do.

When we started back to rejoin them, we went through the woods, not the road. We decided to go up on a hill and see if we could stop the approaching German tanks and keep them out of Malmedy. We felt that we could blow the tracks off the tanks, slowing them down so they couldn't reach those guys on the road. This is what we did as long as it was dark, but we knew we didn't have a chance against those tanks in daylight.

Before sunrise, we took off through the woods. A few hours later we heard a bunch of machine guns go off. We learned afterwards that the tanks caught up with the fellows we'd left on the road. The Germans took them out in a field and just mowed them down.

We kept walking through the woods, working our way south and west. We traveled during the night and slept during the day, sometimes in barns, or in haystacks. We liked the warmer haystacks, for the weather was right at freezing—foggy, with some snow. One guy was always on guard wherever we were. On the fourth day, we decided to cross a river. The water was deep, and we felt almost frozen as we crawled later into a haystack.

When I saw an old cow go across the barnyard, I thought, "There's a warm meal." I milked the cow into my helmet, and the warm milk really tasted good.

The next morning when the farmer couldn't get any milk, he called his wife, who also tried unsuccessfully to milk the cow. The poor cow was the subject of much conversation, which of course, we couldn't understand since none of us knew their language. But we got a good laugh from their bewilderment. They milked the cow that night, but she was mysteriously dry the next morning. We stayed in that haystack two days to get thawed.

Paul Brunelle, Avon, MA
Company G, 2nd Battalion, 8th Infantry Regiment

Christmas Packages from the Sky

From the book Company G, 2nd Battalion, 8th Infantry Regiment, 4th Infantry Division *by Shirley Devine. Reprinted with permission.*

A few days before Christmas we boarded trucks. I looked back behind us and saw the clouds of dust that our two-and-a-half-ton trucks were throwing up and wondered if there were German observers out there. Boy, they must have known exactly where we were because as soon as we got off the trucks in this forest of enormous trees, the artillery started. The most amazing part of it was that even though the artillery was intense, not a person was hit by the enemy fire.

We moved beyond that hill to another hill. There was a valley in front of us and at that point we dug in. There were snipers up on that hill. I was standing up in my foxhole, and I heard a bullet go whizzing right past my ear. It popped as it went by, and I knew it had missed me by a fraction. I was very lucky. The next morning we moved down into the valley, and Theodore Rupack was hit. When the troops went down the hill, I was behind a very large tree and I didn't see them move out. All of a sudden, I realized I was alone. I crawled and walked down the hill until I came to the other troops. But just before I came to the troops, I found Theodore lying on the ground. He was delirious and talking to members of his family. I regretted there was nothing that I could do. I did tell the officers when I got down to the bottom about him being there. He was removed from the front a short time later, but died en route to an aid station.

We were relieved and went back to Luxembourg. This was the day before Christmas. I can remember on Christmas day, watching planes—a huge flight of planes flying over—huge bombers dropping bombs on the enemy, way to our forward position. You could actually see the bombs coming down. It was quite a sight. We all cheered and wished the Germans a Merry Christmas, and hoped that the packages they were receiving from the bomber would do what they were being asked to do. Again, I remember the cooks brought us a wonderful Christmas dinner. So here we were into December.

- -

Jack Cunningham, Manteca, CA
Battery C, 29th Field Artillery Battalion

Luxembourg Observation Post During the Battle of the Bulge

During the Battle of the Bulge I shared duty at an observation post (OP) in Luxembourg with Bill Cole. We used that post from mid-December, before the German attack began, to mid-January, 1945. The OP was near the edge of a high bluff overlooking the Sauer River and the Siegfried Line pillboxes across the river, from which the enemy looked back at us. The position was held by a single squad of infantry and the ground behind us was empty, not occupied, for a distance of about a mile.

Bill and I exchanged letters in 1993, when he was trying to spot the OP on a map. He has written a story about his radio operator, Sergeant Glenn Warren who was wounded at the OP. That story appears elsewhere.

I will borrow from my letter of December 15, 1993, in the account that follows.

I remember going through the town of Lillig on the way to the infantry at the front, so the battery must have been located to the West or southwest of that town. My first visit to the OP was with Captain Jim Hurst. We drove to the point where the road was nearest to the OP and then had a half-mile walk to the infantry outpost there, which consisted of only three or four men at that time. The last quarter mile of that walk was through a clearing, which made us uncomfortable because we felt exposed. The outpost was above a big canyon through which the Sauer River flowed near its confluence with the Moselle.

There were pillboxes across the river, and when we exposed ourselves for any length of time, the Germans fired their rifles at us. The distance was so great that the odds of a hit were terrible. I don't think we depended on the odds very often.

At a later date I was on duty at the OP when Jim Hurst and the division artillery commander, General Blakeley, along with the division artillery staff officers, came to the OP to fire and observe the bursts of new shells having "proximity" fuses. They exploded in the air just before impact, producing air bursts, which were very effective. Later the fuse proved to be very successful in night interdiction fire on Trier, which was just over the hill about ten or fifteen miles from our OP.

During the Battle of the Bulge there was a prolonged period of bad weather that prevented the air corps from bombing Trier or helping the ground forces. When the weather cleared, the American and British bombers would come over us and bomb Trier. As I stood at the OP I could see shock waves coming through the air, and my pants legs would quiver from the concussions. I was glad I wasn't in Trier.

Before the Bulge started, I believe we went back to the battery at night, but when things heated up we spent nights at the infantry command post at either Moesdorf or Mompach. Every night two guys came into the village with a jeep and trailer and yelled, "Champagne Call!"

They had "liberated" the stuff in Grevenmacher, which had big ware-houses of champagne aging, and the area was not occupied by the enemy or us. The stuff we got was very "green" and not very good, but it tasted a bit like the finished product and contained some alcohol. I took some of it back to the battery when I had a bit of a break from duty and drank some one evening. I didn't try it again. It was three days before my system returned to normal.

Conrad "Frenchy" Adams, Gulfport, MS
Company E, 2nd Battalion, 8th Infantry Regiment

Outpost in the Snow

Company E was very short of men as the Battle of the Bulge went on. Many men had been killed or wounded. As a machine gun assistant, I was told to go on a 24-hour stakeout. At that time, the snow was knee deep—and that was a lot of snow for a country boy from Louisiana, who had only seen snow once in his life—and I had to walk three quarters of a mile down a ravine to get to my post. As night fell, I started to expand the foxhole that someone before me hadn't finished. I hit rocks, and the German soldiers started firing 88s at the place where the sound was com-ing from. I had to stop digging and set up my shelter half. It started to snow harder during the night, and my shelter half fell on me. I couldn't move until the next night because the Germans would have seen me if I had moved.

With the snow on me all night, I became hoarse and could not talk for a month. Although I couldn't talk, I was never taken to the rear for a checkup. As I said, we were short of men, short of new replacements, and that was a hell of a feeling…but we kept on going.

Also, I remember one time the GIs were drinking cognac or schnapps, and I didn't drink. We hadn't taken off our shoes for a couple of months, so I put some of the liquor in my helmet, after removing the liner, took off my shoes and soaked my feet in the helmet—boy did that feel good.

Marvin A. Simpson, (Deceased) Baton Rouge, LA
Company D, 4th Medical Battalion

A Pretty Girl

I had my first taste of Calvados at a pub that catered to the American soldiers.

During late December and early January 1944, we were stationed in the wing of a hospital on the outskirts of Luxembourg, where we received many casualties from the Hürtgen Forest and the Battle of the Bulge. This was during the Christmas holidays, and I had my first taste of Calvados at a pub that catered to the American soldiers. I must admit, I was attracted to a very pretty girl and was a good dancer. Her father was a banker in downtown Luxembourg and the family invited me for dinner one Sunday, which I enjoyed very much.

Wayne Brown, Marshalltown, IA
Company F, 2nd Battalion, 12th Infantry Regiment

Back to Active Duty

I was wounded on July 12, 1944, in Normandy, so I missed the St. Lô breakthrough and the taking of Paris. My shoulder wound was so serious I was sent to a hospital in England for recovery, which took until early September. I was sent back to my original unit but didn't recognize anyone. Most had been killed or wounded. Some of the wounded returned later. We continued our push through the Siegfried Line and into Germany.

In November we encountered one of the worst battles of the war—in the Hürtgen Forest. We were down to three or four men to a squad before I was wounded a second time on November 30, 1944. A bullet struck me in the chest but must have struck a tree first and entered my chest sideways, just to the right of my breastbone. It didn't hit my lungs or any vital organs. I was sent to a Paris hospital where they removed the bullet.

I was in a convalescent hospital when the Battle of the Bulge breakthrough came. We were helping the nurses decorate the tent hospital for Christmas, which we assumed would include us. On December 24, a group of doctors came through the tent asking every man that could stand to do so. A doctor looked at my chart, and I told him that I still had stitches, which he quickly removed and said, "Back to active duty."

That afternoon, we were loaded on "forty and eight" railroad cars and sent back to our units in Luxembourg and Belgium. What a way to spend Christmas. I missed most of the battle Company F had at the Parc Hotel in Berdorf but knew a lot of the fellows who were there, such as Master Sergeant Ed Potts from Hudson Falls, New York, and others. From that day on, the weather was horrible. I thought Iowa winters were bad but when someone is trying to kill you, it is worse. I went days without taking off my combat boots, which were wet. No wonder so many men had trench foot. Walking through a foot or two of wet snow with a heavy army overcoat on was very tiring and also made us good targets against the white snow. We didn't receive any white camouflage suits until well into February, after most of the snow was gone.

I was wounded the third time when our own artillery shelled a house we had taken in Germany. We had lost our radioman so didn't know we were supposed to pull back before they shelled the town. A shell came through the roof of the house and exploded, wounding several of us as well as the eight Germans we had captured. I was hit with shrapnel at the belt line. It went through my army overcoat, field jacket, cartridge belt, web belt, and long johns. It embedded about one inch into my back, just right of my spine. If it had been an inch or two higher or lower, who knows what would have been the outcome. I still have the piece of shrapnel, the web belt and the helmet with a bullet hole in it that cut the liner strap but didn't draw blood. This happened later in Germany in a forest battle.

Anyone who lived through the Battle of the Bulge should give thanks every day. Everyone thought that after the Battle of the Bulge the Germans were done, but a lot of soldiers were killed in February, March, and April 1945.

Ed Burgess, Las Vegas, NV
Company E, 2nd Battalion, 8th Infantry Regiment

Prisoner of War

I was at Fort Meade, Maryland, for Thanksgiving Day, 1944. Then on to Camp Shanks, New York. I embarked on the USS Marine Devil on

December 12, 1944. We disembarked at Marsiller, France, on December 24, 1944. My first airplane ride (C-47) touched down at Lyon, France, landing at Air Base Relfa, France, between Nancy and Metz. We had Christmas Dinner on December 26, 1944. We mounted large trucks that night, going by General Patton's Headquarters in Nancy, France. We arrived at Luxembourg City after midnight. We were lined up in the snow and deposited our extra large, duffel bag-sized backpacks. Much foul language came from those who had purchased cartons of cigarettes and had to leave them in the snow. I joined Company E, 8th Infantry Regiment, 4th Infantry Division in Luxembourg City on December 27, 1944. I was wounded twice, captured and taken as a prisoner of war by the German Wehrmacht at 0500 hours January 13, 1945. Our position was on the outskirts of Hinkle in the Rosport jurisdiction. We were captured near the Moselle River, which is the boundary between Luxembourg and Germany.

Marcus Dillard, Largo FL
Company M, 3rd Battalion, 12th Infantry Regiment

In God's Hands

I was assigned to Company M, 3rd Battalion, 12th Infantry Regiment, 81mm mortars. I served with them from the start to the finish—all five campaigns and the landing. With the help of God, I came through it all without ever being wounded. Three different times really stand out in my mind; I came so close to being a casualty in these particular events.

The first was in Normandy. We had our 81s dug in. It was a beautiful sunny afternoon, and you could not hear one shot being fired—like the war was over. We were by our guns doing nothing, and then we did what we were always taught never to do. We all ganged up around one gun pit and started talking. After a few minutes I said, "I am going back to my mortar."

I turned and had walked maybe fifty feet when all of a sudden, out of nowhere came an 88mm shell and hit the edge of the gun hole. It killed two of my buddies and wounded five others. All was quiet again.

The second time was in Germany. We had a salient into the German lines. Just like a finger sticking in there. We had to be on alert most of the night as the Germans sent patrols out, and they came to our area and planted mines and booby traps almost every night. This one night was my turn to go to the rear in our jeep to get hot chow. My buddy, Joe Peel, from Cleveland told them to let me sleep, that he would go in my place. They had gone about half a mile when the jeep ran over a mine that had been planted that night before. Joe was not killed, but he never came back.

The third time was during the Battle of the Bulge. We had been in Luxembourg supporting Company I. After fighting the Germans, we were out of Dickweiler and went back to Herborn where our company was.

As my buddy and I left the house we were in to go to the chow line for supper, I noticed I did not have my canteen cup. I told my buddy to go ahead, that I had to get my cup. While I was in the house, I heard a big boom like a railroad gun, and all of a sudden, the shell landed right where they were serving chow. My buddy was wounded, but not killed.

I believe in all cases that God was guiding me, and guiding all the battles, also.

George Knapp, Westchester, IL
Chaplain, HQ, 12th Infantry Regiment

The Three-Man Quartet

During the Battle of the Bulge when we were in Luxembourg, one of the first shells severely injured the first sergeant of our 3rd Battalion, 12th Infantry Regiment as he stood near me. I took off my belt, made a tourniquet for his leg, and he was sent at once to the hospital. We never saw each other until our National Association Reunion in Pittsburgh about twenty years later. He was OK, but it was hard for me to think of him as the same man. He had changed a lot.

On Christmas of '44, in a small town close to the river separating Luxembourg and Germany, I conducted a candlelight service in a barn alongside the road leading to the front line. Candelabra and candles came from a bombed-out church in town. Men of all faiths attended. We only had a trio to sing as the other member of an intended quartet had been captured with others from Company K. Men from another outfit were going on the road past the barn, on the way to relieve our men up in the foxholes at the front. I was glad for my men, but sorry for the replacements getting into those front-line foxholes on Christmas Eve. The next morning, my Christmas Day Services were conducted in a two-lane bowling alley in another town a bit farther away from the front. Other services were held that Christmas Day of 1944.

When we eventually left Luxembourg, the officer in charge of a chateau in Luxembourg City said to me, "Chaplain, everything is cleaned up, but here is a set of golf clubs. Can you take them?"

He knew that I had a jeep and a trailer, so I did. I still have that set of golf clubs. We went on again into Germany into some of the same towns we had been before—this after the war passed through twice leaving nothing but rubble—no streets visible, etc. Since the war was winding down, we were coming from the south into Munich and heading out east from the center of the city. As we were proceeding outside the city limits, all of a sudden, my assistant let out a yell, jumped out of the jeep from the driver's seat without putting it into neutral and ran on ahead faster than the column was moving. I slid over and brought the jeep to a halt. Why had he jumped out? He had seen his buddy from Company K coming to us after he and others who had been captured at Echternach, Luxembourg, had been freed from a POW camp by another outfit up ahead. What a reunion! His buddy was the fourth member of the quartet that was to have sung at Christmas time.

Frank Douglas, Janesville, WI
Company F, 2nd Battalion, 8th Infantry Regiment

Hold at All Costs

We could see the open plains leading right down to the Rhine Valley—open country in front of us—after our fight through the Hürtgen Forest. The 83rd Division relieved us, and Captain Reborchek was glad to get us out of there. There were 28 left in our company that day as we got onto trucks to head out to get some rest and be regrouped. I'll never forget our truck ride out of those woods. My word! What memories of all those we left behind.

Once on the trucks (only to haul what was left of Company F) we headed south to Luxembourg and ended up in a sixteenth century chateau. We were in reserve. We slept on the floor of the second story of the building. Chapman, Moody, Rene, and others were to get passes to Paris.

I loaned Chappie twenty dollars. That night, a rifle sergeant, Peter Ramsey, had an appendicitis attack, so off he went to the hospital. Back at the chateau we were informed that all passes had been canceled. The next morning, Saturday, December 16, we were told there was a big emergency. We wondered what the past few months had been. Of course, we soon found out. The Battle of the Bulge was on.

The next day we moved out and climbed up on a rocky bluff along a ravine. The following day we went further along that ravine, and in an open field we set up the guns. The field was on two levels with about a five to six foot ridge down the middle. At the base of this steep ridge, we dug in. We also dug in the guns, a few yards away from our holes. Because the ground was soft we were able to dig down quickly and deeply.

The next day we were ordered to attack. Since Company E had fifty men, they led this futile attempt. In short order the plans were changed to "hold at all costs." That's different. The mortars fired hundreds of rounds on the Krauts on the next ridge and down along the road in a ravine near a small river. One lucky shell knocked out a Kraut tank. Engineers put mines on and near the road. Jerry knew where we were, so they sent over 88s via direct express. The shells screamed right over our ridge and landed in the nearby woods.

We built up our pillbox-like foxholes and made them deeper. We filled empty shell boxes and tubes with dirt and mud. Then one night, it got very, very cold. Everything and everybody froze solid. The fog lifted, and the air corps now had perfect targets. They really went after the Krauts. During the afternoon of Sunday,

December 24, the 5th Infantry Division moved up to relieve us. They had men.

The Krauts really did lay on the 88s. I felt sorry for them as they really didn't have holes dug, and we had only a few.

It didn't take long for us to get on trucks and haul out of there for the rear. What a Christmas present! I will never forget that moonlight ride through the snow-covered trees and woods…just like a Christmas card scene. The quietness was overwhelming. That night we bedded down on the floor of a feed mill in Berdorf, Luxembourg. On Christmas Day, we moved into a house and set up housekeeping. Jake, Moody, Chappie, and I shared a room. They managed to serve us a real dinner—turkey and the works. What a miracle.

We also got bags of mail, packages, letters and cards. I got seven or eight boxes plus letters and cards, as it had been weeks since we'd had mail call. However, the joy was tempered by the sight of all those addressed to KIAs and those who were wounded. I helped "Hollywood" (Moody's nickname for Meyers) sort out those letters to be forwarded to the hospitals. We decided not to return those for the KIAs. That would have been too much for the families. We later took our own surplus stuff, plus the other men's, over to the nearby orphanage for the children there. We'll never forget the looks on those poor kids faces. They never had chocolates.

William C. Montgomery, Long Beach, CA
Company A, 4th Medical Battalion

The Survivor

In January 1945, when the infantry was pushing the Germans back out of the Bulge, the 4th Infantry Division began recovering ground we had held four or five months before. That was in the fall, after we and the French 2nd Armored Division had liberated Paris. The glow was still there, things were pretty good, and the war was going to be over by Christmas.

Then came the Hürtgen Forest and now the Bulge. Everything was miserable. The countryside was buried in deep snow. The temperature was unbelievable. The terrain was much steeper and rougher than my native Ozarks. My litter squad and two others were jammed into a tiny wayside railroad station with some of the 1st Battalion, 8th Infantry Regiment's command post, when a runner pushed in looking for medics to pick up two casualties.

We decided all three four-man squads should go—two to carry and one to break trail. It was a good decision because when the runner finally found the casualties, we were on a steep ridge covered with evergreens in snow up to our waists.

The casualties had been hit by shrapnel the night before and were lost in the dark. One man had frozen, poor guy. The other was a real Survivor—with a capital "S."

His leg was shattered, but he had made a tourniquet of his belt. He burrowed down into the snow and covered himself with his shelter-half, lit an alcohol cube with his Zippo lighter, and shoved his rifle butt into the small flame. When the fumes got to him, he put out the flame, flapped the shelter-half and settled down for a while, then started over again.

We strapped him securely onto a litter and began a rough mile-long litter haul, with one squad breaking trail in the snow, one carrying, and one following along catching its collective breath. We wanted to make sure this survivor got to the aid station and eventually home.

I remember him well because he was such a vivid example of the hell riflemen had to live through every day. Even now, fifty-five years later, I'm still in awe of what guys like him did. My squad and I carried a lot of them off the line—enough to know it was the infantry who won the war.

A Letter from General George S. Patton

General George S. Patton wrote to Major General Raymond Barton of the 4th Infantry Division—

"Your fight in the Hürtgen Forest was an epic of stark infantry combat; but, in my opinion, your most recent fight—from the 16th to the 26th of December—when, with a depleted and tired division, you halted the left shoulder of the German thrust into the American lines and saved the City of Luxembourg and the tremendous supply establishments and road nets in that vicinity, is the most outstanding accomplishment of yourself and your division."

Germany 1945 through the End of the War and Deactivation in 1946

After holding the southern shoulder of the German thrust and saving Luxembourg in the Battle of the Bulge, the 4th Infantry Division retraced their footsteps from September 1944, re-entering the Siegfried Line at the same location they had crossed in the fall. After breaking into Germany, the remainder of the winter and spring of 1945 was spent pushing the stubborn German army deeper and deeper into their homeland. When hostilities ceased on May 8, 1945, the 4th Infantry Division was soon on its way back to the States to prepare for the invasion of Japan. Fortunately, that did not happen. This section covers the last five months of hostilities in Europe and the final chapter of the Division after returning to the States to wind down their WWII experiences.

Chronology of the 4th Infantry Division 17 January 1944—4 May 1945

Courtesy of Robert S. Rush, Ph.D.

17 January. Luxembourg: XII Corps completes preparations for attack; 87th div takes over 4th Div zone along the Sauer from Echternach to Wasserbillig, with 4th Div now on left and 2nd Cav Gp on right; 4th Div takes responsibility for portion of 5th Div zone.

18 January. XII Corps opens offensive at 0300 when 4th and 5th Divs attack abreast N across the Sauer between Reisdorf and Ettelbruck, surprising enemy. 4th Div, attacking with RCT 8, reaches heights commanding Our R between Longsdorf and Hosdorf.

19 January. 4th Div gains heights overlooking the Our NE of Bettendorf; in conjunction with 5th Div clears Bettendorf but is unable to reduce strongpoint across the Sauer from Reisdorf.

20 January. 4th Div, committing RCT 12 on left of RCT 8, continues attack N of the Sauer, clearing angle formed by junction of Sauer and Our Rivers, bypassing Longsdorf to gain positions just N and occupying Tandel.

21 January. 4th Div captures Longsdorf but is unable to take Fuhren.

22 January. 4th Div gains ground along W bank of Our River and takes Walsdorf but is still unable to clear Fuhren.

23 January. Fuhren falls to 4th Div.

24 January. 4th Div consolidates along W bank of Our River from Vianden to confluence of Our and Sauer Rivers.

26 January. 4th Div withdrawn from XII Coprs and line.

28 January. 4th Div attached to VIII Corps and enters line between 87th on N and 90th on S, occupying Burg Reuland-Maspelt sector.

29 January. 8th Inf of 4th Div is held up near Lommersweiler, but 12th bypasses Hemmeres as it drives across Our R and advances into Elcherath.

30 January. 4th Div makes little progress but does clear Lommersweiler and Hemmeres.

31 January. 4th Div clears Elcherath and Weppeler.

1 February. 4th Div, in center, advances almost 4 miles into Germany to positions overlooking Bleialf.

2 February. 8th Inf, 4th Div, drives to high ground W of Radscheid; 12th gets elements of 2nd Bn into Bleialf.

3 February. 8th Inf, 4th Div, clears Halenfeld and Buchet; 2nd Bn 12th Inf completes capture of Bleialf.

4 February. Brandscheid: In VIII Corps area, while units on corps flanks consolidate and regroup, 4th Div, attacking with 8th Inf on N and 22nd on S, breaches outer defenses of West Wall along the Schnee Eifel ridge NE of Brandscheid.

5 February. Brandscheid: 22nd Inf of 4th Div takes stubbornly defended crossroads in the Schnee Eifel NE of Brandscheid, where strong opposition is overcome; another column moves E from the crossroads and clears high ground overlooking Sellerich. 8th Inf attacks NE along Schnee Eifel ridge and secures crossroads in Schlausen Bacher Wald.

6 February. Brandscheid: 8th Inf of 4th Div, in conjunction with S flank elements of 87th Div, continues to clear the Schnee Eifel ridge. Relief of 3d Bn 22nd Inf, 4th Div, in Brandscheid by 1st Bn 358th Inf, 90th Div, is interrupted by determined enemy counterattack toward that time, but attack is repulsed after some hours of fighting; other elements of 22nd Inf attack at noon and seize Hontheim, Sellerich, and Herscheid.

7 February. Prüm: 4th Div drives SE toward Prüm: 8th Inf seizes Wascheid and reaches outskirts of Gondenbrett; 22nd secures Ober Mehlen and heights overlooking Steinmehlen.

8 February. Prüm: 4th Div arouses even greater resistance as it presses toward Prüm, but 8th Inf takes large part of Gondenbrett and 22nd clears Ober Mehlen; 12th Inf is committed on div S flank.

9 February. Prüm: On 4th Div N flank, 8th Inf completes capture of Gondenbrett, clears Hermespan, and crosses elements over the

Prüm; 22nd seizes Nieder Mehlen; 12th partly clears Steinmehlen.

10 February. Prüm: 8th Inf, 4th Div, consolidates bridgehead E of the Prüm and 22nd Inf pushes a short distance toward Prüm; 12th Inf completes capture of Steinmehlen and gets a bn to the river line across from Nieder Prüm.

11 February. Prüm: 4th Div readjusts positions before defending Prüm R line from Olzheim to Watzerath, relieving elements of 345th Inf, 87th Div, to N and elements of 358th Inf, 90th Div, to S. 8th Inf in bridgehead E of the Prüm and elements of 12th Inf on W bank of river opposite Nieder Prüm are withdrawn. 3d Bn 22nd Inf enters Prüm and starts systematic search for enemy within the town.

12 February. Prüm: 4th Div completes capture of Prüm.

18 February. 4th Div zone of action is extended slightly S as elements of 12th Inf relieve elements of 358th Inf, 90th Div, near Pronsfeld. 4th Div sends out combat patrols as diversion for 90th Div attack.

28 February. To S, corps attacks across the Prüm River in force, starting before dawn.

4th Div's 8th Inf takes Kleinlangenfeld while 22nd captures Dausfeld.

1 March. 4th Div makes limited progress in bridgehead E of Prüm River and crossed 12th Inf into it.

2 March. 4th Div, with 3 regts in assault, is slowed by terrain and lively opposition E of the Prüm and makes negligible gains; efforts to take Weinsheim, Gondelsheim, and Nieder Prüm are unsuccessful.

3 March. Enemy continues stubborn resistance to 8th Inf of 4th Div in and about Gondelsheim; good progress is made to right, where 22nd Inf clears Weinsheim and positions W of Fleringen and with 12th overcomes negligible resistance in Nieder Prüm and takes Rommersheim.

4 March. 4th Div presses eastward all along line, overrunning Gondelsheim and Schwirzheim and mopping up resistance bypassed by 11th Armd Div at Büdesheim and Wallersheim.

5 March. 4th Div drives NE clearing Duppach and Oos; one of two hills N of Oos is secured at request of 11th Armd Div.

6 March. 4th Div, after completing capture of high ground N of Os and taking Roth early in morning, follows CCB of 11th Armd Div to the Kyll, with 22nd INF on left and 12th on right; during night 6-7, crosses to relieve CCB and expand bridgehead.

7 March. Expanding bridgehead secured by 11th Armd Div, 4th Div's 22nd Inf takes Hilleshiem while 12th secures Bolsdorf, Dohm, and Bewingen. CCB, 11th Armd Div having been relieved E of the Kyll by 4th Div moves S toward Lissengen.

8 March. While 22nd and 12th Regts improve current positions, 4th Div drives rapidly NE with TF Rhine (8th Inf, reinf) to Honerath area.

9 March. Passing through 87th and 4th Divs, both of which are then out of contact with enemy, 6th Cav Gp drives E without opposition and establishes contact with 11th Armd Div. TF Rhine completes 4th Div's mission, clearing Honerath, Adenau, Rodder, and Reifferscheid before being passed through.

10 March. 4th Div is detached from VIII Corps and attached to Seventh Army. 4th Div refits.

30 March. 4th Div attached to XXI Corps 7th Army. 4th Div completes its crossing of the Rhine and advances E through elements of 12th Armd Div.

31 March. In XXI Corps area, 12th Armd Div spearheads corps attack toward Würzburg-Schweinfurt-Kitzingen region and is followed on left by 42nd Div and on right by 4th Div.

1 April. XXI Corps continues E and NE with 12th Armd Div spearheading, 42nd Div following on left and 4th Div on right. 101st Cav Gp, screening right flank of corps, is attached to 4th Div.

2 April. CCR 12th Armd Div, reinf by 2 bns of 22nd Inf, 4th Div, overcomes opposition in Königshofen.

3 April. 8th Inf, 4th Div, completes its crossing at Ochsenfurt and CCB, 12th Armd Div, also crosses after bridge is repaired. CCR, after closing in Sonderhofen assembly area and releasing attached elements of 4th Div, drives rapidly E, forward elements reaching N-S railway line at edge of Herrnberchtheim.

4 April. 8th Inf, 4th Div, presses northward in Ochsenfurt bridgehead in conjunction with CCB. 22nd and 12th Regts launch attack in Königshofen area make slow progress on wooded heights.

5 April. After CCB 12th Armd Div, seizes bridge at Kitzingen, 8th Inf of 4th Div establishes small bridgehead there. CCR clear Seinsheim and Ippesheim. 22nd and 12th Regts, 4th Div, continue to clear region E of Königshofen.

6 April. Bad Mergentheim: 8th Inf, 4th Div, mops up in Main bend N or Ochsenfurt. 22nd and 12th Regts clear Königshofen area and start SE abreast toward Bad Mergentheim. Corps prepares to pivot SE about 4th Div.

7 April. Bad Mergentheim: 22nd and 12th Regts, 4th Div, continue SE on right flank of XXI Corps against scattered resistance; 22nd Inf clears Bad Mergentheim while 12th Inf drives to Tauber R line.

8 April. 22nd and 12th Regts, 4th Div, patrol actively SE on right flank of XXI Corps. 9 April. 4th Div activity is limited to patrolling on right flank of XXI Corps.

10 April. Renewing offensive on right flank of XXI Corps, 4th Div's 22nd Inf pushes SE to line Bartenstein-Niederstetten while 12th, to left, overruns Laudenbach. RCT 324, 44th Div, is attached to 4th Div.

11 April. 4th Div, reinf by RCT 324 of 44th Div, opens drive SE toward Rothenburg. 12th and 22nd Regts, 12th on left making main effort, reach general line Baldersheim-Röttingen-Laudenbach.

12 April. 4th Div continues SE astride the Tauber toward Rothenburg with 12th and 22nd Regts abreast while 8th and 324th Regts mop up on left and right flank of div, respectively.

13 April. XXI releases 101st Sq to 4th Div. 4th Div, with 12th, 22nd, and 324th Regts from left to right, in assault, advances to line Freudenbach-LichtelSchrozbertg-Blaufelden on right flank of corps.

14 April. Rothenburg: 8th Inf shuttles SE on 4th Div left flank to follow CCR 12 Armd Div, closely while other elements of 4th Div push closer to Rothenburg.

15 April. Rothenburg: 8th Inf, 4th Div, attacks SE toward Ansbach in conjunction with CCR of 12th Armd Div. 12th and 22nd Regts push a little closer to Rothenburg against stronger resistance.

16 April. 8th Inf, 4th Div, continues toward Ansbach while 12th and 22nd Regts gain positions just N and W of Rothenburg, respectively, and 324th drives SE on div right.

17 April. Motorized TF of 8th Inf, 4th Div, thrusts to outskirts of Ansbach while rest of regt works southward through woods to Ober Felden area. 12th Inf takes Rothenburg. Other elements of div clear villages in region SW of Rothenburg.

18 April. 4th Div continues southward and begins relief of 324th Inf with 22nd Inf.

19 April. 8th Inf, 4th Div, reaches Rödenweiler area; 12th reaches line BottenweilerWildenholz-Theuerbronn; 22nd completes relief of 324th which is detached from div and corps, and pushes S to line Michelbach-GailrothSchönbronn-Rossbürg-Schainbach; 4th Rcn Tp clears Rot am See and maintains contact with 63d Div.

20 April. Crailsheim: 4th Div gains 6-8 miles against disorganized resistance; elements of 22nd Inf reach outskirts of Crailsheim.

21 April. Crailsheim: 4th Div continues S, gaining 6-8 miles along entire front. 8th Inf, heading for Ellwangen, gets advance elements to Stocken. TF Rodwell (12th Inf, motorized), 4th Rcn Tr, and supporting units) is formed for attack on Aalen and drives S through 22nd Inf to vicinity of Jagstell, between Crailsheim and Ellwangen. 22nd Inf clears Crailsheim with little difficulty.

22 April. In 4th Div zone, TF Rodwell thrusts to outskirts of Aalen; 8th Inf reaches Ellwangen but is unable to clear it; 22nd drives to Adelmannsfelden area, W of Ellwangen.

23 April. 4th Div gains it objectives and is ordered to continue to the Danube. 8th Inf drives through Ellwangen to Westhausen. Aalen falls to TF Rodwell, which also takes Unter Kochen, 22nd Inf reaches objective W of Aalen.

24 April. 4th Div speeds S toward Danube, TF Rodwell reaching Giengen. 25 April. Forward elements of 4th and 63d Divs reach the Danube and start crossing. Most of 8th and 12th Regts, 4th Div, are across at Lauingen by end of day.

26 April. Danube River: 8th and 12th regts, 4th Div, push S from the Danube to Dinkelscherben-Horgau area; 22nd, leaving elements to guard Lauingen bridge, assembles S of the Danube.

27 April. 4th Div's 8th and 12th regts continue to follow armor SE; 8th Inf secures bridgehead across the Lech at Schwabstadl with 2 cos.

28 April. 8th Inf, 4th Div, maintains Lech bridgehead at Schwabstadl while 12th continues southward toward the Lech in same area and prepares to cross upon completion of bridge. 2222nd Inf moves SE to cross the Lech.

29 April. 22nd and 12th Regts, 4th Div, cross the Lech in Schwabstadl area and drive E to W bank of Amper R; 8th Inf maintains Lech bridgehead and sends elements to Augsburg to relieve elements of 3d Div.

30 April. Isar River: 22nd and 12th Regts, 4th Div, drive quickly to the Isar; 12th Regt takes Loisach and Isar bridges in vicinity of Wolfratshausen.

1 May. Isar River: 12th Inf, 4th Div, drives SE to Thankirchen and Hechenberg; 22nd Inf gets 2 cos across the Isar in Unter Schäflarn area; 8th Inf (-) shuttles forward to screen left flank of div W of the Isar.

2 May. Against disorganized resistance, 12th Inf, 4th div, drives to Tegern See while 22nd crosses newly completed bridge near Unter Schäflarn and drives SE to Miesbach-Gusteig area.

3 May. 4th Div remains in place, mopping up and preparing for relief by 101st A/B Div, which is moving into its zone.

4 May. 4th Div is relieved by 101st A/B Div, which completes movement into corps zone and is attached to corps, and starts to Neumarkt area for occupation duty within 3rd Army zone; 8th Inf and 101st Cav Rcn Sq are attached to 101st A/B Div.

Norm Chapin, Jenison, MI
Companies A and B, 1st Battalion, 22nd Infantry Regiment

German Soldiers, Loaded For Bear

I joined the 22nd Infantry after the Battle of the Bulge as a brand new Second Lieutenant coming from the 100th Division. My battalion commander, Lieutenant Colonel George Goforth, was a great officer. I was called into the CP one night and given orders to go to a town called Elligen and hold it until the battalion came in the next morning. Captain Claude Ecabert was my CO, and Captain Willis Williams was our S-3.

I felt—being called that late—that I would probably get my liquor ration. What else would we do at that time of night? I was given my mission and soon found out.

I selected one squad comprised of twelve men and took off down the road. On the way I heard a noise, so I stopped my squad. Here came two German soldiers on bicycles. I stopped them and determined that they were two snipers going down the road to shoot at our battalion in the morning as we advanced. I still have the compass one of them carried, plus a pair of field glasses and a sniper's rifle one of my squad leaders gave me. As we proceeded down the road, we heard more noise. I still had part of my squad on both sides of the road. To my amazement, here came at least two squads of German soldiers, loaded for bear. Not knowing just what to do, I stepped out in front of them and indicated I had a lot of men with me. They surrendered, and then I had the problem of just what I would do with them. As luck would have it, a half-track came up behind me and took them off my hands.

The funny part of the whole escapade was the last incident. As we proceeded into the town of Effigen, we encountered another German soldier. He was riding a bicycle and headed in our direction. We stopped him and found out he was the squad leader of the squad ahead of him. Drunk and very belligerent, he became one of us.

Clive Clapsattle, (Deceased) Ransomville, NY
22nd Infantry Regiment

Looking for my BAR Man

I joined the 4th on April 6, 1945, or about then. I know the last town we were in was Kircheim, and that is where this story begins.

When we left Kircheim the platoon took over the hill. We "did in" two Germans, and as we continued on I told my BAR man to be my backup as there were more Germans close to the road where HQ was going to be. I went around a tree and ran into a German. He swung his rifle, so I had to shoot him. That is when I was shot in the neck (a half-inch from my artery) and part of my left ear. My BAR man was not around—gone—and boy, did I swear.

I fixed myself up with sulfa and tried to decide what to do. The platoon had already gone over the hill, and I could not connect with them, as there was a German behind me somewhere. Well, I loaded up and started firing to about where I thought he was. He finally said, "Camerade!" and surrendered. I took him prisoner. Going down the road into town, I picked up five more Germans. I had to take them about a half mile and tried not to pass out, which I did about one hundred feet from a forward aid station. Medics fixed me up, and I wanted to go back and have a talk with my BAR man, if not shoot him.

They sent me to a MASH unit where they operated on me and then sent me to a hospital in France. I came back to the unit in Ausbach. I signed in with Staff Sergeant Ivan Johnson and then started looking for my BAR man. I found him and was mad, but I passed it over.

Before this, I was connected with SHAEF and in charge of perimeters when Ike, Churchill, Marshall, and others were meeting in little towns outside London. I was in intelligence and security. I was hooked up with G2 and had the job of seeking out Germans dressed as GIs. I followed all outfits, including the 4th Infantry Division, to Paris where I set up a HQ. I worked with both the 3rd and 7th Armies all along the German border.

Harper Coleman, Tucson, AZ
Company H, 2nd Battalion, 8th Infantry Regiment

London

While in England, I got to leave the hospital on occasion. The local people would give afternoon tea parties, and some of the hospital patients would be invited. We would go by truck to the homes. Also, there were several tours to town and one to a park with canoe rides.

On December 26, 1944, I was transferred to a replacement center near the hospital. I was there several days. While there, we were required to do guard duty at the POW camp in the area. I had several of these tours of duty during my stay.

From there, we went to Le Havre, France, where we were put on boxcars. We were on them four or five days going across France. It was winter time and very cold during this trip. There were a number of rest stops along the way with hot meals. Very soon in the trip someone came up with an old bucket of some kind. With a little coal from the engine and some wood along the tracks, we had a fire going in the middle of the car. We also burned a hole in the floor.

I was back with the 4th Infantry Division by the first week in January of 1945.

It did not seem like the unit I had left. Almost everyone was new, and I knew very few of them. The gun crew that I served with was gone. I was told that they took a direct hit on their position sometime during the Battle of the Bulge.

This time, the snow seemed to get deeper—several feet deep in most places. Roads were almost impassable with the mud, snow, and rain. This was during the time the division was pushing the Germans back after the Bulge. We were on line for more than a week in the rain and cold. We were issued "Snow Packs" (rubber bottom shoes with leather tops). I had gone for about a week without being able to change socks or to dry out my shoes. After about a week of this, and being so cold, I came down with a bad case of trench foot. By the end of January 1945, I was back in the hospital in Paris, unable to walk, where I stayed for about a week. After this time, they decided to send me back to the rear. I was put on a hospital train and sent to England for the second time. This time I was in a hospital about an hour's ride by train north of London. I stayed there until after VE day, May 8, 1945.

While in the hospital in England and after I was able to walk, some men were given passes to go into London on a number of occasions. We could be away from the hospital for three or four days if we wanted to. We would stay at the USO club in London for several days at a time. The hospital was located a mile or two from a small town and the railroad station.

Several things happened while at the hospital. On one occasion, on our way back to the hospital and on a very foggy night, we had to crawl in the ditch by the side of the road to find where to turn to get to the hospital. Another time, four or five of us decided to take a cab back. When the cab was within several blocks of our stop, someone said to stop here, and we all jumped out and ran. We still owe the driver. If I ever find him, I will pay up.

In London I was sad to see the destruction of the city. The air raids had done quite a bit of damage. During this time, they were being bombed by V-2 rockets and Buzz Bombs. I was very close to the V-2 rocket explosions on several occasions. There were bomb shelters all over the city, but you could not always get in when the sirens would sound. The buzz bombs started sometime in October or November while I was still on the front lines. We would hear them going over every night. However, they were going on past us, and we did not get too concerned about them at that time.

It was the policy at this time that if anyone had a given number of days stay in the hospital, they were automatically to go stateside. With a little help from several nurses, my records disappeared for several days. With the end of the war near it did not make any difference. I was sent by hospital ship to the States. I entered the hospital at Camp Butner, North Carolina. After a thirty-day leave, I received a medical discharge on September 6, 1945.

Albert Schantz, Reading, PA
Company A, 1st Battalion, 22nd Infantry Regiment

Pay Raise

On March 7, 1945, I arrived in Prüm, Germany, and was assigned to Company A, 22nd Infantry Regiment, as a replacement rifleman. The 4th Infantry Division was pulled back from the front line of battle to rest and take on replacement troops. The 4th Infantry Division had suffered many casualties after 199 consecutive days in combat and required about a fifty percent replacement base.

We did some retraining and reorganizing, at which time I was asked to be the assistant 60mm mortar gunner in the 4th platoon.

After retraining, we boarded army trucks and journeyed south through Luxembourg, on to Metz and Nancy, in France. Then east to Luneville, France, and north to Worms, Germany, where we crossed the Rhine River and engaged the enemy on the front line on March 29, 1945.

In school I had read about town criers. Well, for some reason we had to hold up in Luxembourg for a few days. There I saw the town crier. He walked through the town and cried out the news. All the people either opened their windows and listened or came outside to hear the news.

During our first battle we were pursuing the Krauts when the 60mm mortar gunner collapsed from exhaustion, and I automatically became the gunner. That meant carrying a 60mm mortar and a .45 caliber pistol in place of the M-1 rifle. The mortar was heavy; it seemed to weigh about sixty pounds with the base plate.

The infantry motto was "Follow me!" I must have performed properly because I was promoted to Private First Class on April 1, 1945, just three days into battle.

The promotion and the Combat Infantryman Badge gave me a raise in pay. I can't remember exactly how much the promotion increase was, but I do remember that the private rating paid thirty dollars per month, and the Combat Infantryman Badge paid an additional ten dollars per month for the rest of my military career. I suppose the promotion raise was about five dollars per month, all of which raised my monthly pay to about forty-five dollars.

During one of our battles we encountered sniper fire. Our platoon leader, a field commissioned second lieutenant, spotted the sniper in the steeple of a church on top of the hill we were trying to take. He asked me to set up my mortar and knock the sniper out of the steeple. I set up and knocked the steeple and the sniper off the church on the first shot and saved a few American lives. The rest of my platoon cheered, but not loud, for fear of revealing our location. I don't remember whether this shot was the reason for earning my first stripe on April 1, 1945, but it may have been.

We were all scared of being shot at and terrified hearing the incoming German artillery shells, especially the screaming meemies.

We were all scared of being shot at and terrified hearing the incoming German artillery shells, especially the screaming meemies. These were a special type of German artillery shell. They made screaming noises as they headed in our direction. I experienced anger, and my adrenaline made me want to fight harder when I saw my comrades receive a hit.

One of my comrades, Harry Campbell, was the most relaxed man I ever saw in the midst of a war. If we stopped for ten-minute rest, he would lean against a tree and fall asleep on his feet. We called him "Sleepy" Campbell. We couldn't depend on him to stay awake for guard duty.

Max Gartenberg, Livingston, NJ
Company E, 2nd Battalion, 12th Infantry Regiment

German Informant

When I tell this story, people look at me sideways, but it's true. How I wiped out a troop of SS…with a little help.

I joined the 4th Infantry Division in March 1945 at a replacement center just west of Metz and was assigned to Company E of the 12th Infantry Regiment. Nothing much happened for a while until the division was moved south, out of General Patton's 3rd Army and to General Patch's 7th Army. Hitler had fooled our intelligence into believing that he had a huge military redoubt in Bavaria, and I suppose the 4th Infantry Division was enlisted to help take it out.

Still, there were Jerries enough to keep us busy, and men suffered and died as we raced East across the German heartland.

My story begins at twilight in early April. We had marched through a wood and came to the edge of a town. We were going to flush houses to get us some billets. It was always better to sleep in a house than in a fox-hole, even if you didn't get a bed and had to sleep on a hardwood floor.

There were three or four of us banging on a locked door, but no one answered. Finally, I bethought myself of my German class and shouted, "Machen sie auf!"

Immediately, as if I had spoken magic words, the door opened and a middleaged man appeared.

"Wir sind anti-Nazi," he said, raising his hands.

The man escorted us into his kitchen, where he introduced us to the members of his family: his wife, two or three kids, and an elderly grand-mother. All of them seemed glad to see us. Then the man asked his wife to get a bottle of wine and some glasses.

It looked like we were going to have ourselves a little party when an-other GI ran into the house and announced: "The captain said we're not to flush any more houses. This town is full of Jerries, and we're not going to do anything more until the morning."

I bade, "Auf weidersehen" to my host and followed the GI out.

The next morning, we resumed clearing the town. Most of the Jerries seemed to have left during the night, and the work went swiftly. I had just gone up some stairs when I heard somebody rush in below.

"Anybody here sprechen sie Deutsch?" "Yeah. Gartenberg?"

As soon as I heard my name, I went down the stairs and encountered a company runner. "There's a Jerry trying to tell us something and nobody can understand what he is saying."

The runner led me down the street to another house. Inside an officer and a noncom were sitting with a big map stretched out between them.

Opposite them sat a civilian. It was none other than my German host from the night before. He recognized me, too, and greeted me warmly.

What he was trying to say, I told the officers, was that in a stone house beside a stream there were SS men. My new friend pointed to the spot on the map. Immediately, I could hear walkie-talkie crackling with the information. I was in a house when I heard the first boom.

It was firing at a building—a stone house. Behind it was a stream. The house was solidly built, and the shells were doing no visible damage. But inside the concussion must have been horrific.

Suddenly the door opened, and men in dark uniforms started running out. A machine gun opened up out of nowhere, and the men fell to the ground like berries shaken off a bush. There were at least a dozen I could see wounded…dying.

I sometimes wonder about the German civilian who helped us. Was he an opportunist or was he truly against the Nazis? Whatever he was, I can't help but be grateful to him.

A few days after this incident took place, while running through a newly plowed field, I myself was cut down by machine gun fire. It was April 15, less than a month before the war in Europe ended.

Robert R. Gable, Upperco, MD
Company I, 3rd Battalion, 8th Infantry Regiment

Knoll's Raiders

Sometime after the Sauer and Our Rivers, Company I was coming out of a wooded area. The word was given to take cover in the woods. After some time, someone came to the first platoon and called out for me to go see the Company Commander, just ahead of us in the woods.

I was told by the captain that I was to be part of Sergeant Knoll's Raiders along with Private First Class Owens, Raymond Lord, Crisfield, Winford Norris, Norman Fritz, and an artillery forward observer. The CO briefed us on our mission, which was to take an outpost on the hill.

Sometime later we were all given white cloth to cover our uniforms, and we set out to take the high ground. We started out in the wooded area to keep cover— until we were about fifty to one hundred yards from the pillbox.

The artillery observer called for artillery fire on the area. At the same time, we would go out of the woods, into the clearing, with artillery going over our heads. Our observer was very good with the shells landing just in front of us. It was now getting late in the day, and the Germans were all inside for safety from the shelling.

As we were able to get close to the pillbox, we could see two houses with Germans who were forming a triangular defense. We had to stop for more artillery. After the artillery barrage opened up on the final house and dazed the few remaining Germans, the patrol moved in to capture them. The Raiders captured forty-six prisoners, of which seventeen were captured without firing a shot. We had zero losses in the raid.

By nightfall the battalion was able to come up to the high ground, set up, and secure the hill. Sometime later, the account was in the Stars and Stripes service publication. Our battalion commanding officer sent each one the clipping describing the fight that Knoll's Raiders took part in.

Carlyle Coleman, Bullhead City, AZ
Company E, 2nd Battalion, 8th Infantry Regiment

Asleep

I would like to hear from anyone who knows where Hill 555 was located. I do know we took it four days in a row and the Germans ran us off it three nights in a row. I also remember a small village of Hinkel, divided by the Moselle River. We initially took the east bank, and the Germans occupied the west side. I have been unable to find it on any map since the war. I was leading a contact patrol that night and was to check all our outposts. At the last outpost prior to Hinkel, we found one of the outposts in an abandoned farmhouse, high on a bare hill. We were not challenged as we approached over open ground. This caused some tense feelings for a while, because we could not raise anyone by calling.

It was a moonlit night, and I was reluctant to go through the only window not boarded. I did not want to silhouette myself in that window if it were occupied by Germans. We finally went to the back of the house, threw a grenade into the cellar and still did not get any response. I had no choice but to go through the window. Upstairs, I found them all asleep. Their excuse was they had not been relieved in forty-eight hours and had passed out from exhaustion.

If we had been the enemy, their sleep would have been permanent. I contacted the Company CP and was instructed to take over so they could get some rest. Later that night, the Germans attacked and killed or captured the platoon-strength outpost in Hinkel. A good buddy of mine named Coulter was taken prisoner, but later we overran a prison camp and released him. He refused to be shipped home and finished the war with us. Every company had one, but he was our company clown. He had the knack of making us laugh in the heat of battle. He was our morale booster and helped us all keep our sanity.

Paul Brunelle, Avon, MA
Company G, 2nd Battalion, 8th Infantry Regiment

Another Shower Story—
On the Maginot Line

From the book, Company G, 2nd Battalion, 8th Infantry Regiment, 4th Infantry Division, *by Shirley Devine. Used with permission.*

February 5, 1945, I was listed as LIA (Lightly Injured in Action) with frozen feet. I was sent to a hospital in France close to the German border. While we were there we were transported to the Maginot Line for showers. As I remember, above ground there was a series of domed forts. We were lowered deep into the earth by an elevator into what looked like an underground tunnel, which apparently joined the forts together. It was all lighted and heated.

The line was thought to be impregnable and perhaps it would have been had the Germans not outflanked and gone around it.

We were taken into a shower room for hot showers—quite a treat after having spent those cold months outdoors.

For a little while we were allowed to walk around, and we were amazed at the extent of it. Now, fifty-five years later, part of the Maginot Line has been preserved as a museum. I would like to go back and take another look.

Denver Sayre, Wildomar, CA
Battery C, 44th Field Artillery Battalion

100-Yard Dash

On February 5, 1945, the 3rd Battalion, 22nd Infantry Regiment, with tank destroyers and medium tanks attached, attacked Brandscheid. I was attached as a Forward Observer for the 44th Field Artillery Battalion. Pea-soup fog came in. As we advanced, a large number of pillboxes were taken, and by late afternoon Brandscheid had fallen. We were to be relieved by the 90th Infantry Division and move to a different sector early the next morning. That night we bedded down in a large stone house on an intersection in the center of town. Early the next morning, just before first light, my buddy, Forward Observer Robert Smith, and

I took our sleeping bags out to a parked jeep about one hundred yards from the building. Just as we were throwing the bags in the back of the jeep, what seemed like a hundred Jerries came out screaming from behind other buildings and sheds.

They were yelling, "Surrender, surrender!"

We had left our carbines in the building and were standing there unarmed. I believe we broke the record for the hundred-yard dash without a shot being fired. Once inside, all hell broke loose. It seems about five hundred enemy troops had taken advantage of the dark foggy night and amid the confusion during the relief, they had infiltrated our lines. Bob and I wanted to get to one of the windows to help ward off the attack, but the lieutenant told us they already had too many riflemen at the windows. He sent us to the basement to assist in caring for the wounded. The firefight lasted for about three hours until the tank crews got enough cover to man the tanks. We almost immediately heard cries of "Comrade! Comrade!" from the ones ordering us to surrender. As we left, we observed the sickening sight of bodies strewn about, some run over by tanks. I give thanks to this day that we made that dash to safety.

Joseph Kraynak, Lansdale, PA
HQ Battery, 29th Field Artillery Battalion

Soldier's Diary

This is another aspect of soldiering that does not fit neatly in the concept the brass had for us. At one point in our move forward, we noticed there were MPs guarding an old barn. I could not believe my eyes. I stopped and talked to the MP in charge, asking him,

"Why the hell are you guarding this gem?"

I thought he was a comedian when he said it was full of barrels of five-star cognac champagne. My immediate thought was to get my hands on some of this so I could help the war effort by sharing this with my friends. After about fifteen minutes I convinced him we could make the next few weeks fun. If he would guard me instead of the barn, while I went inside to confiscate some of this "gold," I would split with him whatever I could get. It looked impossible because it was all in full-sized wooden kegs, row after row. But I noticed cases of empty bottles with old-fashioned caps attached to them. My lights came on. In about one hour, we had about six or eight cases of bottles filled. The rest is history. I gave the MP his share, and we took off.

Needless to say, I had more buddies in the next month than I knew what to do with. This sort of experience, I am sure, will not be in the record of great deeds, but it is truly in a "Soldier's Diary." It made our lives bearable for the approaching five weeks of the war. I'll say in our defense, we rationed it out so we could still perform our necessary tasks.

Stan Tarkenton, Virginia Beach, VA
Company M, 3rd Battalion, 22nd Infantry Regiment

Taking a Break

Battalion Reserve is a holiday with capital letters. In simple terms, that rare occasion means you and your guys may have ten or twelve or more hours off from the war. The adjoining battalions continue with the nasty war business while you may have the chance to catch up on some sleep. Sure! Or, you may even have the opportunity to sew a few stitches in the rags you are trying to keep together…sometimes, a shave.

There were not any quick trips to paradise to soak up a few rays, but there were some precious few hours away from the shooting war. I remember seeing the movie, Meet Me in St. Louis, in a barn in France while in reserve. It was a fair movie. Not really, but it was a diversion to escape from the reality of the times.

On one brief reserve, we were so far in the rear there were rear echelon-type people walking all around us in the town. These GIs looked like real soldiers compared to our ragtag crowd. Some even carried weapons, which I doubted they knew how to use. They wore nice, new, clean-looking uniforms; they shaved and probably took a bath every week or so. They were impressive looking. They seemed to act as though they thought they knew what they were doing. Our guys were wearing an assortment of tattered and torn clothes, muddy and cruddy looking. Our boots looked like they had been rejected by the Goodwill people. We were not only dirty to look at, we were dirty. Since shaving was an almost unknown luxury, everyone sported ugly beards which had the appearance of something thrown out of the Persian glue pots.

One of the rear echelon dandies approached us asking, "Hey, do you guys want to take a bath?"

"Bath?" was the response, "Hell, yes!"

I could not remember the last time I had soap and water on my scroungy hide. "Where can we get this bath?"

Directions were given. Second invitations were not necessary. Even though my feet were worn and hurting, I hurried along with everyone else. On the way, I was thinking about how much I was going to lie back in the tub with plenty of hot water and soapsuds.

Since it was one of those blue-cold days without sunshine and with dreary winds blowing off the snow, I decided I just might spend the rest of the war reposing in that hot tub of water. I could almost feel the heat again, already.

In our obvious eagerness, one would have thought someone was giving away free beer. We arrived en masse at the park, but I did not see a bathhouse. What's this? Someone's idea of a joke? There were no bath facilities in this park. Some of those clean-uniformed jokers were prowling around in the park area. One of our men corralled one of the official-looking, clean-uniform types, with chevrons up and down his sleeves, saying, "Hey, Jack, where's the freaking showers?"

"This is it," he beamed proudly.

"Yeah? This is what?" demanded one fairly short-tempered individual.

"This is the shower," he said, pointing to a series of overhead pipes that had the appearance of an extended child's gym set—without the swings.

One man assisted the clean-uniformed man by grasping him about his necktie, saying, "Listen to me, you smart ass. We came over here to take a shower. You start talking "perlite-like," or I may just kick your butt inside out."

"I told you," he says, "This is the shower."

"WHAAAAT?"

The sergeant-type goes on to explain they would heat the water via some kind of a heating contraption, and the warmed water would be pumped through the pipes while we washed under the flow.

"Are you nuts! It's freezing out here!" shouted another man. It really was a blue-cold day.

"It will not be cold under the warm water," the sergeant-type allowed.

"What about our clothes?" someone said. "We sure as hell can't strip down in the buff here in the middle of this town. Them are Krauts walking all around out there. Some of them are women, too."

"They don't care, if you don't," Sarge said. "Heat up the water!"

After about a half hour, the sergeant calls, "OK, boys, your shower is ready.

Here's some soap and towels."

So about twelve of us pile our weapons in a heap and promptly shuck off our dirty rags down to our bare-assed skin. We soap up our beards and our hides under the warmed water flow while trying to see the color of our skin again.

Some of the German females walking by the park smiled or outright laughed and pointed. We sure as hell did not care. "Eat your heart out."

Elmer Klaus, Columbus, OH
HQ, 22nd Infantry Regiment

Shangri La

As you know, not too many war stories were fun and games, especially if you were in a line company and would always be looking for ways to stay alive for another sunrise. The following incident has some humor and took place in the vicinity of Brandscheid, Germany in February 1945—just beyond the Siegfried Line, and the weather was terrible.

I wasn't feeling well while on guard duty, and the sergeant of the guard said we were short of men and had to continue on duty. Shortly thereafter, I doubled up in pain and was transported to an aid station, which was a huge barn that looked like Shangri La to me. It was away from the misery of the front lines, and I was hoping I could stay there for a few days. No such luck. I was diagnosed as having the GIs, given medicine that had a horrible taste, and, lo and behold, I was back at the front the next day—all cured. I found out the miracle drug was Kaopectate— 'nuff said.

Merle P. Davies, New Baltimore, MI
Company F, 2nd Battalion, 12th Infantry Regiment

Christmas Hymns

Sometime after the battle for Nieder Prüm, Germany, I was vacationing in an unremembered military hospital. Each morning the major commanding the nurse brigade would sneak into the wards, one by one, swagger stick under her arm. She was on the prowl for any erections among her male domain. Down the rows of beds she would proceed, smacking down all who "stood" in her way. After your first experience with this lady in the morning, it became our first activity of the day. One patient challenged her as to the purpose of this mission, to which she replied, "I do not want my young nurses to be embarrassed."

During a Christmas Eve service, the choir and parishioners were to join in the singing of the hymn, "Silent Night, Holy Night." As the first words of the selection were delivered, my mind flashed back to another evening many years ago. A group of "still alive" soldiers were singing those same words. In unison with that hymn was the delivery of a fire mission by a nearby artillery battery, interlaced by the sounds of a firefight off in the distance. What a contradiction of ideas and feelings in those times. That particular experience and many others were purposefully blocked from my mind for over fifty years. The singing of a Christmas hymn triggered a long-forgotten experience. The months of November and December have always produced at least one nightmare relating to those turbulent times. I was once called a "foxhole hero," but I consider myself only a survivor.

Milt Bremer, (Deceased) Sherman Oaks, CA
Company K, 3rd Battalion, 22nd Infantry Regiment

An Imperfect Map

In the early spring of 1945, the 22nd Infantry Regiment was beginning to move fairly quickly across new terrain in Germany. One day the company commander put a map in front of me and pointed out a hill with a clump of trees about halfway up. I was to take my platoon into that clump of trees and see if I could reconnoiter further, finding out what was ahead. Movement was fairly easy at first; there was a long draw and some trees and bushes that provided concealment. As we got closer to our objective, I started looking for the clump of trees. No sign of trees, and by now all we had for cover was tall grass. I was beginning to wonder if I was lost, but other features were readily identified. Finally, we were at a point where we were on a long slope with nothing ahead but grass. Off at two o'clock, about one thousand yards away, was the beginning of a pretty dense pine forest. I moved back down to where my radioman was waiting, and called back to the company CP.

When I told the CO that the clump of trees didn't exist, he said, "What are you talking about? The trees are on the map."

"I see them on the map," I said. "That doesn't make them on the ground.

There is no sign that trees were ever in that spot."

After several minutes of arguing, I got instructions to try to move across the open area toward the distant trees. I got the platoon up and we began to move out. Just as we came out into the open, a German 88mm opened up on us from those woods. But it couldn't touch us. Its flat trajectory and the slope of the hill kept the projectiles over our heads; however, the concussion of the shells passing over was enough to knock us down. Even worse was the ringing in my ears. I could hardly hear for a while, and to this day, I have a constant ringing.

We finally pulled back and the firing stopped. In reality, there were only a few rounds fired at us—it just seemed like more at the time. And the forest was so thick we could see nothing at that distance. We never did find out how those trees showed up on our maps.

Jesse Stadler, Mt. Morris, MI
Battery B, 29th Field Artillery Battalion

Peppering a Plane

Sometime in the spring of 1945, the 29th Field Artillery Battalion was in position on German farmland. Stadler and Smolens were serving on Gun Number 2 of Battery B. This gun was used to sight in fire missions, and when on target, it was to be followed by the other guns. "Possen fuses" were being used, which would explode within twenty-five feet of any object. This particular mission was being observed by an overhead Artillery observation aircraft that was, unknowingly, within twenty-five feet to the trajectory of the outgoing rounds. One round exploded and peppered the airplane wing with shrapnel (unknown to the gunners). The plane moved swiftly away and was not seen again.

Lon Murphy, Jr., Columbus, OH
Company L, 3rd Battalion, 12th Infantry Regiment

They Were All Around Us

We were advancing near Crailsheim, Germany, in April, 1945. Our objectives for the day were three sets of woods. We didn't encounter any enemy opposition in the first two woods. It was overcast and getting late in the afternoon when we entered the third set. There was a slight misty fog hanging around, and visibility was not great. Schuler and Carter were near me as we entered the edge of the woods. I heard a "pop" and saw a body fall from out of the shadows beside a tree in front of me.

Schuler said, "They're all around us, Murph," and he fired again—and another body fell.

I couldn't see any Germans in that gray misty forest, but Schuler kept hitting them. Soon, rifles and machine guns were popping all around us. The muzzle flashes would light up in the mist when people fired, and that gave me an idea of where to shoot.

Schuler said, "Come on, Murph. Get up here by me."

Just then, a Kraut machine gun opened up, cutting Schuler across the thigh. If I had been up where he was, I would have been right in the line of fire myself.

My eyes adjusted to the low light, and I noticed there were Germans all around us. We had obviously surprised them, and we were intermixed with them in the woods. In the confusion, I lost sight of where the rest of the company was. The only GIs I saw were Schuler, Bacon, and myself—and Schuler was out of action.

He was crying out, "Help me, help me!" but we couldn't help him.

We were too busy keeping the Germans off us. I was letting that BAR rip as fast as it could. I was burning up the ammunition. I know the barrel was hot because it started to rain, and the drops of water would hiss and steam as they hit the barrel. Adrenaline was pumping, and I was reacting to events around me with split-second actions. Out of the mist, I noticed the upper half of a human form sticking up out of a foxhole pointing a rifle right at me. Reflexively, I held down the trigger to the automatic rifle and swept it from right to left across the midsection of that image. The bullets kicked up the dirt directly in front of the German, and he disappeared from view.

I noticed a few more GIs in the area now, and they took care of the machine gun nest. The firing quieted down, and many Germans came out of their firing positions to surrender. We took a count and had twenty-seven prisoners. We were searching them and checking them for maps and papers when the shells started falling. Apparently, the Germans who withdrew started sending mortars and artillery in our direction in preparation for a counterattack. All of the prisoners and GIs dropped to the ground. German prisoners were crawling around looking for shelter. We made it clear to them that they were to stay put or suffer the consequences. We then found holes to get in for shelter. I was standing in a hole during the shelling, keeping an eye out for more Germans to counterattack. I saw their dark, shadowy, images coming toward us, and I started letting the BAR rip again.

Shells were exploding around us, and one landed a little closer than the others did. It felt like somebody pounded my arm with a sledgehammer. I felt a burning sensation in my upper right arm. I glanced down and saw that my field jacket was torn, but I didn't see any blood. I kept firing. This was no time to let up and get distracted. Once again, the firing quieted down, and the Germans withdrew. I didn't know what happened to Schuler.

A medic came over to look at me and said, "We're sending you back to the aid station, buddy."

I checked myself out and discovered that the front of my field jacket was torn from left to right with a large hole in the upper right arm. A piece of shrapnel had ripped across my jacket and hit me in the arm, pulling the jacket material behind it and into the wound. This was fortunate because it helped reduce the bleeding. Two people were needed to escort the prisoners to the rear. Since I was wounded and going to the rear anyway, I was one of them. I gave my BAR to Carter and took his M-1. As we started walking down the road with the prisoners, shells started coming in. We made the prisoners run all the way to the rear. I believe they were as happy to be leaving the front as we were. We left the prisoners with Company M. I walked to the aid station and passed out as soon as I entered the door.

I regained consciousness about thirty minutes later. I was lying on a hospital cot with my arm bandaged up. The nurse came by and talked to me a little bit. Later, a doctor came by and told me that I was lucky. The jacket material that was with the shrapnel in my arm had prevented a lot of bleeding. The fragment had entered above my bicep, spun through the muscle, and came to rest around my elbow. They cleaned out the wound, bandaged it, and placed me under observation for a few days. I found Shuler in the hospital. His legs had been torn up by the machine gun. He had also been hit by shell fragments while lying on the ground waiting for help. He seemed in good spirits. He said the doctors told him they were going to send him back to England for more surgery. He wrote us later saying they had to remove the leg.

There were also some wounded German prisoners in the hospital. There was one German with a badly wounded leg. Two orderlies were giving him a rough time. They dropped him off on one side of the room and were making him walk to his bed on the other side on his own. I could see by the look on his face that he was in severe pain and was afraid. He could hardly manage. Each step reopened the wound in his leg a little bit. I couldn't take it anymore. It turned my stomach. These two orderlies had never been on the front lines and had no idea what this German soldier had already gone through. I had been there. My face got red and I yelled at them with all of the fury I could muster.

I said, "Cut that out and help that man to his bed. It's your job."

Also, in the hospital, I ran into Private Moore. In those days, you had to be on the front lines and under fire for thirty days to get a Combat Infantryman's Badge. Private Moore was a rare individual. He had two Purple Hearts and no Combat Infantryman's Badge. On his first trip to the front, the truck he was in hit a mine before he got there. The second time he was on the front lines for three days before being wounded.

Since I was able to walk, I would help the nurses out. I would carry bedpans, get bandages from the supply room, or do whatever else I could to help. The field hospital was a very busy place. The nurses never rested. I don't think most people realize how hard the nurses of an army field hospital work. I appreciated everything they did for me and for all of the other wounded and dying soldiers.

Infection set into my arm, and the doctors had to go in again and clean it out. It turned out to be a more complicated wound than they had previously thought. I ended up staying in the hospital for about thirty days. When I returned to my unit, the war was over.

Milt Bremer, (Deceased) Sherman Oaks, CA
Company K, 3rd Battalion, 22nd Infantry Regiment

The Fly of Your Pants

In the early months of 1945, we were following a tank unit, making sure there were no pockets of the enemy hiding out where they could harass us. I was assigned a hill and the area on the other side. With my men spread across about seventy-five yards, we started up on what seemed an easy task. However, the hill was covered with wet leaves, and it was like climbing a sheet of ice. We had to dig in our heels and rifle butts to make any progress. Even though the weather was cool, we were soon drenched with sweat.

I kept saying, "Come on, let's keep moving. It's all downhill on the other side." I was hoping there was some level ground where we could catch our breath. Eventually we did reach the crest and discovered to our dismay that it dropped away as precipitously as the slope we had just climbed. To stand required that you use one foot, ankle bent, on each side of that knife-blade ridge.

If there had been any enemy around, we could have been picked off like targets in a shooting gallery.

Finally I gave the order to start down. The descent was worse than the climb with men sliding into each other or sprawled on a sled of wet leaves. When we hit bottom we sat, breathing hard, while I decided to find an easier way to return to the company CP. One of the men scouting around came back with word of a railway tunnel. So, off we went. Near the exit at the other end, some of the men discovered a stack of wooden cases. It turned out to be a cache of beer. Of course, there was no way to keep the hot and thirsty men from sampling. There was one problem though: as one of the men put it, the beer was pretty good, but if you were going to drink it, you better do it with the fly of your pants open.

Stan Tarkenton, Virginia Beach, VA
Company M, 3rd Battalion, 22nd Infantry Regiment

The Pain Will Ease

Along about April, 1945 we were going through southern Germany like cow chips through a tin horn. Perhaps the newscasters were reporting there were pockets of heavy resistance, but the command element of the Third Reich was breaking down. The Luftwaffe and the Panzers had almost run out of gasoline, and the onetime fearless Wehrmacht was reduced to arming old men and children as the home guard. The war was winding down....The German soldier was merely doing the job assigned to him, just as we Americans were doing our job. I do not believe any of the soldiers on either side wanted to be where they had to continue to perform in battle. All were battle weary.

Men were still being killed and wounded. I was with many of my brothers when it was their time to leave us. Always an emotional hit, it hurt. There were those that I did not even know were gone until I missed them after a particular engagement with the enemy.

"Where the hell is Eddie?" someone would ask.

"He took a hit about a half hour ago," might be the reply. "Is he OK?"

"No... He bought it...." "Damn! Damnit! Damn..."

Then I would try to blink away the tears, all the while trying to breathe again with that severe shortness of breath, the excruciating pain of loss of a trusted friend and the tightness in my chest. Breathe deep, the pain will ease....

By the last week of April we were less than a hundred miles from the German-Austrian border and closing fast. Heavy numbers of those of the German military were deserting their units to try to return to their homes in peace. Almost every night now, small groups of approximately six to eight to ten men, in ragtag civilian clothes, would unwittingly stumble into our positions. When we detected the deserters coming through the woods at night, rifle shots would be fired in their direction, but well over their heads if we were the least bit uncertain as to their identity or their intent.

"Comrade! Comrade!" they would cry out in a plea, hoping they would not be hit by random rifle fire.

"Kommen sie hier!" was the usual American response back to them. They would troop in single file with their hands on their heads. They did not carry weapons nor did they have papers to identify themselves. Their civilian clothes, obviously picked up somewhere along the way, looked as though they were purchased in depression days' flea markets. Always they denied they were deserters. They were simply farmers going home. Sure, farmers always go home at three in the morning.

We knew they were lying, and they knew that we knew, but who cared? They were worn-out wretches of all ages. They were sick and tired of a war they did not want and did not start. They were polite enough gentlemen and grateful to be still alive. The poor bastards were only trying to make it back to their homes and their families. They were fearful of capture by the Americans. They were informed by their officers that the Americans were ruthless killers. They feared us, but they were more fearful of falling into the hands of the Russians.

If we had any food, we would give them some of ours. After all, our food came from that last German town we had just secured. We gave them some of our cigarettes. If some were suffering from wounds, our medic would render first aid or we would treat their wounds. We treated them as needy human beings.

I remember a conversation one night with several deserters who spoke and understood English fairly well.

"How many soldiers are in your company?" they were asked. "We are farmers," was the response.

"Sure. How many farmers are on the farm you are farming?"

They forced smiles and tried to look perplexed. Why must we continue searching for military information?

"Listen to me," I explained. "Stay out of the woods at night. Travel only by walking on the open roads in the daylight hours. Tell the other men. You could be killed creeping up in the woods at night. Tell 'em now—mach schnell."

He translated to the other deserters and you could see their faces light up in smiles of relief. Looking at me, they nodded their heads up and down as though they were soliciting confirmation of what was said to them.

Maybe, it is just possible, they would learn that we Americans were not as evil as their Nazi officers had informed them. Maybe, in time, the surviving Nazi officers would realize the Americans were not so bad, and we were pretty good guys, after all.

Dominick Huster, Morris Plains, NJ
Company A, 1st Battalion, 22nd Infantry Regiment

Hairy Escape

After crossing the Rhine, we were advancing on a small town by going through a large, open field when we came under fire from snipers in a small clump of trees in the middle of the field. We all hit the ground and started shooting in that direction. Suddenly, a rabbit jumped out and headed off to our right. Everyone in the company stopped shooting at the snipers and started shooting at the rabbit. I was a mortar gunner and fired my .45 caliber pistol—the barrel needed cleaning anyway. The rabbit escaped the hail of bullets unharmed. We took the town unopposed. Our marksmanship wasn't tested by the Germans.

Frank Bradley, Medford, MA
Company G, 2nd Battalion, 8th Infantry Regiment

Change of Scenery

My army career had been spent in the Signal Corps where I was stationed at Headquarters in London, in a spit and polish outfit. We worked three shifts around the clock and were stationed in British homes in what was known as Montague Square, just down from Marylebone Station. We stood inspections every three weeks on the Saturday morning when we were completing our turn on the day shift. Our buttons and shoes were polished so you could see your face in them. Our uniforms were spotless and pressed to perfection. We were clean-shaven and had military haircuts. Our Enfield Rifles were in top shape; our bayonets gleamed, and we knew the numbers of all our equipment.

After Paris had been liberated, I was assigned to the advance party and sent there. In February I was reassigned to the infantry and sent to some place in France for Advanced Infantry Training. I believe it was sometime in March when I joined Company G, 8th Infantry Regiment, somewhere in Germany. What a surprise! Never had I seen soldiers who were exactly the opposite of my garrison idea of what a soldier should be. In short order, I became just like them. I became a really tough, hardy, weather-beaten infantryman. I was stocky, strong, and stupid in the ways of the infantry, and the last man in the squad. As a result, Sergeant

Gibson assigned me to carry the Browning Automatic Rifle (BAR). My assistant was Forrest A. Downs from Riverhead, Long Island, New York. We carried about twenty pounds of ammunition in twelve ammo pouches, plus the usual two bandoleers and a couple of hand grenades. He had an M-1 rifle rather than the BAR.

My first day in combat was some baptism of how things were going to be. We moved forward in a skirmish line with tanks. That is where a long horizontal line is formed consisting of a tank and two or three infantrymen, another tank, and two or three infantrymen, so that the company covers quite a wide stretch of ground. As we moved forward, the tank on the extreme left at a crossroad ran over a mine, which disabled it by blowing off a track. It also blew Private Patsy Pagano of Newark, New Jersey, to his death. His legs were blown off, and he seemed to fly up into the air for fifteen feet before dropping lifeless to the ground. A sergeant who was standing near him suffered from the concussion. He was bleeding from the eyes and ears and crying with pain and distress. A medic came up and helped him. I did not know his name.

The skirmish line moved forward and stopped on the crest of a hill overlooking the town. The tank commander fired a shell through the steeple of the church in the town we were attacking. When that cannon fired I must have jumped ten feet. Immediately we moved forward down the slope in that skirmish line, with the tanks firing their 20-millimeter machine guns over our heads as we approached the town. These 20-millimeter machine gun bullets went in one side of the roof or building, passed through the interior, and came out on the opposite side. Never had I heard so much noise nor seen such confusion. The tanks finally stopped firing, and we proceeded to go through each house in search of enemy soldiers. Now we were formed in files, one on each side of the street with the right side watching the houses on the left, and vice versa.

Usually, three soldiers would enter each house and proceed to search each room to make sure no enemy lingered. When we finished clearing the town, headquarters troops would drive through it, stirring up clouds of dust as they proceeded to the next town to wait for us. We did not use the road but formed up into that skirmish line, keeping in sight of each other. We made our way over hill and dale or through heavy underbrush until we hit the next town where the same procedure was repeated.

I learned that the tanks fired that cannon through the steeple because it was a German observation post from which they could watch our every move. Since they had everything zeroed in and fields of fire to use against us, it was important to eliminate that steeple.

One night we finally stopped in a beautiful barn filled with lovely brown cows. What a splendid spot to spend an evening, we thought. It was nice and warm, and we immediately stretched out on some straw on the floor. After about five minutes in those plush surroundings, we were politely requested to move our weary bodies out because another company, which was to be in reserve the next day, was to occupy the premises. Since we were to lead the attack, it was important for us to be up and at them bright and early, and up front where the action would be.

On another occasion we walked in blinding rain for about three days. We were in thick woods, and the water dripped off the trees as well. It also squirted in and out of our combat boots like a pump with each step that we took. We finally stopped around midnight. Every stitch of clothing and anything else in our possession was as soaking wet as we all were. Around 0200 hours my teeth began to chatter, and there was no way they would stop. Our medic, Doc Reilly, carried two canteens. One of them he filled each morning from a barrel of cognac that the cook carried with his supplies in case he needed to flambé one of his gourmet delights.

Since I had been in the Signal Corps prior to joining the infantry, and had sent many messages stateside that "so and so" had suffered death, blindness, or what have you, from drinking poison alcoholic beverages, I was reluctant to drink anything other than water. Doc Reilly prescribed a large drink from that special canteen for my chattering teeth. I took one large gulp with no results but the second swallow produced the desired effect. Not only did my teeth stop chattering, but also my whole body suddenly felt a welcome warming from the top of my head to the tips of my toes.

My worst combat action with Company G was in Elwangen, Germany. I had fired my Browning Automatic Rifle and was not quick enough in moving to another spot. A German shot me through the helmet behind my left ear. The helmet must have turned the bullet enough to keep it from taking the top of my head off, and I escaped with a nine-stitch scalp wound on April 22, 1945. After a few days in the hospital, I rejoined Company G. We continued slogging along through Germany, fighting sporadically and liberating the concentration camps (whose hideous sights and rotten stenches are ingrained in my memory) until the war ended in Europe on V-E Day, May 8, 1945.

We moved around after that to a German armored training camp where we had double-tiered beds. A few days later we were taken to the Archives Building in Bamberg, Germany, where we were relegated to sleeping on the coldest and hardest cement imaginable. Most of us were on the slim side, and our lack of flesh made us feel that our bones were protruding through our skin. It was a common occurrence to hear moans and groans during the night as buddies turned in their sleep. In my own case, my weight was down to 120 pounds. I had been surviving on a D-bar, a special chocolate bar contained in one of the K-rations. I had one half for breakfast and the other half for supper and never suffered any pangs of hunger.

We were now on occupation duty, and as a Technician 4th Class I was in charge of a squad assigned to guard an Italian prisoner of war camp. Our schedule required us to be on duty from 1400 hours to 1800 hours, and from 0200 hours to 0600 hours. The afternoon shift was not too bad, but that 0200 hours to 0600 hours shift was brutally cold and uncomfortable. Our first day and night on the job went without incident. On the second day, we made sure that those Italian prisoners had plenty of wood available for a comforting fire during our dog watch. We told them to get plenty of wood or else. Well, they tore down the Burgermeister's wooden fence to provide us with warmth. The Burgermeister became very hot under the collar when he discovered his fence was gone, and we received orders to cease and desist. In a very short time, we moved back out into a field and woods before we went to camp "Old Gold" in the vicinity of Marseille, France. This was prior to returning to the good old USA.

After thirty days R & R, we journeyed to Camp Butner (near Durham, North Carolina), until we were discharged on October 20, 1945. How come I never forgot that date?

I cannot remember the names of any of the concentration camps that Company G liberated, but I will never forget the starved and worn look of the people— so skinny and so decrepit and so happy to see the Americans. Especially do I remember the stench, dirt, and squalor of the camps. The sights and smells were enough to turn the stomachs of men who had seen horrible sights of wounded and dead soldiers. Such disconcerting things are part of war and combat and, while upsetting, are generally viewed as such. That people could be subjected to such base living conditions and still survive seems incomprehensible to many Americans. Perhaps that is why some deny the horrors of the Holocaust. It is indeed incredible that men could be so inhumane and so cruel to their fellow men.

All combat infantrymen are familiar with the smell of death and destruction as buildings are blown apart, and years of dust and the accumulation of years of dirt are suddenly dispersed through the air. One familiar sight was that of farm animals—horses and cows, usually out in the fields, lying dead on their backs with their legs sticking straight up in the air, their stomachs bloated and distended.

Occasionally they burst open as the gaseous by-products of decay and putrefaction exceeded the holding power of their dead bodies. Such scenes and smells in war may become common, but it is hard to accept man's deliberate cruelty to man.

Bud Whelan, Silver Spring, MD
Company M, 3rd Battalion, 22nd Infantry Regiment

On the Job Training

I was inducted into the Army on October 3, 1944. Basic infantry training at Fort Blanding, Florida lasted thirteen weeks.

"You will get more training up north," the army advised.

I spent ten days at home, went to Fort Dix, New Jersey, and got all new uniforms and equipment.

"You will get more training overseas," someone in charge said.

I went overseas on the Queen Mary. "You will get more training in England…"

I got off the Queen and onto a train, which took me to a boat and then to France. We took a long hike up a steep hill—by this time, we were leaving three tracks.

At an old farmhouse, I was told I was now in Company M, 3rd Battalion, 22nd Infantry Regiment, 4th Infantry Division.

"Pitch tents, set up guards—don't go into any other fields because they have not been cleared of mines," we were told.

The next morning we bitched because the GIs in the next field didn't pitch tents…until we saw some dead men in body bags. This was the start of my on-the-job training. We were sent into a town called Prüm, for "intensive training by foreign instructors."

I spent my nineteenth birthday in the small town of Hillshiem. While celebrating in the basement of a house, some of the uninvited instructors knocked the upper floors off the building. What a party—I will never forget it.

While waiting for a new bunch of "trainers" at Worms, on the Rhine River, with a bunch of other GIs in tanks, half-tracks—all kinds of things—across the river on a large hill, five deer suddenly appeared. Every man saw them at the same time, and they all fired at once. The deer, the forest and half the mountain disappeared—and maybe some of my new trainers.

Bad Mergentheim: My next trainers were out for their masters from the SS Munchen OCS. They brought out the best in us. All of this training was beginning to pay off. Near the end of April we crossed the beautiful blue Danube. Boy, was that named by a tourist guide. We were now on our way to the Austrian border. I saw lots of my trainers, but they didn't seem interested in me anymore; they just put their hands on their heads and walked by. Then the training was over, and we shipped to Camp Butner, NC. We almost had another chance to get more training in Japan, but Harry Truman thought we knew enough.

All kidding aside, I can sit and write this because of the training, love, devotion, courage, bravery, and caring of our own 22nd FBI (Forgotten Bastards of the Infantry). Bless them all.

Sydney Krause, Kent, OH
Company K, 3rd Battalion, 12th Infantry Regiment

Remembrance of a River Crossing

I recall what it was like to be sniped at by an 88 and the reaction of Sergeant MM, who shared the scare with me. He was a guy we looked up to as the most combat-savvy and gutsiest man in our Company, known to all as just plain "M," his nickname.

During the drive to push back the breakthrough, we were brought up to a jumping-off point just west of the Our River. Once off the six-by-sixes, we started our trek toward a hill just above the river. We had to trudge across a broad open slope, cursing the knee-deep snow that made it slow going, especially with us being such inviting targets. There we were, a string of lumpy black figures against that white background, minus so much as a sheet for cover. But as we'd drawn no fire half way to the wood ahead of us, we relaxed a bit and just concentrated on making it across. About ten feet in front of me was M, and walking along a fence in the draw below was another line of guys. In among them was the "Mad Russian," who had been hit some time before and was just back from the hospital. He was in high spirits, having put some Schnapps in his canteen so it wouldn't freeze up on him—not a thing we'd want to do going into the attack. Joker that he was, the Russian had spotted some of our light tanks on the road, and, noting their 37mm guns, he laughed, "What do they think they're going to shoot with them—mosquitoes?"

Carrying on the way he was, I thought he'd probably missed Hürtgen. For a long time, none of us had done any laughing.

Before I knew what was happening, I saw M suddenly throw himself down, and I did the same. In that instant the air was split by a familiar ripping sound from an explosion that hit just below us. The shrapnel was zinging inches over my head as I dived into the snow. As we all knew, the 88 was so lightning fast that by the time you heard the report the darned shell was on you. Down by the fence, the Russian was strangely dancing around in pain, bleeding, his helmet blown off. He threw his M-1 away, and with his arms flailing and knees pumping he was starting to grope his way back when the second round came pounding in. M and I had crunched ourselves further down in the snow waiting for the third round we knew would be coming, after which we made a mad dash for the wood. It occurred to me afterwards that if the 88 rounds were point detonating we might have been saved by the snow we had cursed.

Having reached the wood, we burrowed down into the snow as deep as we could get and waited, hearts beating in the back of our mouths. You could be vaporized by a direct hit from an 88; it had happened in the mud of Hürtgen. I could just picture that forward observer following us with his binoculars and in a foul German rage growling back to his gunner, "Du Arschloch! Zwei rechts, eins runder, und mach's schnell!" (You @$*=#!, two turns right and one down, and be quick!)

He evidently had something to show the first time around (our Russian probably wasn't the only one he'd snagged), but it must've burned him that we got away. I had the feeling he'd looked into our very faces, tight with fear, and said he had to get those gutless swine.

We didn't have to wait long for the damned things to come bearing down on us like so many banshees crashing through the trees. We shook with each boom as if it was right on us. Thanks to the observer's rage (half a turn down and he'd have had his wish) the shells landed just ahead of us. As we moved on up, M said something to me about how scary it was—an 88 coming after us like that. And, dammit, the way he followed us. This stuff was bad enough without them going for you personally. It made me feel a lot better to know how he took it.

We spent the rest of the day in place, sort of huddled against the snow, and broke out our K-ration while we waited for orders. The sunless air was getting icier by the minute. As luck would have it, I had the lunch ration and, already frosted to the bone, that meant eating a chunk of cold cheese with a lemonade chaser. But I was alive.

At dusk, we finally proceeded up a kind of winding trail and just off the trail at the top of the slope I came on a sight I hadn't seen before—a frozen mound of four GIs curled up on one another. They were the guys in Company I who had taken the 88s intended for M and me. How they got heaped that way, I didn't know. Would they have sort of clung together protectively when they heard the stuff coming in? It was one of those things you tried to put out of your head. I felt bad for them and bad that we had brought it in on them.

It wasn't long before we arrived at the top of the hill above the west bank of the Our. Somebody thought he heard some small arms fire in the distance (a patrol?), which didn't seem to make any sense. We knew where they were, and they us. A kid who had come up with the last batch of replacements said maybe it was guys from Company I wanting to get even. Oh, sure.

We finally made our way down to some well-dug foxholes, nicely built up— German style—with logs on the sides and top. Next morning, at first light, the stuff was hitting all around us. Some thought it might be coming from behind, our own artillery supposedly wanting to soften up the Germans over the river and falling short. Others thought it was the Germans wanting to take some casualties and hold us up. The runner stumbled into our hole, white in the face, holding his stomach. I got the medic, who gave him a morphine shot and put a bandage on him. A piece of shrapnel had made a hole about the size of a half-dollar in the middle of his gut. It scarcely bled. Maybe it was the cold. Anyway, it was the classic million dollar wound. As we moved out he asked the medic to make sure somebody knew he was there.

When we started peppering the hill on the other side of the river, the most active fire was coming from one of our machine guns. The gunner, "E," a ruddy, hoarse-voiced kid from Minnesota (they liked to have a guy his size lugging the barrel), was about twenty paces to the right of me. The night before we got on trucks we were having a smoke together, and E had taken off his knit hat and was scratching his head with his trench knife. I didn't say anything, but I didn't like the looks of it. Jinxed for sure, I thought. Anyway, just as we were getting the order to move on over the river, I heard a sharp metallic pop. E had stuffed his canteen inside his field jacket, and a sniper had hit him right in the canteen covering his heart. The red water gurgled out, and he fell face down on the ammo box. I thought I heard the chatter from M's angry grease gun, but it was more likely to be accurate at closer range. The kid said he'd seen a Jerry come out from behind a tree trunk and steady his rifle on a low branch....no telling. M had sprayed in that direction.

The snow was pretty deep on top of the frozen river and our haste only made us stumble all the more as shells started falling in among us, breaking holes in the ice. We stopped firing when we noticed it had become quiet on the bank. Once there, we found that the Germans who hadn't been killed or wounded had taken off. We yanked several of the wounded out of their holes—pathetic-looking guys—wet-faced and calling out in spasms, "Nicht schiessen! Bitte, nicht schiessen! Keine Gewehr." (Don't shoot. No weapons.)

They'd cast off their helmets and their gray uniforms were torn. One guy was bleeding down both sides of his face. Another had a bloody hand over his side, and the third was holding his thigh. I did a little scrounging in their hole. It was not above their comrades to leave a booby trap or two to reward the scrounger looking for a Luger. Next to the helmets and rifles was a half-eaten tin of Baltic sardines—Spruten. The image of it hit me as kind of sad. Nothing else to eat. Sure enough, life in the infantry was as lousy for them as for us. My father had told me he used to eat Spruten—poor man's caviar. Only he had them with black bread and beer.

M was about to march these guys around to the other side of the hill, but he paused as if he had second, second thoughts. He looked around for someone to take these guys back. I didn't want to be the one. That forward observer might get his wish. Besides, I had to be scouting out a hole or digging one, since the Germans were usually zeroed in on a position they'd just abandoned. I went looking for somebody to dig with me and found a lone guy who had apparently lost his buddy. I didn't especially like him, but no matter…He would be OK and besides, he happened to have a strong arm. I was thinking M had better get with it and do some digging of his own.

Later on, when I asked around, I got word that rather than being knocked off trying to take care of those whimpering clowns, he'd had second thoughts. At least that's what I heard. If that's what happened, M had probably considered it a necessity (him for them, potential victims of their own incoming anyway?)—for which it would be hard to fault him.

M was the soul of our Company. He was not a big guy—at most, five-nine, skinny, with a gimpy walk—far from imposing. But he had a forceful personality, and everybody saw him as a natural for his role as leader. Whenever a new second lieutenant came up—which was often enough—M would tell him what he had to know. Wanting to see to it that the Company made its objective and maybe a little more, M was a CO's dream. Eventually it would cost him.

Back in Normandy, he took a burst from a burp gun that got him up the side of the leg, and when the Company pulled back, M lay there in pain behind enemy lines, playing dead until the hedgerow was retaken. Sometime after crossing the Our, the Company had taken a certain town. But a remnant of Germans were holding out in a house at the far end. M and B, his right-hand man, a wiry little squad leader in M's platoon, went out to get rid of that remnant. At about the time M and B called back that they had flushed the Germans out and had taken the house, our artillery came in on it and killed the two of them. But that's another story.

Lon Murphy, Jr., Columbus, OH
Company L, 3rd Battalion, 12th Infantry Regiment

The Fight Goes On

As we advanced toward the Our River in early February, some companies adjacent to us had already crossed the river. They had advanced so rapidly that some German units were bypassed and remained on the west side of the river. We were proceeding down a draw toward a paved road just west of the river. I was at the front of the column with the lieutenant. The temperature was just below freezing, and there was a light snow on the ground. The sky was gray and overcast. The lieutenant, my BAR assistant, the radioman, the company runner, and I crossed the road to the cover of some trees on the other side.

The lieutenant shouted, "Heinies!" and jumped into the road firing his carbine. A German heavy weapons platoon was walking right down the side of the road with their weapons broken down and slung over their shoulders.

The remainder of our column was still coming down the draw. They fanned out to the right and formed a skirmish line coming down the hill. It was all over in a couple of minutes. Germans lay dead and dying in the road. Many were screaming or crying. They never had a chance to fire their weapons. They were taken completely by surprise.

We proceeded through the woods to the river bank. The Our River wasn't a very impressive river. It was narrow and not very deep. The water was murky. It was flowing swiftly with runoff from some melting snow. Ahead and to the right crossing the river was a one-lane bridge with wooden planking.

Our objective was to cross the river and take the large hill on the other side. The lieutenant called for smoke to cover our crossing but was told we had already used our daily smoke ration. Since we had just wiped out a German platoon, the lieutenant decided we should be clear to cross the bridge.

The lieutenant called for the radioman, Carter, and another GI to be the first to cross the bridge. Just as the radioman and the GI cleared the bridge and set foot on the east bank, a machine gun cut them down. The radioman fell to his knees and slumped forward. Carter spun around and ran back to us. The machine gun kicked up dirt around his feet as he ran, coming closer and closer. Carter dived through the air and rolled as he hit the ground with bullets ripping all around him. He rolled into the brush at the edge of the woods. He wasn't touched by any of the bullets. We knew the Germans had the hill defended and the bridge zeroed in.

The lieutenant called for other GIs, including Esposito and me, to go across the bridge next. The first man made it across. Splinters were flying from the wooden bridge as the machine gun raked across it. As I was running, I could see Esposito under the bridge, hanging onto it with his hands and his feet in the water. I decided running across the bridge would mean certain doom.

I ran full speed toward the river about twenty yards upstream from the bridge. When I got to the bank, I leaped as far as I could. I couldn't swim, but the river didn't look very deep. I hit the ice cold water and immediately sunk in over my head. I kept running under water. The current was swift, and I was swept downstream towards the bridge. I managed to get to the east bank about ten yards upstream from the bridge.

I was completely waterlogged. My boots, cartridge belts, bandoleers, pockets, and helmet were all filled with water. I found it very difficult to get up the river bank. I was water soaked and it was very muddy and snowy. I pulled myself up to discover there was an open area to cross to get to the cover of some trees.

I ran as fast as I could but felt like I was in slow motion. The extra weight of the water slowed me down a lot. I heard the machine gun open up. I could see dirt kicking up from the ground in front of me. I saw tracers pass eight inches in front of my eyes. If I had been dry and running one step faster, I would have been dead. I could hear guys from my company cheering for me as if it was a football game. They were shouting, "Run! Run! Run!"

As I ran for the trees, I noticed a four-foot tall wire fence topped with barbs stretched as a barrier between me and the safety of the trees. There was no way I was going to clear that fence as waterlogged as I was. Out of the corner of my eye, I noticed a spot where someone had dug a hole under the fence. I dived for it and made it through.

The machine gun couldn't shoot at me anymore. Due to the contour of the terrain, it couldn't sweep any further in my direction. While all of this was going on, some of our guys were able to set up a machine gun on the west side of the river and lay down some suppressing fire. The

German gun fell silent. More GIs got across the river, and we assaulted the hill. By nightfall the hill was ours.

It was a dark, cold, winter night in Germany. I was soaking wet and had no change of clothes, and we were sleeping outside. The guys found a blanket and gave it to me. I wrapped myself up in the blanket and before long I was dry.

Rations had been brought up from the rear by truck but had been left on the other side of the bridge. There was a call for volunteers to follow a guide-wire through the dark, down the hill and back to the bridge to get rations and bring them forward. Each volunteer would get one extra ration. Esposito and Sergeant Roe went along with me.

As we approached the bridge we noticed some soldiers coming down the road. One of them shouted out, "Bist du Deutsches soldat?" (Are you a German soldier?)

"Hell no!" replied one of us, and a firefight broke out.

Apparently there were still some Germans around that we had by-passed in our advance. Sergeant Roe asked for some grenades. We gave him about four grenades, and he crawled off to the right. He tossed the grenades on them, and that ended the encounter. Esposito was badly wounded with two bullet wounds in the side. He was helped to the rear, and I never saw him again. We got the rations and returned to our fox-holes.

We had taken the crest of the hill and began to dig in. As we were digging, the Germans counterattacked. They were coming through a hedgerow and then a small clearing. We killed several of them. Company K was on our right flank. I was the last man on the right of Company L and Sergeant Ramsey was the last man on the left of Company K. He was our point of contact. He was about ten feet away from me during the counterattack when he was shot in the head and killed. We walked by some of the German bodies the next morning. It was a gruesome sight. Their eyes were wide open and staring at us. Some of them had frozen with their hands stretched upward and fingers spread apart.

The next morning I was part of a patrol that was sent down the hill again. There was a railroad tunnel through the hill, and it was feared that the Germans would use this to get behind our positions. We were pre-pared for the worst as we crept into the tunnel.

We encountered no resistance, but we did find the remnants of an abandoned German machine shop. They had excavated rooms into the sides of the tunnel and installed machinery for the manufacture of small arms. Apparently the shop had been evacuated in a hurry. The only German found was a civilian. He was an old man and worked as a custodian in the shop. Some of my fellow soldiers held him at gunpoint and searched him. They went through his personal items and found a pocket watch that looked as old as he was. It was probably given to him by his father or grandfather. I could see the fear and sadness in his eyes and tried to talk the guys out of taking his watch. I was unsuccessful. My heart was filled with sympathy and compassion for the old man.

We made contact with the rest of the company at the east end of the tunnel and proceeded to press the Germans back. Three straight times we advanced against the Germans and were pressed back. Each time, we ended up at the same position we held at the crest of the hill. Sergeant Ramsey's body was still lying there.

Frank Douglas, Janesville, WI
Company F, 2nd Battalion, 8th Infantry Regiment

Send Our Bodies Home

From January 17, 1945 on, we were basically in combat. Our rest and recovery was over and the one hundred new replacements were "baptized." We old timers felt sorry for them, but such are the ways of war. On the 18th we were attacking across the Sour and Our Rivers. Company F was going down a rather steep, wooded slope to the river. The engineers were to get us across in boats. Most of the company crossed, but we mortars were bringing up the rear when the Krauts sank the last boat. We moved back up the hillside a bit when the Krauts started working us over with screaming meemies rockets. One exploded in the top of a tree that I was under. I was knocked out cold, and my mortar barrel was cut in half by a big piece of steel. Everybody assumed I was dead. Eventually Chapman came over to get my wallet and watch to send home to the folks. Thank God he did—otherwise I'd have frozen to death during the night.

About this time, Lieutenant Bacon had fallen into the river and was soaked. He told us to hole up in some nearby foxholes, post guards, and wait for him to return from the Battalion CP, where he'd gone to get some dry clothes, if possible. Several hours later, the Germans really shelled the hillside. During the confusion, a tree burst really did a job on Moody. He was really bloody with a cut in his gut area. Bacon came back, found him and Theil, but claimed he couldn't rouse any more of us.

The next day we waited and waited, but there was no sign of Lieutenant Bacon. We stayed the night there again. The next morning Rene and I found a CP and were told how to get back to our company. Captain Reborchek was dumbfounded to see us. He'd been told we were dead. Our suggestion to send our "bodies" home got nowhere, so we went up the street and rejoined the rest of the weapons platoon that had originally gotten across the river.

Frank Douglas, Janesville, WI
Company F, 2nd Battalion, 8th Infantry Regiment

Thinking About the Battle of Prum

An excerpt from his book, Oh So Young, *used with permission.*

MONDAY, FEBRUARY 26, 1945

Something new has been added to our diets. They've put us back on 10-in-1's, the first time we've seen those things since last July—which is at least seven years ago. The first order of the day was to fill up several empty 105 and 81 ammo boxes with dirt and plug up the windows of our room. The krauts have decided to shell this town in the usual way—only more so. We laid low most of the day, played cards, looked over the joint, gabbed, sorted out the 10-in-1 rations left by the 3rd Battalion, and just waited. I expect Chap to be back any day now. Nobody stuck his big toe out of any of the buildings, for the jerries are in everything across the river. Especially the railroad station. We have run up against a solid line again and it looks as though we're in for trouble. This is it for the krauts as they haven't got much land left on this side of the Rhine River. There's an OP and machine gun located in the railroad station. The 105's bounced off that place most of the day, but couldn't do much damage to those inside. I slept alone tonight as I expected Chap to come in after dark; however, he didn't show. Hope nothing happened to him.

We set up a .50 caliber machine gun on the second floor before turning in for the night.

TUESDAY, FEBRUARY 27, 1945

The first that that we did this morning was to bluff the krauts with a feint attack. In short, we fired everything we had; Jake had a field day with the 50 cal.—its barrel got red hot before he quit firing. The object was to draw jerry fire to find out their positions. In this purpose we were successful. Too damn successful, for the 88's came in by the dozens; so, we all hauled our little asses down to the fruit cellar under the house until things cooled off. We weren't there alone, for the two old krauts left behind to take care of the cattle were there also. No comment! But, we'd better keep an eye on them. After a breathing spell and an all quiet, we went back upstairs. My but they sure changed the appearance of this rubble heap with their 88 special delivery mail. Greek has been fixing our 10-in-1's, he even made a batch of chocolate pudding. Hollywood came through with an 8 ounce package with a large Hershey bar in it, as well as four letters. I answered and asked for more air mail stationary, cookies, handkerchiefs, etc. At times I wonder if the folks realize that any of these letters could be the last one? I wonder myself. This game is beginning to wear my nerves down. Kennedy just came back from the CP with the hot poop. C Company is to come in on a left flank and wipe out the railroad station and F Company is to go the right, break the line, and then with E Company go up to the top of the hill. That isn't much, so sleep good tonight.

WEDNESDAY, FEBRUARY 28, 1945

The hot poop says this is to be the real thing. Surprise is to be the major weapon. "What? No 1,000 bomber softening up process? They can't do this to us. The hell they can't." Well, anyway we had a light breakfast, stacked our rolls, got our K's and water, and left early. It was about 6:00 AM, rather dark out yet, and the sky is very overcast. We are in luck. This is one deal Chapman is going to miss. "Now isn't that just too bad." Lord only knows that he's had his share of this crap. I wonder how the rest of us will fare in the deal? We're off! In a single column we went up the road to the right, followed an 8 to 24 inch wide path along a slight ridge, over the railroad tracks, and into the first trenches. So far, so good. We've caught the bastards with their pants down. Just about this time the 22nd opened up and all hell breaks loose on the right flank. The element of surprise is kaput! We have been lucky so far, for all we've run into was a couple of characters for some POW pen. Kennedy has kept this thing going and moving forward (shades of Lt. Dooley). In short, we've been moving upward in a ravine in the woods. Unfortunately, the jerries either saw us coming or figured that we'd be there, for they started to toss over some 120mm mortars. Kennedy kept us moving, so we manage to stay just ahead of where they landed. However, a few managed to do some dirt. One got Greek. What a low blow! He was the next to last of the original 26 replacements to this outfit. I'm the 26th. The spirit in me just died. What sort of deal is the fickle finger of fate going to give me? Time and time alone will tell.

The general purpose of this whole picnic is to capture the hills around Prum. This is known as task force Rhino or the next step is the mighty Rhine of song and history. Without too much trouble, the rifles and machine gunners managed to get to the top of the hill. We started to dig in along a road about 100 yards to the rear of the front line. The new guy and I, Al Holter and Aaron, and the rest in a big hole dug by the Krauts. As we were digging, my partner says, "Look over there, Sergeant!" I did and dropped—for standing there like a big bird was a jerry paratrooper with a burp gun. He missed us, but sure as hell was a close call. Then the war really let loose. The kraut landed behind a tree and I with my M1 tried to at least scare the bastard. Old Joe Domino yelled from the hole, "Duck, here comes a grenade!" It bounced through the trees and that was the last of that bad guy. Just then there was a terrific explosion next to our hole. The new guy is badly cut under the arm, so I'm trying to patch him up. Just then another series of grenade explosions in the big hole. We looked up horrified to see a big column of smoke and hear screams from that spot. Things sure moved fast after that. The bastards thought they had us and started to move in for a killing. They are never satisfied, it's got to be all or none. Just then Al Holter cut down a couple running in from the flank to finish off the job. Good for him. It's for sure that I didn't see them coming—what with watching the road and trying to stop the new fellow from bleeding too much—and they sure didn't see Al behind that tree stump.

About this time, Kennedy comes back on the double to see what's going on with the mortars. We've having our own little war; whereas, the rifles and machine gunners aren't doing anything up front. Kennedy knocked off a couple more swine with his carbine and high tailed it up to get some riflemen to bail us out. About this time I looked over to the big hole and I see Tenn running like a streak of crap through the woods for the rear. Other than that, all I hear are groans. With Kennedy and his reinforcements things really opened up for a while. It seems as though the krauts have sucked us into a real trap. However, we shot up their flanks; so, we still have a way out of here. When things finally calmed down there were about 15 dead krauts cluttering up the woods and a few wounded ones here and there.

The medics moved in and we moved up to the top of the hill. It's better all around. Besides, there is only Aason, Holter, Jake, Joe and me left of our 60mm mortar section. Banks, Sugar, Peters, and Tenn got hit in that big hole. Jake and I dug in up at the top of the hill—it didn't take long either. This has been the roughest going that we've had since December 16 and 17 (first days of the Bulge). Then Jake said, "My God, Doug, what happened to you?" "I don't know." "Well, the left side of your helmet's all beaten to hell and there's blood all over your face." Feeling with my hand confirmed this. Nothing serious. The medic put a bandage on it and Jake and I finished setting up housekeeping. You know, this is beginning to get a little bit tooo rough. I feel like the tenth little Indian; but I'll be damned if I'm going to get on a fence if I don't have to.

The show now began to get a little hot up in the front; so, we sent over a few mortars and got plenty of everything right back. "They don't play fair, I'm going home!" Poor Tucker, gunner on the machine gun got it right through the head. His poor wife and three kids. Meanwhile, Mike Donovan is loading some of the wounded down the hill and on the way he knocked out a machine gun nest. However, a jerry killed Sugar as they made a break for back into town. The old fickle finger of fate sure is messing with them today. The rest of the boys got through to the aid station.

Jake and I now moved the guns over fifty feet to a small ditch in a clearing. We dug them in and then ourselves. That's four holes so far today. "We've got to keep in training, you know." All of these arrangements are tied together with sound power phones. So, the day went. We paid plenty on a section and company level for this damn hill and it's for sure we ain't finished either, for we're on top and they're all over the rest of the place. About this time Chapman comes up with the rations and some doughnuts. It sure was good to see him. He was quite upset to hear about Greek and how things had turned out. However, we told him to stay in the rear if he could. He did. During the early evening Peters died before the aid men could get him out. He really wasn't hurt bad. Just a small wound in the leg. In short, he killed himself from pure fear. That's really getting a screwing!

Guard was long, lonely, cold as hell, and very unpleasant tonight. We were each on for a total of six hours. In the moonlight on this frosty night and in these cursed woods (we have been in them since last September), a lot of things passed through my mind. It can all be summed up as follows: Your luck is still with you; for how much longer? What is the purpose of all this crap? This life sure is an uncertain affair; and God Bless those who paid so much for all of this real estate.

Robert Williamson, Lakeland, FL
Company F, 2nd Battalion, 12th Infantry Regiment

A Million-Dollar Wound?

Our first lieutenant of Company F phoned back and asked what our company was supposed to do. The CO said that we were supposed to take a town. Just the second squad of the second platoon was supposed to take this town.

This was madness, but orders are orders. We waited until dark, and then we moved up to the edge of this town where two of our Sherman tanks had moved up. These tanks left us as soon as we got there and we were left there by ourselves, just twelve men to hold off the Germans. The next morning it got awful hot. The Germans threw everything but the kitchen sink, and I think they threw that, too. The artillery came so close to the two houses we were in that the shrapnel was coming through the windows. Then to top it off, the Germans started attacking, and it really got hot. I was shot in the right wrist from a Burp gun. I had to fire my rifle from my left shoulder. The lieutenant wanted me to go back to the battalion first aid station, but I said I would stay and fight it out with the Germans. The men needed all the help they could get. I was given orders that I was supposed to stay in this house with our medical man and a few other men. They sent the prisoners for us to take care of. They all came back after taking the town and that night at dusk, another fellow and I took the prisoners over to the MPs. Then this fellow and I went to the battalion aid station and got our wounds taken care of. We were then sent back to the rear, to the hospital in Whexham, England. When I got back to the outfit, the fighting was just about over.

I had been back to the outfit for about two weeks when I got an explosion in the face. I was blind in both eyes. I looked like I had been cut up with a knife. The ambulance took me to the battalion aid station, and they put me on a C-47 plane to Paris. I was put in the hospital, and they operated on my eyes. The doctors saved my left eye. Then I was put on a C-54 plane to the United States to Crile General Hospital in Cleveland, Ohio. This is where I stayed from June to October 12, 1945.

Marvin A. Simpson, (Deceased) Baton Rouge, LA
Company D, 4th Medical Battalion

Afterward

In March 1945, stationed near Prüm, Germany, I was given a three-day pass back to Paris. This happened the day after I had won $300 in an all-night poker game. Wow, was I ever excited and happy. I boarded a train with other comrades and arrived in Paris. Suddenly, I was in a different world. I took in all the sights, peed in an outdoor latrine on the sidewalks of Paris, rode in a two-seat taxi pulled by a bicycle and took in the shows and nightclubs. I had come a long way from the farm in Iowa to the streets of Paris. It was a tremendous 72-hour pass.

On VE Day our camp was near Starnburg, Germany. What a day to remember. We thought the war was over. A month later, however, we were on our way across the Atlantic for a thirty-day leave before going to the Pacific for the invasion of Japan. After arriving back in the States and traveling by train to Cedar Rapids, Iowa, I waited a long time for my wife to appear. It was there I realized I was getting a "Dear John" letter in a very subtle way. I was right—the marriage that began at the beginning of the war for me was over at the end. VJ Day came during my furlough, and I was discharged soon after with the rank of Staff Sergeant.

I went to Chicago and lived with my wartime buddy, Jim Saxton. I married the sweetest, most wonderful girl, Mary Fellmer. During our fifty-two years of marriage, I have experienced many breathtaking moments. Our first son, James, was born in 1949, then our second son, John, in 1953. My wife and I attended the 50th Anniversary of D-Day, lived with a French family in Normandy who called us "liberators," walked through the rows of white crosses at the Normandy American Cemetery, and, with tears in our eyes, we prayed.

Lon Murphy, Jr., Columbus, OH
Company L, 3rd Battalion, 12th Infantry Regiment

Keeping the Germans on the Run

By early March, we had been attacking for two months. We had to keep pressing the attack in order to keep the Germans on the run. If we slowed down or stopped to rest, it gave the Germans time to dig in and prepare defensive positions. We remembered what a well-prepared German defense had done in the Hürtgen Forest. The impact on the foot soldier was serious fatigue and nastiness. There was no time to sleep, bathe, shave, or change clothes. Our clothes were crusted and dirty and stank like garbage. Our hair was shaggy, and our beards were thick and scruffy. We lived in the holes in the ground through snow, sleet, rain and cold. When it rained it streaked the dirt in our faces and made us look even dirtier.

As for me, my leather boots were cracked and split open. My shoulders were rubbed raw from the cartridge harness that carried clips full of ammo for my BAR. My feet were calloused and swollen from month after month of freezing, thawing, and walking through all kinds of terrain. I had been requesting new boots for weeks, but the army didn't care. The Army was interested in maps and objectives, not in the peripheral needs of a foot soldier.

After taking Prüm, we had to stop to set up defensive positions along the west bank of the Prüm River to allow our supply lines to catch up to us. Since I was a BAR man, I was part of the outpost rotation. The company was dug in about two hundred yards from the river. There were three advanced outposts placed along the river bank. Each outpost had three BARs and a bucket of grenades. Outpost personnel were rotated every twenty-four hours. It was dark by 1800 hours. The crew that was due for rotation would replace the previous crew each evening. Twenty-four hours later that crew would be relieved.

Our turn came, and it was time for Dwight Larrowe, Sam Carter, and me to pull outpost duty. It was a scary and lonely feeling. If the Germans attacked or a German patrol discovered us, there was no support within two hundred yards. With three BARs and a bucket of grenades, we knew we could hold out for a while and take a lot of Germans with us. We all hoped it wouldn't happen.

Larrowe was an excellent artist. He took an envelope out of his pocket. He sketched Carter and me in the dugout with our weapons and surroundings. I was impressed, and he gave me the picture. I sent it in a letter to my brother, Walter, who was on a destroyer in the Pacific. He carried it with him all the way through the war and gave it back to me in 1990 when I was visiting him.

The Germans were dug in on the other side of the river. We could hear the clanking of their mess kits as they ate, and some occasional chatter. We would even spot the top of a German helmet moving through their trenches once in a while. It was an eerie feeling to be closer to them than to our own lines. Even though we could see them once in a while, we would never snipe at them. There were two reasons for this: First, they weren't sniping at us, and second, it would give away our position.

We kept in touch with the company command post by phone. A wire was strung from each outpost back to headquarters. During the night the Germans would shell us sporadically to keep us from sleeping regularly. We did the same to them. Exploding shells would frequently cut the wire. One of us would have to leave the outpost, trace the wire to the point of disconnection, find the other end of the wire and splice them back together. This was extremely dangerous because you were outside of the safety of the dugout. Encountering a German patrol would mean certain doom.

One night we received word from the command post that the battalion raiders would be going on a raiding patrol that night. The patrol would cross the lines by one outpost and reenter by another outpost so as not to give away any positions. Their mission was to harass the enemy and keep them guessing about our intentions.

As they passed our outpost, I thought about how glad I was to be in a nice safe outpost instead of going with them behind enemy lines. Later we heard small arms fire and exploding grenades from behind the enemy lines. This was surely the work of the battalion raiders.

Later we caught sight of the patrol reentering our lines near the outpost to our left. I noticed one GI being helped by his buddies. His leg was missing from just below his knee. I was jealous. The war was over for him and he would be going home alive while I remained in this frozen, muddy hell wondering if I had a future or not. I would have accepted the loss of a foot or leg to get out of my current situation. I heard a few days later that the soldier died because of blood loss.

After eight days of holding, the attack was called off. The Company Commander told me that this was my opportunity to get some new shoes from the quartermaster. The quartermaster was a few miles behind the lines, and I asked if I could have the jeep driver take me back. The commander said that wouldn't be necessary because we would remain in position for a few days, which gave me plenty of time to walk. I found it annoying that I had to walk three miles down a muddy mess of a road to get new shoes.

After I had been walking for a short time, along came a jeep with a major in it, and he offered me a ride. As I walked into the supply area it was obvious that I was out of place. The GIs in the rear had clean haircuts, clean shaves, and they were altogether clean. The quartermaster sergeant didn't even ask me what I was looking for. He took me to the supply room and made sure that I got two of everything. I received new uniforms, underwear, socks, boots, gloves, and an overcoat. He directed me to the showers. It was a wonderful feeling to take a nice hot shower. I was then showed to the mess tents where I had my first hot meal in three months. I was so grateful for those things. I never took anything for granted again for the rest of my life.

Our next objective was to take a town located in a valley. McCullough told me to keep an eye on the company and provide supporting fire if they got into trouble. At first, I felt good about not having to participate in the attack of the town, but after the rest of the company left, I wasn't so sure I liked the idea. There were just the three of us alone on this hill. I thought of all the times we had bypassed pockets of Germans and what would happen if a squad of them showed up. We couldn't see our column advancing from where we were, but we did notice when a German machine gun opened up about five hundred yards away from us. They must have seen some of our guys. I opened up with the BAR, and this gave the rest of the guys the opportunity to get into position and return fire themselves. After the machine gun was silenced, Carter said he thought we should be moving since I had attracted attention to our position. About five minutes after we swung around to the other side of the hill, a mortar barrage peppered the area we had just left. I'm glad Carter was thinking. The idea had not crossed my mind.

Dr. Lewis L. Jacobson, Eagle River, WI
Company G, 2nd Battalion, 22nd Infantry Regiment

A Major Contribution to the Second Platoon

As long as bath stories are being told, I thought I may just as well add my experience although it is nowhere near as poignant as Colonel Lum Edwards's and Fred Stromberg's adventures. Stromberg's story epitomizes the phrase, "dirtier than dirt."

When the 4th Infantry Division was relieved shortly before war's end on May 3 and moved back to a rear area, we were provided field showers. I believe they were about three minutes long and barely halfway through that time period, I dropped my soap into the deep trough of draining water. I spent the remaining time trying to find and reclaim my soap. I pleaded for extra shower time because of this accidental debacle but was drummed out of the shower tent.

Following this sad experience, it turned out that I might have owned the only towel in our depleted second platoon of Company G. I had always worn this towel around my neck, perhaps in anticipation of baths or showers. Two other GIs, including my platoon leader, used the towel. I had a couple more requests for the towel, but at that point, it was thoroughly wet.

As I look back on my memories of combat with G Company, I wonder if this might have been my major contribution to the second platoon.

Francis W. Glaze Jr., Clearwater, FL
HQ, 8th Infantry Regiment

One Scary Night

I believe it was in April 1945; the 8th Infantry Regiment was in reserve and the Division was headed toward Munich, straddling the Autobahn. I had set up the Regimental HQ in the local bank—a sturdy two-story building in the middle of the village. The main street was typical German with two-story houses walling the street with an occasional alley or cross street. The houses had the typical large barn-type double doors fronting on the street. One of the large doors had a normal size "people" door for everyday use.

The I&R Platoon was responsible for security at one end of town, the communications platoon was responsible for the other end, and the security platoon was responsible for the immediate vicinity of Regimental HQ. I had been Duty Officer at HQ until relieved at 0200 hours. I had nothing much to report to my "relief," except some patrol action between us and the 2nd Battalion as well as a firefight in front of the 3rd Battalion. It was a relatively quiet night.

My Company CP was set up on the second floor of a private home down the street from and close by Regimental HQ. We had not made the German civilians evacuate although we did make them go to the cellars of the homes we had commandeered. I had gotten to my CP about 0215 hours and was taking off my shoes just prior to crawling into my sleeping bag. Just then I heard a Schmeiser machine pistol firing in the street up in the I&R area. I alerted my Company CP group, which consisted of the Company Executive Officer, the First Sergeant, two drivers, a radio operator, and my "dog-robber." We could hear firing, explosions, and all sorts of German noises in the street, so we headed down the stairs for the defense of the Regimental HQ.

I was leading, and when I got to the door we could hear hobnailed shoes marching by. It was pitch dark and as I opened the door, a German soldier just passing by stopped. He knew somebody was there but not who. He asked, "Sind sie ein Amerikaner?" I didn't want to say yes, or lie and say no, so I said nothing—just closed the door. I assume the German didn't want to go alone into the dark, so he kept on going. By now we had assumed that the 2nd and 3d Battalion's had been overrun, the Regimental HQ erased, and we were the sole survivors—so far. We went briefly into the inner court to find a route over the roofs and out of town to report the loss of the Regiment. Luckily, we couldn't get to the roof, so we very quietly went back upstairs to look out the windows at the street fighting.

We were no sooner there when there came a knocking at the front door accompanied by much shouting in German. It wasn't my house, so I felt it inappropriate to answer the door. Luckily the lady of the house and her grandfather came out of the cellar to open the door to greet the officer and his detail. He said one of his men had seen someone in the doorway—was it an American? She said that Americans had been there, but she had heard us come down and go out, so we were long gone. She was obviously on their side, so they continued on—mopping up stragglers.

They had no sooner left than the field phone rang—loud enough to awaken the dead or get us killed—whichever came first. I had to stop the ringing, but I was scared of who might be on the other end. I picked up the phone and said, "Hello."

From the other end came, "Hello." (You can see our repartee was not up to par.) I responded, "Who's this?"

The response was, "Who's this?"

I could see someone had to break the impasse so I said, "Captain Glaze." The response was, "You don't sound like Captain Glaze."

It is alleged that my response was, "If you were as scared as I am you wouldn't sound like me either."

That must have been a clincher because then we got down to business.

The platoons were all on a party line, so they all started checking in. All the platoons were basically intact; fighting was going on in the street, but only the outposts seemed to be involved. They were evidently looking for a Regimental HQ, but they weren't strong enough to attempt a house-to-house search. It began to sound more like a raid than a general assault, so we decided that we should join the dance. In one minute, each point on the party line (there were about six) would send four to six grenades to the party, then cover the street while "me and mine" went out in the street, across and down an alley, to come in behind the Regimental HQ. Everything went as planned until we got to the end of the alley. Then I remembered that there was no recognition signal, and when we rounded the last building we would be in sight of our outpost behind the bank.

The real problem was that if the Germans had taken the HQ and held the outpost we would be shot; or if our people still held the outpost and we came running up, we would be shot. There was still some shooting going on in the street, but I couldn't see any action inside the bank, so I decided to earn my keep. I left my gun with the first sergeant and walked slowly forward with my arms in the air and softly saying, "Captain Glaze, Don't shoot," over and over, until I suddenly had a rifle muzzle in my gut.

It (the rifle muzzle) was then was taken away with the comment, "It really is you, Captain. I'm damn glad to see you, Sir."

I went on by and through the back door of the bank to the stairs going up to the second floor. None of the staff was down at ground level; they were all on the second floor, twittering around, knotting sheets together, and close to panic.

As I went up the stairs I shouted, "What the H--- are you stupid sh--- doing? Get the H--- over to the street windows and shoot anything that moves until I tell you to stop!"

By then it was about all over but the shouting, and shortly we went about the business of counting the cost and paying the piper.

Harry Kuhn and two others were killed on our side versus four Germans; they took their wounded with them, and we had three wounded. We had over thirty jeeps, and the Germans had immobilized eighteen to twenty of them. By that time in the war, our mechanics were so experienced that fifteen jeeps were back in service by 1500 hours and the rest by 2400 hours. I always suspected that they stole or exchanged for two of the worst jeeps, but who was counting?

As I remember, the scariest moment of my life was crossing that street and then going up to the back of the Regimental HQ hoping that I wouldn't be shot by friendly fire. That's what happened, to the best of my memory. We didn't cover ourselves with glory, but most of us did survive.

John K. Lester, Stone Ridge, NY
Battery B, 29th Field Artillery Battalion

A Dud 88

I can't remember names of the many small towns and villages that we overtook. Time and places didn't register. I had close calls, saw many of our soldiers, the enemy, and civilians that had been wounded or killed. It really bothered me at first, but after a few weeks it seems that you start to get used to it. You try not to let it bother you anymore. I was very fortunate that I was able to survive the 337 days of combat without injury. One time I thought I was hit bad by German artillery. I was seeking protection under my jeep during a German artillery barrage when I was jarred by a deafening explosion. My head (I was wearing my steel pot) and shoulders were splattered with what I instantly thought was shrapnel. Thanks possibly to some of the forced labor that had to work in the German munitions factories, I was splattered with dirt and debris. The 88 shell had landed about five or six feet from my jeep. It was a dud and sprayed me with the dirt it had dug up when it landed. If that had been a live shell or had traveled a few feet farther....

I always had to be on the lookout for any signs of land mines. I had to be very cautious at crossroads because the Germans almost always had them zeroed in by artillery fire. Booby traps, open areas, artillery tree bursts, snipers, etc. kept you on the alert at all times.

A radio operator, a second lieutenant, and I comprised our observer party. We alternated with another similar group. When we were back from the infantry, if telephone communication lines were needed, I would use my jeep for running telephone lines from the artillery to the infantry. I had a large reel of wire mounted on the back of the jeep. I would also be involved in keeping the lines operating. One thing I want to mention is that I had a good buddy who was a member of one of the 105mm gun crews. He always had a foxhole ready for me if it was needed when I returned to the battery area. His name was Richard E. Showalter.

Another important member of my unit was William (Bill) R. Cook. He distributed one of the most important things that we looked forward to—mail, and occasionally a package from home. I still see Bill a couple of times a year.

Paul Brunelle, Avon, MA
Company G, 2nd Battalion, 8th Infantry Regiment

Not Old Enough To Vote

From the book, Company G, 2nd Battalion, 8th Infantry Regiment, 4th Infantry Division, *by Shirley Devine. Reprinted with permission.*

Well, things went along then from December 1944 into the end of the war in May. I recall going through towns, but I never knew where I was. I do remember going through woods, going through fields, and going through villages. At the end of the war, when the Germans knew everything was lost, they were taking these young people, giving them guns, and having them defend some of the small villages. It got to the point that if we received enemy fire in those closing days of the war, the company commanders would pull the troops back, and they would just flatten the towns. They knew the war was over, and they weren't about to sustain casualties when there was no need. If these people hadn't been so thickheaded, they would have given up rather than have this fanatic defense at the last.

I was twenty years old on April 29, 1945, and for my birthday present I was given a couple of shots. One of them was a flu shot, which didn't really knock me off my feet, but I was rather uncomfortable for a few days. That was the way I celebrated my twentieth birthday. Because I wasn't twenty-one years of age when I came home, I had to go to the school committee and get a working certificate. At the time, if you were not twenty-one, you could not be employed unless you had a worker's certificate from a school committee. I had spent just about a year overseas and wasn't eligible to work. If fact, there had been an election in 1945, and I couldn't even have voted because I wasn't twenty-one. I arrived back home, strangely enough, about July 1, 1945, which was just a year to the date that I had left the United States to go to Europe. My total time of service in the army was, I figure, a total of one year, eleven months, and twenty-five days. A year of it was pretty active.

George Peterman, Cinnaminson, NJ
Company B, 1st Battalion, 22nd Infantry Regiment

A World War II
Infantry Replacement's Diary

On June 6, 1944, I was seventeen years old and a senior in high school. By the end of June, I had graduated, turned eighteen, and registered for the draft. In September of 1944, I was drafted. In October, I began the 16-week basic Infantry Replacement Training course at Camp Robinson, Arkansas. Upon completion, I took the usual route to Europe: a ten-day leave en route to Camp Meade, Maryland., then to Camp Shanks, New York—a five-day trip on the British liner, Aquitania, to Glasgow, Scotland—an express train to Southampton, England—

Channel crossing by ship to LeHavre, France, a 40 & 8 boxcar ride, and finally to Metz, France. I was assigned to the 22nd Infantry Regiment, Company B, in Loonville, France.

The receiving officer told us that if we lasted the first day of combat we would be awarded the Combat Infantryman's Badge and made Private First Class. I didn't fully realize what he meant by "if you last the first day of combat." Nevertheless, I consider my Private First Class stripe a battlefield promotion.

I lasted five weeks in the light mortar section before I was caught in a screaming meemie tree-burst barrage. The concussion was terrifying and so was the shrapnel and my broken leg. The other three wounded in the platoon, though more seriously wounded than I, were able to leave the area on their own. My fractured leg was bleeding badly. Fortunately, one of those courageous medics came to get me in a jeep. He gave me morphine and bent the vial needle around my dog tag chain. He also reduced the bleeding. Strange how we recall small details. From there it was to the battalion aid station; 11th Evac; 187th General Hospital in Rheims, France, then my first C-46 airplane ride, to England to the 188th General Hospital in Cirencester. As the war ended in May, I returned to the U.S. on the hospital ship Goethals in June. We were given a grand welcome home in Boston. I'll never forget that attention.

I finished my army career of one year and twenty days at Camp Pickett, Virginia, on the 18th of October, 1945, with a deformed, scarred, and partially paralyzed leg. But I was only one of 1.2 million U.S. casualties of WWII. Over 300,000 of these were KIAs. Based on the cases I saw in the hospitals, I was very fortunate.

Philip W. Tawes, Crisfield, MD
Company G, 2nd Battalion, 22nd Infantry Regiment

My German Prisoner

In the spring of 1945 we were chasing the German army. The 2nd Battalion, 22nd Infantry was ordered to secure a hill on the right flank of our army's route of advance. We carried out the assignment with problems.

Our platoons were digging foxholes in the event of a counter-attack. I was on my way to the Company CP and had to cross a wooded area. I broke out of the heavy stuff into a man-made clearing. Sitting on the ground cross-legged was a German soldier, a pack and rifle beside him, a hunk of bread in one hand and a hunk of cheese in the other, and the friendliest grin on his face one could imagine. I took him prisoner and walked him to the next firebreak. Seeing movement at the bottom of the hill, I pointed him in that direction. I thought it was our CP, but he told me, "Nicht, nicht!" (No, no.)

I pointed on down the hill and then I got it when he said, "Comrades!"

I looked again, and there was a mess of German helmets. I hurried through the woods to the next firebreak. When I looked around, there was my prisoner, an even bigger smile on his face. I slung my rifle, shook his hand, and we walked down the hill side by side. We found the Company CP, and I remember how bad I felt turning him over to the prisoner guard detail. If I had his name and address, I would be sending him a "thank you" card every month.

Gordon Gullikson, Onalaska, WI
Company A, 1st Battalion, 22nd Infantry Regiment

No One Wants to Be the Last Man to Die

I don't think this qualifies as a war story, but it kind of showed me the attitude of our commanders, especially Lieutenant Colonel George

Goforth. We were to attack this German-occupied town in the morning. We took off to find that German soldiers had left during the night and had the old men of the village cut down trees across the road as they left. (This was toward the end of the war.) Colonel Goforth had the same old men cut up the trees and haul them off the road so we could advance with our vehicles. If you ever heard swear words in German, this was classic—work all night to impede our progress and all day to help our progress.

We kept pushing the Germans in retreat and came to a small river. Goforth called Regiment and told them he would have to find a way to get across.

I said, "Colonel, there's a bridge about a half mile downstream."

He said, "Gordon, the war is about over. If we close on the Germans, they will have to stand and fight. We will just keep pushing them back as they retreat. No one wants to be the last man to die for his country."

That was a great lesson to me—I carried that over to Korea as a company commander—get as much support firepower from battalion and regiment to help you take your objective with the least amount of casualties.

Fred Stromberg, Concord, CA
Company G, 2nd Battalion, 22nd Infantry Regiment
Hit With a Milk Bottle

Towards the last few months of the War, tanks rushed across Germany twenty to thirty miles per day clustered with soldiers riding on top. We faced backwards with legs dangling over the end so a quick exit could be made if we encountered fire.

One such day, nearing dusk, we were traveling on a road through low hills when gunfire sprayed the tank. Bullets snapping just over my head caused me to jump off and roll to the side of the road for cover. My helmet fell off, and the tank behind ran over it.

Our CO came by in his jeep and pointed to a house some fifty yards or so away and told me to take the wounded over there and make it the CP for the night. I made my way over to the house. I opened a little white gate and then closed it behind me as I walked up a few steps to knock on the door. After I knocked hard, the door opened. A baby crying in the background made it hard for the welldressed man to hear me. I shouted in the best German I knew, "Amerikaner Soldaten schlaffen hier." (American soldiers sleep here).

"Nein. Heraus mit Ihnen," (No. Go away,) he replied and slammed the door.

"Amerikaner Soldaten schlaffen hier."

"Nein. Heraus mit Ihnen."

Again, I pounded on the door. The door opened and before I could say a word, the man hit me on the head with a milk bottle. My basic training instructions of "always wear your helmet" came to mind.

I walked back to the tanks, told my story to the tank lieutenant and asked him to bring his tank over to the door of the house. This he did as I stood on the steps and watched that giant tank crush the gate and stop at the steps. The huge monster swung its ugly cannon around and lowered it to a few inches above my head.

Once again I pounded on the door. It opened slowly. The Kraut peeked out and looked right down the muzzle of that cannon. "Gott im Himmel!" (God in heaven!)

We took over the upstairs for the CP. There was too much glass in my head from the broken milk bottle for the medics to remove, so I was driven to the battalion aid station. I was soon bandaged and sent back to the Company. No, I did not receive a Purple Heart for this, as the battalion did not prepare a casualty report. They felt the army would not take it lightly for the cause of injury to read, "Hit on the head with a milk bottle."

Lewis Jacobson, Eagle River, WI
Company G, 2-22 Infantry

War can be hell

Near the end of WWII, we would commonly mount up on tanks and toward evening occupy homes overnight. On one occasion my squad rapidly dismounted, running up the walk to the house, looking for positions of comfort. As a result, the lady of the home fainted.

When I checked a bedroom, two of my men were on the bed. Across the room was a crib which I stretched out on, with my legs dangling over the side.

Shortly a toddler arrived, screaming because I was in his bed. The situation was so unbearable that I had to retreat to the kitchen. As a member of the 22nd Infantry, it marked the first time I had to retreat in the face of an unrelenting verbal onslaught by a two year old German toddler.

John C. Ausland (Deceased), La Crosse, WI
Headquarters Battery, 29th Field Artillery Battalion

Waiting Angrily for the War to End

This article, written by John Ausland, appeared in the International Herald Tribune *on April 11, 1994.*

One reason people born after World War II find it difficult to understand why the final days of the war were so destructive is that they do not realize how angry we Allied soldiers had become—and to some extent still are.

Once our forces crossed the Rhine, it was clear that Germany was doomed. But Hitler, in his madness, vowed to fight on. German generals and admirals, whatever they thought, supported him. Their soldiers and sailors continued to fight in the misguided belief that they were defending their fatherland.

Anger became outrage and horror as our forces began to overrun concentration camps. As General Eisenhower emerged from one of them, he asked an American guard if he still had difficulty hating Germans.

Shortly before the 4th Infantry Division crossed the Rhine on March 29, at Worms, I went from artillery liaison officer with an infantry battalion to command of the 29th Field Artillery Battalion's fire direction center. I was in no mood to see any more of my friends in the infantry die. When our troops came under fire from a town, we would shell it heavily.

We were, as always, well aware that we could be causing civilian casualties. The fact that these would be the German enemy, and not French or Belgian friends, made our task easier. The glum faces we met even in the towns we did not destroy reminded us that we were not being welcomed as liberators.

With our forces sweeping eastward across Germany toward a Russian offensive even more ruthless than ours, the 4th Infantry Division advanced on a line of attack that took us west and south of Munich. Not far from Munich, the 8th Infantry Regiment ran into determined resistance in the town of Ellwangen.

Ellwangen was an SS military training center with a model defense. Its commander decided that his four hundred troops should defend it to the last man. When the commander of the 8th Infantry Regiment suggested by telephone that the German commander avoid a useless battle, he was rebuffed with an obscenity. With the 8th Infantry Regiment's staff planning an attack for the following morning, I suggested we try to force the town's surrender. On the night of April 22-23, the 4th Infantry Division and supporting corps artillery fired 1,500 shells into the town. We used delayed fuses so the shells would penetrate buildings before exploding, and we followed these with white phosphorus incendiary shells. Other shells scattered leaflets about how to surrender.

For many years I wondered what went on in Ellwangen that night. In 1992 the town archivist, Immo Eberl, sent me a lengthy account.

The military commander rejected the recommendation of the town's deputy mayor that he and his men leave the town. But after our bombardment began, the German commander had second thoughts. Changing into civilian clothes, he and his men quietly disappeared.

A tragic comedy then ensued as the civilian leaders tried to figure out how to communicate their wish to surrender. A proposal to send an emissary in an ambulance was abandoned when it was noted that a key bridge had been destroyed. A plan to raise a white flag on the church tower was delayed; no one could find the key to the church.

We ceased the bombardment early in the morning to see what the response was. An emissary soon appeared carrying a white flag, and our infantry took the town without an Allied casualty. The civilians had taken shelter in deep cellars. Fortunately, only a few were killed. Damage to buildings, however, was extensive.

A few days after Ellwangen, I visited a concentration camp that had just been taken near Landsberg. It is hard for me, even today, to describe what I saw there without crying. Hundreds of bodies, I wrote to my parents soon afterward, were laid out in neat, efficient rows. Some were burned. Some were shot. Some had been tortured and maimed. Others may have just died. All were unbelievably emaciated.

"This can never be explained or pardoned," I wrote, and "the leaders who caused, and the men who performed these crimes must die."

Shortly after that, we learned that Hitler was dead—a joyous moment—and the war in Europe finally ended. The rumors that Hitler would make a final stand in an Alpine retreat having proved wrong, we observed those beautiful snow-covered peaks in the distance and congratulated ourselves on not having to fight in them.

Our assumption that the war was over for us, however, proved wrong. Not long after VE Day, we learned that the 4th Infantry Division would be returning to the United States. There, after an intense training period, we were scheduled to go to the Pacific to participate in the conquest of Japan.

Having survived the fighting from Utah Beach to south of Munich, I could not help but wonder how long my luck would hold out. I am not inclined to question Harry Truman's decision to destroy Hiroshima and Nagasaki. Had the fighting in the Pacific been prolonged with the death and destruction that would have ensued, it would have been even more difficult than it is proving now for Japanese and American veterans to escape their bitter memories and bury the past.

William G. Cole, Tacoma, WA
Battery C, 29th Field Artillery Battalion

Memory Fragments from a Strange Two Days in Combat

Late in the war, perhaps in April of 1945, my forward observer party was with an infantry company of the 8th Infantry Regiment and we were all involved in what seemed to me to be a bizarre series of combat events, which, for whatever reasons, I recall clearly and likely won't forget. Writing about them will help me clarify my memory and will be the first step in identifying the location. I have few clues to identify the time or place.

I recently told a friend that I had a dozen strange stories connected with the two or three days involved. He replied, "It was the Twilight Zone."

We were in the 7th Army in southern Germany. There was little resistance from the German forces. We moved very rapidly in the latter stages of the war in what was called a pursuit situation.

We entered a small German village early one day. It had been captured earlier that morning when an advance party, in a stealthy action, surprised the garrison and cleared the few buildings. Apparently, there was not time nor communication facilities for the Germans to inform their headquarters that the village had been occupied by us.

The village was in the valley of a small stream with rather steep hills on either side. It was on the side of the valley toward our rear areas and across the valley from our next objective. One narrow road along the valley passed through the village from our left to our right, crossing the stream as it entered and as it left the village.

The first action I remember was the sudden appearance of a German jeep type vehicle entering the village from the left. An outpost had tried to stop the vehicle, but the occupants tried to make a run for it. The vehicle had the top in place and side enclosures, which largely concealed the occupants. I was standing in the road at about the center of town as the vehicle approached. The people around me started firing at the jeep. I emptied the clip of my .45-caliber handgun but didn't hit anything. Someone hit the driver, who was dead when the vehicle left the road and stopped. The only passenger, a young officer, had bailed out as soon as the shooting started and was not injured. I may have fired my pistol at the enemy on other occasions, but I cannot specifically recall doing so.

Later, another small German vehicle approached, this time from the opposite direction. Our outpost was in a structure of some sort that I remember as a small farm building located at the sharp bend in the road as it turned to cross the bridge on its way into town. The vehicle was not moving fast as it passed our outpost and the infantrymen there fired a bazooka into the side of the vehicle. I don't think they gave the enemy any warning, but apparently they did not try to kill the occupants. The projectile hit the side of the vehicle just below the passenger-side front seat. It disabled the vehicle, burned a big hole in the seat of the passenger's uniform and burned his butt somewhat. He was lucky—he was able to walk. He limped up the road ahead of his GI captors. I can still see it—a junior SS officer in a black uniform coming toward us, a very unimpressive little guy with the seat of his trousers burned out—a very satisfying sight to see. He spoke English, and later as he sat in the company command post, I asked him what he knew of the concentration camps. He professed total ignorance of such camps. I had nothing else to say to him. He didn't seem to be too unhappy. His war was likely over, and he had just survived in a close encounter with a bazooka shell.

The large wooded hill to our front was our next objective. It must have been the first day that we arrived in that area at a position far up on the hill where the infantry, having encountered some opposition, was digging in. I don't remember going up the hill—I guess nothing much happened then. We were not with the lead elements of the company.

There appeared to be no great urgency to advance. The company commander was busy and didn't have time to tell me what he was being told. We were basically in a pursuit situation, the enemy in a rear-guard delaying action. If we didn't clear the hill, their position would be outflanked soon. I was available and ready to get artillery fire if anyone wanted it. Artillery is not much help in such cases. You don't have a target other than a few enemy infantry close to you in the underbrush, and you don't dare adjust your artillery fire that close in. "Friendly" shells bursting in trees over one's infantry and oneself is to be avoided, if possible. Even if you can get the impacts a short distance ahead of you where they may be effective against the enemy (who may be a short distance behind his outposts), you are still shooting blind and still have the hazard of an occasional shell which falls short. (Every artillery shell that is fired, because of a number of variables, has a small probability of falling a significant distance too long or too short. Fire direction personnel have tables that have parameters by which the variation in range can be judged.)

An infantry NCO decided to fire mortars in the general direction of the enemy. I expressed my doubts to him. The first mortar rounds fell behind us. That was sufficient confirmation of my warnings, and no more mortar rounds were fired.

We spent one night on the hill and left it the following night. My memory retains the unusual events, and I'm not sure of the sequence. Our few skirmishes with the enemy probably took place on the second day. Panzerfaust projectiles were fired into our position. They are hand-held antitank rockets. They didn't do any damage, but they sure got our attention.

A German soldier, identified by his uniform as a paratrooper, got careless, I guess, and was taken prisoner. I was nearby when he was marched along ahead of his captor. A few yards from where I stood, the German saw a chance and ran for cover. The GI shouted at him before firing at him. By that time, the prisoner was moving fast in the underbrush and on his way to escape. I guess he preferred fighting to being a prisoner.

After dark on the second day, we came down the hill and back to the village. We moved along in single file, stopping often. At times, we heard German voices, but, presumably, neither side wanted a fight that night, and after minor exchanges of fire we were disengaged.

The next day the outpost personnel in a small house about two hundred yards in front of the village found a large bomb in a crate, which the enemy had placed against the house, but abandoned when the outpost was alerted to their presence and drove them off.

I guess it was the infantry command who told me that an air strike—dive bomber—had been arranged against the village, which was about a mile down the valley to our left and partially visible to us. It may have been our fire direction center that let me know they were going to fire a red-smoke shell to mark the target for the P-47. I can never forget how badly I wanted to have the opportunity to adjust our gun on the target before it was marked with red smoke, but for whatever reason, I did not get the opportunity to do so. Where do you guess the red smoke shell landed? It fell in the valley, remote from any built-up area, but nearer to our village than to the target. The house containing our outpost was as close to the smoke as any other structure and the 500-pound bomb from the P-47 was placed somewhere in the vicinity of the smoke.

Later, I talked to an infantry officer who was at the outpost at the time. He was standing in the doorway of the building when the bomb exploded and was knocked across the room by the blast.

I don't remember the sequence—I just remember the explosion. Our guys fired mortars at a target in the vicinity of that same outpost and the mortar shells detonated some large amounts of explosive, perhaps bombs in crates.

An enemy tank appeared in a clearing well up on a hill, which was off to our right front, and began busting up our village. I was able to adjust artillery fire close to him, and undoubtedly we fired white phosphorous incendiary shells. We didn't get a direct hit, and he soon moved on to other things.

In the evening as I sat in the infantry command post in a village building, Captain Joe Gude, CO of Company C, 8th Infantry Regiment, came in and sat down. I had known him since early in the fighting and had been so impressed with him that I had mentioned him in letters I wrote during the war. Captain John Ausland, in his personal memoir of his experiences in our field artillery battalion, the 29th Field Artillery, had a lot of good things to say about Joe Gude.

Joe was prepared for the cold night. He had a bottle of Scotch inside the front of his field jacket. I asked him what he was doing there. He said he was taking his company up on the hill that night. He was cool and all business. Whether he started up the hill that night, I do not know.

I left the area that evening when I was relieved by Lieutenant George DeMeyers. I presume George was of Dutch ancestry, but it could have been Belgian. In either case, he had reason to hate the Germans. He never expressed himself to me on the subject, but he was very intense in his approach. I was told later that early the next morning the Germans mounted a counterattack across the open flood plain toward the village. DeMeyers was up to the challenge as was the artillery he called upon.

As I remember the story, George's first transmission was, "Counterattack— request division artillery."

The artillery evidently was up and running because my memory of what I was told is that they adjusted their fire by battalion; that is, they fired all twelve guns of one battalion without delay on the location they had been given. This fire was sensed by the forward observer, which is a report of the location of the impact area in relation to the desired target. This is followed in turn by fire from twelve other guns of a second artillery battalion and then a third. This would make thirty-six 105mm howitzers pumping shells while, perhaps, the twelve 155mm howitzers of the division remained silent. Whatever the details were, the message I retain is that a massive amount of artillery fire was put on the target very quickly with much credit due the forward observer and the whole artillery command. The Germans got out of the area as best they could. One can thank God that he was not where the Germans were that morning.

I was always very glad that I had been relieved and didn't have to fire that mission and that George De Meyers did an apparently flawless job of it. If I had been associated with it, something would have gone wrong. I never fired such a mission and never saw one conducted in an emergency situation.

In thinking about it now, I wonder if such a large amount of artillery was justified. I don't really know all the facts, but if it accomplished the desired results, who am I to quibble?

It is very strange, considering the overall strategic situation, that the Germans would expose themselves to significant losses, which a counter-attack across an open area would have produced. Maybe there was a local reason to buy a little time, or maybe some macho German paratroop officer had something to prove, as has been known to happen in our army. At least the survivors can, fifty years later, swap stories.

Henry "Hank" Strecker (Deceased)
Company C, 1-12 Infantry
The war is coming to an end, and I get wounded...

Submitted by his daughter, Leslie Strecker Weisner

It was early April and the Germans were withdrawing from a little town. In the afternoon, the unit went on patrol in the woods across a river. After about an hour they met German rifle fire. The patrol, with Sgt. Joe Juarez in charge, had met the Germans head-on along a firebreak. The startled Germans yelled, "Kommen Sie hier." And Joe snapped back, "Du kommen Sie hier". Joe was fast on the trigger and shot two Germans. The others ran.

That night they spent in the houses of a small German town. Lil and Ellen, his sisters, had sent Hank a package of dry chicken noodle soup which he fixed on the stove. It tasted really good after a steady diet of rations. The next morning the men moved out at 10:00, crossing the river and getting into the corner of some woods where they could see the Germans on the ridge moving around among the bushes. An artillery officer came up and sent in some rounds before the men dug in for the night.

The next morning, the company attacked again, moving about one fourth of a mile. Support was called for and one or two light tanks came up and cleaned out the Germans. The tanks left and the infantrymen moved on. A wounded German was picked up as they headed along the woods and stopped at a clearing. Hank plopped down at the end of the column since everything had come to a stop for the moment. It was a beautiful spring day, bright and warm.

Someone was talking and moving in the woods behind him and he looked out of curiosity to see who was coming. Five Germans were creeping through the forest. Hank grabbed his rifle and fired at the first, second and third German, eight times before emptying it, as the Germans dashed off in all directions.

Henry noticed a coal shuttle helmet on the ground and what looked like a German coat lying in the ditch. Hank aimed and fired, but was startled by the spray of a burp gun over his head. One of the Germans had sneaked back up on him. Hank ducked behind a tree and hurried to the front of the column to see what was holding them up. As he started back he heard four or five shots and asked what had happened. The Germans had prowled back and were sniping—Germans ahead were holding things up, too.

It was April 12. They moved up and dug into a night defensive position. Hank heard an explosion in the rear and the TD's moved into their night lager. Only one TD lieutenant made it through and asked if a couple of squads of men could get the Germans out and clear a path for his TD. The patrol crept down to the edge of the woods and spotted two or three figures lying low, but they were afraid it might be their own men. A bullet snapped past Hank's helmet and he yelled, "Let 'em have it boys."

The GI's raced into the woods to get more cover. Hank emptied his BAR at them as the Germans behind the road bank jumped up and ran along the edge of the woods. He felt something hit his leg and thought that his trousers were torn by a branch as he ran in pursuit, but as he looked down it dawned on him. He must have been hit. He hobbled back and slumped into his hole until an aid man came and gave him a shot of morphine. He was thirsty and his squad buddies gave him some water, but water and morphine don't mix and he got sick.

The squad was mostly replacements, younger than him and they were extremely upset that their experienced staff sergeant would have to leave them. They were saying things like, "how will we make it through without you?" and "don't leave us." Mortars carrumped in on them. Hank felt terrible— his squad was upset and here he was in a front line hole— knowing he would be out of it after all the unbroken months of combat—if he could live to get out of it—by dusk.

They moved back to the firebreaks and were sitting in the woods. Hank was half asleep and froze with fear when he saw what he thought was a German on the skyline above him. It was a GI. Jeeps came up, Hank climbed into one and they rolled back along the firebreak where the Germans still lurked, before getting into the town where the battalion aid station was located. An aide Lieutenant asked what the 12th Regiment boys were doing to the Krauts because the ones he was caring for were shot up so bad. The next day Hank was put in an ambulance and taken to an airfield. The GI's had to wait while some Germans were loaded in the first plane, ahead of the Americans. He had waited a long, long time to fulfill his childhood dream of an airplane ride and now, at last, he could hardly enjoy it.

They were flown to Rheims and processed by hospital train to Nancy. His bandage slipped and the wool blanket grated against his open wound along the way. It became infected and was drained with a tube and sewn up. Several days later the stitches were cut out—and the wound opened into a wide crescent scar above his knee. V-E Day dawned with Hank still in the hospital. To celebrate, the French set off dynamite behind the hospital. He was grateful but remembered, there was still the Pacific. While in the hospital, he was given the Purple Heart and one of the nurses gave him her Presidential Unit Citation pin, saying she wanted him to remember them when he wore it and tell people about the work the nurses had done.

Back in the States, his family (father, two sisters and two younger brothers) were told by the neighbors that there was a telegram for them at the drugstore. No one wanted to retrieve the telegram, fearing the bad news that came in those days. Edward, who was just about to go into the army—and to the Pacific, was persuaded to ride his bike and pick up the dreaded telegram. It is still in the family keepsakes and the terse form provided some measure of relief as it announced simply, "wounded in Germany." (The two other brothers, Edward and Alan, also became sergeants during their army service. At age eighty-four Henry still wore his original wool uniform with insignia and medals to Veterans and Memorial Day services).

On recovery, Henry was sent to Worms and then back to the squad at Nuremberg and south to Zuggenheim on the way to Bamberg. Hank was happy to see his buddies again and catch up on the news. He had last seen them on the road to Crailsheim and Rothenburg. Fred Jackson told Hank about how he had captured two German soldiers and some civilians in the basement of a German house after a fight. The two Germans had come out of the basement with their hands up high and, as if to justify themselves, kept saying "Vee ver schleeeping..."

The guys gave Henry a wooden pipe, stamped with a skull and crossbones, as a gift on his return. They had found it with boxes of others in a German military warehouse. Army detail began to creep in as combat became a memory. The Lieutenant wanted the sergeants to sew on their stripes and the men were scolded for wearing their wool knit caps or for not wearing the proper uniform.

It seemed odd, after only two showers and two hot meals, from Normandy to the end twelve months later...

In Henry's words...(these memories were preserved by his daughter)

Over the years, especially in November when the snow fell, I would remember Brownie Means, the man from Big Sky country, Montana and often wondered if he was ever able to ride horses again, which was mostly what he had talked about of home. It was sad, not knowing if he even lived through the war. In 1992, I attended my fiftieth Mt. Healthy High School reunion. During the celebration dinner, different people stood up and told a little about themselves. There were only about 200 of us in the school and one woman got up and mentioned that she was originally from Broadus, Montana. I remembered by a strange coincidence, that was the place Brownie was from, and later asked her if she knew him or his family. She said she knew a Ward Means and the next time she was home in Broadus, she would try to give him my phone number and address.

A few months later she met Brownie, who she only knew as Ward, in the hardware store in Broadus. He had moved to Sheridan, Wyoming but was also paying a visit when they met. Ward called me and he and his wife drove all the way to Ohio to visit us. It was a very emotional meeting. Ward has a truly lovely wife and family and his grandchildren are riding horses just like he did. The distance between our homes is far on a map but very close when measured by the heart.

On May 25, 1994, my wife Dee and I went to a mini-reunion of the Fourth Division at the Radisson Hotel in Columbus, Ohio. It was a four-day get together and there were several other conventions going on in the same hotel. On Friday evening, we were in the hospitality room on the second floor. Dee and I always like to welcome new members. I had just met a first-time fellow and while we were talking, a man with a gray beard and wearing a business suit walked in and then left. After I finished talking to the man I had just met, I asked the bartender if he knew the name of the man who just left. He said he thought it was Angle or something like that.

A light bulb lit up in my head as I said, "Was his first name Richard?" He said he didn't know. I ran straight down to the nearest elevator and down to the lobby. One of the men organizing the reunion was coming toward me and I asked him if he had seen a man with a beard. He said yes, he tried to get him to join the Fourth Division Association. I asked for his name and he replied, Richard Engle. I was frantic. I thought after forty nine years of wondering if this man had lived, he got away from me.

I went to the girl at the desk and asked if she had a listing for Richard Engle. She said yes, but she could not give me his room number or phone number. I explained my situation and she said she would try to call his room.

After about an hour, I gave up. I figured he had gone somewhere and I would try to reach him about nine the next morning. The next morning I called the operator and she connected me to his room. I said, "Richard, you won't believe who this is." After I explained, he said he would come right down to our room. We had a wonderful conversation for about an hour.

They had sent him right back after he got hit in Normandy. The doctor told him that if he would have coughed on the way back from the front, he would have bled to death. Needless to say, we were two happy buddies. Richard had become a priest in 1956 and I had become a convert upon marrying my wife Dee in 1947. He was only at the Radisson that day to attend a Catholic convention and had seen the Fourth Division convention notice by coincidence. Father Engle had spent much of his life working with the VA. He is a close friend of our parish priest and visits whenever he is in town. He still has the bullet I handed him in 1944.

Henry Strecker earned the rank of Staff Sergeant. He received a Bronze Star for combat on the Siegfried Line, a Purple Heart and five battle stars along with the Combat Infantryman's Badge and Presidential Unit Citation. He thanks God every day for seeing him through the war and continued to correspond with Father Engle, Ward and Dora Means, and Herr Hubert Gees, who served opposite him in the Hurtgen Forest, until his death.

Jim Roan, Fenton, MI
Company H, 12th Infantry Regiment

The Beginning of the End

As we went further into Germany, the destruction of cities was awful. We had to feel sorry for the civilians, especially the children. There was a lapse between the time that a city was taken and the time the army-trained civil administrators took over. The people needed food, shelter, and medical help. We always set up shop in the best structures available, and we had plenty of rations for our own needs and some left over. The roads were full of GI flatbed trucks crammed with what was left of the German army. Prisoners of war were crowded into these vehicles with little room to sit down. Some were wounded, and they spent a day or two traveling to their destinations. When they exited these vehicles, they had a hard time walking, and some died during transport.

We noted that there was always a crowd around. The civilians would cheer as they were transported by our troops. The U.S. Army did supply them with boxed rations, usually C or K rations, which we were being fed most of the time. We occasionally were treated with a hot meal when the kitchens caught up with us, and I can still picture the civilians patiently waiting in line with their buckets to dip into the slop that we dumped from our mess kits. We always took more food than we could consume just so they would have something to dip into.

Tom Reid, Marietta, GA
Cannon Company, 22nd Infantry Regiment and Company I,
3rd Battalion, 22ndInfantry Regiment

Last KIA in WWII, PFC Carl Baker

You can imagine my surprise upon reading the 22nd Infantry Regiment Society newsletter for September 1996, and learning that Private First Class Carl W. Baker of Item Company was the last official KIA in the 22nd Infantry in WWII on May 3, 1945—for I was the last Company Commander of Item Company in WWII.

Ever since the end of the War, I had always thought that the Regiment was in action on the following day, May 4, 1945. But with the passage of 51 years, I am willing to concede that my memory may not be as accurate in this respect as are the official records of the War Department.

No meaningful mention of Item Company, 22nd Infantry Regiment can be made without a reference to the contributions and outstanding leadership of two previous commanders of the company, Lieutenant General (Retired) Glenn Walker and Major Joe Samuels, who as a captain brought the company ashore in the first wave of D-Day, June 6, 1944 on Utah Beach, Normandy. Joe Samuels commanded the company longer than any of the other Item Company commanders in combat. Glenn Walker commanded the company in its training days at Camp Gordon, Georgia, and then went on to successful command positions in the 22nd Infantry in WWII, fought in Korea, was commanding general of the 4th Infantry Division in Vietnam, and now resides in Mississippi.

Their magnetic leadership left an indelible imprint on I Company. I was walking in their footsteps and trying to fill a large shoe size.

All through April 1945, we could see the end of the war in Europe coming. Our advances were swifter, more prisoners were being taken, and some days troops riding on tanks were making five to ten miles per day.

Everyone had talked about not wanting to be the last man killed in the war, but no one knew when that fateful day would arrive. On May 3, 1945, (May 4, by my recollection) Item Company was given the mission to seize the small village of Agatharied. We were now in southern Bavaria, about sixty miles south of Munich. Snow was still on the ground in the foothills of the Bavarian Alps.

Resistance was slight, the company had moved through the town, and I was ordered by the battalion commander to hold where I was. Suddenly a shot rang out and Private First Class Carl W. Baker, my company runner, fell. He was only a few feet away from me and was still alive. I took my radio and maps out of my jeep and told the driver to get him back to the aid station as fast as possible. He died on the way.

In a few minutes, I received an order to dig in where we were. The War was over, the Germans had surrendered, and PFC Carl W. Baker had become the last KIA in the 22nd Infantry Regiment.

Carl Baker was from Portland, Oregon, and wanted to be a forest ranger when the war was over. He was an outstanding soldier and could always be depended on to carry out any task he was given with dedication and dispatch. We often shared a cup of coffee or a K-ration. His death came hard to me.

Through the years since, I have often thought of Carl Baker, the gallant soldier of World War II who wanted to be a forest ranger and instead became the last KIA of the 22nd Infantry Regiment in WWII. He truly exemplified "Deeds not Words!"

Bill Boice, Phoenix, AZ
Chaplain, 22nd Infantry Regiment

Letter Home as Hostilities End

From his book, History of the 22nd Infantry Regiment in World War II.

When the announcement of cessation of hostilities was heard, Chaplain Boice sent down a letter to the men of the Regiment to be addressed to their families and mailed home. The letter read:

This evening Admiral Doenitz has announced to the German people the unconditional surrender of all German fighting forces. Had this surrender occurred the 1st of September on our wave of optimism when we hit the Siegfried Line, or immediately after the defeat of Von Rundstedt and the successful crossing of the Rhine, we would have been wild with joy. The news of Germany's surrender was received by all of us with a calmness very nearly approaching indifference about the feeling deep within our hearts.

There was no revelry last night, no drunkenness, no shouting, no flag waving, no horns blowing; there was a sober realization that it was all over, at least so far as Europe was concerned, and that we, by the strength of our arms and by our own courage, had, with the help of God, completely and finally defeated everything that the warped and twisted soul of a perverted nation could hurl at us.

We take no undue pride in what we have done, for we are sobered by the blood of our comrades, which cries up to us from every foot of ground from Normandy to Berlin and from Holland to Italy. We have done what we have had to do for you, as well as for our own peace of mind.

I am proud of my officers and fellow soldiers in the 22nd Infantry Regiment.

There is not one single fighting day of which we must be ashamed, or for which we must make excuses. No regiment in the ETO has more right to hold its head high and to march with shoulders back, colors streaming, than this one. Its record, its casualties, its achievements, and the respect it instilled, and the terror it struck in the heart of the German Army speak for themselves.

Bill Boice, Phoenix, AZ
Chaplain, 22nd Infantry Regiment

The Men Who Were Not There

From his book, History of the 22nd Infantry Regiment in World War II.

And so, the war was over. It was a fact far too deep for us to grasp fully, and we realized somehow that we should be more grateful than we were, that probably we should do all of the little things which we were expected to do, like blowing horns and tooting whistles and perhaps getting drunk. But we didn't. We simply thought of the hundreds and hundreds of our friends who had given everything they had in order that we might see V-E Day. The men who were not there—the memory of them, the years we had trained with them, knowing their families, or perhaps the brief moments we had known some of them who came to us as replacements, the insight we had had into their very souls which can come only to a man who sees his soul laid bare and lives a thousand lives or dies a thousand deaths in a single day of combat.

Stretching back to the Turgen Sea to Bensheim and from Bensheim to Hamn, from Hamn to Henri Chappelle, and from Henri Chappelle to Marigny and from Marigny to St. Mére Eglise were rows of even white crosses dotted with occasional Stars of David, where school children on their way home left flowers on the graves. And always flying proudly, but somberly, were the Stars and Stripes, symbol of the devotion of the men who rest beneath.

The men were not there. Never completely gone from our minds were the little things we remembered—funny, crazy things they did, premonitions they had, ways they fought or talked, or maybe even things about them we hadn't liked; we supposed that we should feel our responsibility and we guessed, too, we were living on borrowed time, time loaned to us from these men who were not there. No more slopping through foxholes half-filled with water, clothes damp, and with such a constant hunger for something that we could never quite place or satisfy. No more of this. No more of it for them either. We had seen the gaping wounds that had sapped their lives.

We had seen the cemeteries; we knew how they were buried. We had seen these rows of lifeless objects, shattered mockeries of that which had been breathing, pulsating men, friends of ours, buried in the soil of France and Belgium and Germany.

Strange that the soil of Germany was no different from the soil of France or America, nor were men any different. Men did what they had to do and hoped they could endure it. If they were lucky, they got back, or sometimes in the hellishness of combat they looked on the body of a soldier and said meaningfully, "Won't nothing bother him anymore."

There were some other men who were not there, men in hospitals in Michigan and Washington, Atlanta and Vancouver, men whose every footstep would bear testimony to war and everything it was and everything it did to men.

And so, the war was over. Perhaps we should have celebrated. Perhaps our celebration was the quiet realization that we were here and they were not, for it was only by the grace of God, by hard fighting, and perhaps sometimes poor shooting that we had lived to see Victory in Europe.

Cal Grose (Deceased), Chapel Hill, NC
Medical Detachment, 3rd Battalion, 22nd Infantry Regiment

My Buddy

The war had ended and we were put up in a tent city around Nuremberg for a little R&R before going back to Paris to turn in our vehicles. The enlisted men had their section in tent city, and the officers had theirs. One day a captain came into my tent and ordered me to give up my cot. Being just a buck sergeant, I did so, but I did ask him why. He said they were looking for someone to be "Officer of the Day," and he wanted to hide so they could not choose him.

You notice I did not mention the officer's name, but I hope after this we will still be good buddies, because he is the brother I never had, and we have remained friends to this day—sorry, Sam Barrett (Regimental Dentist).

Albert Schantz, Reading, PA
Company A, 1st Battalion, 22nd Infantry Regiment

Coming Home

We continued to force the Krauts back toward the east: First, to Rothenburg, then south and southeast through Crailsheim, Heidenheim, across the Danube River on April 25, 1945, then on to Wolfratshausen and Bad Tolz near the Bavarian Alps. We were six miles from the Austrian border when we received word that the Germans surrendered on May 8, 1945.

Morale increased when we learned about the surrender. There was a party mood, but we were glad the war was finished. We were looking forward to going home. Plus, there were no party "fixins" available anyway.

May 8, 1945, was declared "VE Day" (Victory in Europe Day). I remember that day very well. It snowed about eight inches, and we were occupying farmhouses. When we took over a house we forced the German occupants to sleep in the barn, and we slept in their beds. I slept in a bed with a straw mattress covered with a feather-filled quilt. The houses were attached to the barn so that the heat from the animals and the manure heated the house in winter.

A few days after VE Day, we boarded army trucks and rode north through Munich, across the Danube River, to Amberg, then west to Ansbach, Germany, where we took control of a German fort. Here we processed German prisoners of war and discharged them so they could return to their homes. I was able to act as an interpreter for Germans who spoke no English, since I knew "Pennsylvania" German.

The worst war damage that I saw was in Munich, Germany. Munich must have been a beautiful city with statues in the middle of each intersection in the center of town. Many buildings and statues were bombed to rubble. It was sad....War is hell. There were very few people on the streets and sidewalks for a city of that size. One of my desires is to visit Munich now that it is rebuilt.

On June 23, 1945, we left Germany for Le Havre, France, in railroad boxcars. This mode of transportation was known as "40 and 8" in WWI. (Forty men or eight horses in a boxcar).

On our way west to Le Havre, our train stopped in a siding in a large railroad yard. I happened to look across several train tracks at another boxcar into a train that was also stopped. There in the open boxcar door was Bobby Walbert from Macungie, Pennsylvania. I knew Bobby from high school. I walked over to him, and we talked for a short time. He was in the 5th Infantry Division and was also headed for Le Havre, France.

Seeing someone familiar from back home was a happy occasion. It eased some of the homesickness.

We arrived in Le Havre on June 30, 1945, and boarded the General James Parker, a liberty ship, for our ride back to the good old USA. The entire 4th Infantry Division sailed on July 3, 1945. We experienced one rough day on the Atlantic Ocean. I didn't miss any meals, but I couldn't keep my breakfast down that rough morning. I wasn't alone at the rail. I was able to eat lunch and dinner without any problems. The ship was crowded, and many of us had to sleep on the open deck under blankets. The night air made us very wet, and we were glad it was summertime.

We arrived in New York Harbor on July 11, 1945. I can still see the Statue of Liberty as she came into view. How wonderful she looked. After we disembarked, the 4th Infantry Division was transported to Camp Kilmer, New Jersey, where a thick delicious steak dinner awaited us. We were then fitted with new uniforms and attended lectures telling us what to expect back in the States.

The army's plans were to retrain us and ship the 4th Infantry Division to the South Pacific to finish the war with Japan. Thanks to President Truman, who authorized dropping the Atomic Bombs on Japan, ending the War in the South Pacific on August 14, 1945 (VJ Day).

Clarence Brown, Buchanan, NY
4th Signal Company

Tent City

At the end of the war I was sent back to somewhere near Nuremberg where we had Italian prisoners digging up cable and German cable men repairing the cable that had been blown apart.

It was from there (with Selective Service points—married, a daughter, Bronze Star, etc.) that they told me that I was on my way home. They flew us from Nuremberg to Metz, France, to Tent City. (It wasn't really organized.) I then found out what they meant by "40 & 8." That was a freight car that would hold forty men or eight horses. We rode them for three days until we got to Le Havre…tent city again.

Then on a ship back to the States. Took four days. On board ship I was with a lot of American former POWs. The biggest thrill of my life came as we entered New York harbor. With the fireboat hoses spraying, tugboats blowing their whistles—we all shed a few tears of joy. We had made it back. It was then to Shanks, Dix, and deactivation. I was honorably discharged on my birthday (June 23, 1945) and went home to my wife and family in Buchanan, New York, where we still reside today.

Jim Roan, Fenton, MI
Company H, 12th Infantry Regiment

Fabulous Reunion

The motor trip to the coast of France was enjoyable. There were designated stops where camps were set up to handle the troops who were on their way home. Most of the time we were served a hot meal and provided a place to sleep. The meals were served and occasionally cooked by German prisoners of war. In a few locations there were tablecloths, napkins, china dishes, and freshly baked white bread. The Germans were very polite and offered us a variety of food that we had not seen for a long time. Breakfast was usually a treat with bacon and eggs and fresh orange juice. We came to the conclusion that the army, in its way, actually wanted us to re-enlist. They were showing us what we had to look forward to.

Picture this: A long convoy of various army vehicles traveling through a city. Regardless of its size, the lead vehicle would spot a pretty girl walking down the sidewalk. The driver would drive right up onto the sidewalk, and the occupants would all stick their arms out trying to pat the young lady on the derriere and each vehicle following would do the same. I think the young ladies liked it, for no one ran; they would just wave and smile. The GIs would throw them chocolate bars or cigarettes, which we had plenty of.

The ride home on the Sea Bass was uneventful. The ship was an army transport, staffed by U.S. sailors and served American food. It was a long trip, or it just seemed long, for we were all excited about returning home. Some of the troops and officers did not have enough points to immediately be discharged, which made me a very popular guy. We were destined to be one of the outfits that were scheduled to invade Japan. They would pigeonhole you on deck or wherever they could find you and insist that they had a wound, that they saw a medic but it was not recorded, and that the wound was worth five points. We were nice to them and convinced each soldier that we would do all we could to straighten things out, which we did.

As we approached the coast of New York, we passed a number of garbage scows dumping in the ocean, which is normal. Those on deck would exchange words; each vessel would blow their horns as a salute. We reached the harbor to whistle blows, large banners stretched along buildings on the waterfront, and line after line of American gals waving and blowing kisses—a sight to behold.

The New York Fire Department had all their boats out spraying streams of water. Fire engines on the dock all had their sirens blowing and lights flashing. As we exited the boat, Red Cross and Salvation Army gals distributed doughnuts and coffee. They made sure that we felt welcomed.

We were transported via army busses to Camp Shanks and were billeted in barracks…those awful army cots felt mighty good. We were fed things that we only dreamed about, even fresh milk. We spent a lot of time at the Post Exchange, most of the time filling up with hotdogs, hamburgers, gallons of milk, and ice cream. The telephone company had installed zillions of phones, and we waited in line to call home. The lines were long, so we only told the folks we were back home and they could expect to see us soon.

We were granted leave with orders to report to camp on August 30. The entire clan met me at the train station, and it was a fabulous reunion. When I arrived home it was hard to get used to hearing a woman's voice—they all sounded so high pitched. Dad took me aside and suggested that I button my pants before I ventured outside. I was leaving the house putting in my shirttail, and then I planned on buttoning my fly. During the first thunderstorm I encountered, my reaction was to hit the floor when that clap of thunder sounded.

Double Deucer Newsletter— Aboard USAT James Parker

The Late Major General John Ruggles sent an original copy of the newsletter produced aboard the transport ship James Parker, the day before the 22nd Infantry Regiment got back to New York City, after the end of the War in Europe. Following are some excerpts.—Bob Babcock

ATTENTION ALL TROOPS! Upon arrival in harbor, all troops MUST remain in assigned areas prior to debarkation. This ship is carrying no ballast and uncontrolled movement would develop a list, which would delay docking. Strict compliance is required if troops are to remain above decks.

22nd TO MAKE COLORFUL ENTRY TO US. When the USAT James Parker sails into the harbor tomorrow with the Famous 22nd Infantry aboard, it will be bedecked in its gayest, which will include mammoth banners and campaign ribbons worn by the men on board. These decorations have all been painted during the voyage by a staff of artists headed by Technical Sergeant Jim Bradley of Company K. Others who assisted in this tedious job were: T/5 Joe Krynski, Corporal Vernon McCarty, Private Chester Janusz; all of K Company, and Private First Class Phillip Koff and Private First Class John F. Hammill of the I&R platoon of HQ Company. These decorations will be put in place this afternoon, but will not be unfurled until the entry into the harbor. Included in the decorations will be two large Ivy Leaves, two Boll Weevil banners, two mammoth ETO campaign ribbons, two Fourth Division banners, one famous Double Deucer banner and one bearing only the name "22nd Infantry." Yes, due to the untiring efforts of Sergeant Bradley and others, the entry will be colorful as well as exciting.

A GUIDE TO THE UNITED STATES. The United States is made up of 47 states, the District of Columbia, Texas, and Brooklyn. To avoid the embarrassment of breaches of etiquette while visiting in this country, the following points should be studied and remembered:

(1) Places know as "hotels" provide accommodations for a night's lodging when one is not staying with friends. The present practice of entering a house, evicting the occupants bodily, and taking over the premises is frowned upon as being too presumptuous.

(2) Natural urges are apt to occur, even at inopportune moments. Do not grab the nearest shovel in one hand and a roll of paper in the other and head for the garden. At least 90 percent of all American homes have one room called a "bathroom," which contains a device designed to meet your needs. All you have to do is look worried—these Americans catch on fast and will tell you where to go.

(3) The current medium of exchange in the U.S. is "money," which consists of "dollars" and "cents." Silver coins and green paper notes are used and you will find that you can't get a week's laundry done for two Tropical Bars and a piece of soap. Cigarettes, however, are reported to be useful in bartering.

(4) In the event the "helmet, steel M1," is retained by the individual, it should not be used as a chair, washbowl, footbath, bathtub, or kettle for cooking. Every home is equipped with these items. Nor is it in good taste to squat in the corner if all chairs are occupied—the host will provide suitable seats.

(5) American meals consist of several dishes, each in its own container or bowl. The common practice of putting gravy on peaches or mixing chocolate pudding with corned beef to improve the flavor is not considered in

good taste. In time, the "separate dish" plan of eating will lose its newness and become enjoyable.

(6) Americans have a strange taste in stimulants, one of the favorites being a mild concoction known as a "Zombie." Drinks common on the continent, such as green wine, alcohol and grapefruit juice, and gasoline bitters with steel filings (better known as "Calvados"), are not suitable for civilian circles.

(7) Whiskey, a fairly common American drink, may be offered on special occasions. It is considered uncouth and ill-mannered to drain the bottle, cork and all. Exercise control and try to make the bottle last three rounds. If you see it won't make it back to you, then snatch the bottle and empty it.

(8) In motion picture theaters, seats are provided and helmets are not worn. If vision is impaired by the person in front, there are usually plenty of other seats. Do not hit him across the back of the neck and say, "Move your head, jerk, I can't see a damn thing."

(9) Upon retiring, if confronted by a pair of pajamas (a two-piece garment worn in bed) assume an air of familiarity and say, "Goodness, what a lovely shade of blue." Don't ever say, "How in the hell do you expect me to sleep in a getup like that?"

(10) There are no air raids or enemy patrols in America, so it is unnecessary to wear a steel helmet. Nor is it necessary to carry a rifle loaded and cocked when talking to civilians.

(11) On leaving a friend's home after a visit, you may not be able to find your cap. Frequently it has been placed in a small room known as a "closet." Don't say, "Don't anybody move; some #@*?$& eight ball has swiped

my cap!" Instead, turn to your host and say, "I seem to have misplaced my cap, could you help me find it?"

(12) Tip your hat before striking a lady.

(13) A guest in a private home is usually awakened in the morning by a light tap on the door. It is proper to say, "I'll be there shortly." Don't say, "Blow it out your B-bag!"

Furlough

Questions about what to do on furlough had been asked many times aboard the USAT James Parker since the 22nd Infantry Regiment left Le Havre, France. It has been answered many ways, but generally speaking, the average man is looking forward to a period of relaxation with his loved ones and of doing things that could not be done in the ETO.

Following are a few of the varied answers, which have been overheard by The Double Deucer:

Corporal Habichit of Company E is looking forward to the meeting of his four-month-old daughter he has never seen. Other than spending a lot of time with his family, he added that his only plans were to do some horseback riding. Before coming into the army, Habichit was a polo enthusiast.

"I wonder how much Canadian Club it will take to last thirty days?" That was a question being asked by Private First Class Clarence Kothman of Company A, whose home is in Dayton, Ohio. Kothman, a D-Day man, added that he was spending time with his wife and might possibly visit friends in Detroit.

"I'm just going to take it easy," was the answer given by Private First Class George R. Scott of Headquarters Company, who hails from Atlanta, Georgia. He added very tactfully that his wife might have already made some plans for his time at home.

"I'm planning to spend my furlough with my folks and friends at St. Vincent, Minnesota," remarked Private First Class Robert Barker of Company G, when asked about his plans. He said he had no set plans for his entertainment.

"I still have time to make plans as I have a long way to travel after reaching the States," was the answer given by PFC George Whaler of

Company A, who will have a trip to Balvoa, Canal Zone, to make before reaching home. Like most others, he added that his furlough time would be spent with his wife. Whaler came to the States and volunteered for army service.

"Boy, it's wedding bells for me when I get home to Buffalo, New York," said Sergeant Bob Kawolski, a squad leader in Company A. Then he added that his furlough would be spent honeymooning.

"First I'm going to Louisiana where my wife is living, and then we are going to Kansas City," remarked Sergeant Good of Company I, who was doing some guard duty on the Sun Deck Sunday.

"With the help of my wife, I'm going home and set up housekeeping, preparatory to an expected discharge," was Sergeant John Gahl's opinion. Sergeant Gahl is a member of Headquarters Company, 2nd Battalion and comes from Cincinnati. He has 91 points.

Sergeant Havercroft of Company C will travel to Eugene, Oregon, for his furlough and he says it will be spent with his folks and "just having fun."

One could notice that Private First Class Joe Smith of Company A, who is planning a furlough with his family in San Antonio, Texas, was already getting nervous. The reason is that the Smiths are "infanticipating" and the event is scheduled during the furlough. His only comment is, "I hope it is a girl."

"I'm just looking forward to a good time with my wife," was the plans set forth by a 94-pointer, Sergeant Bagley of Headquarters, 1st Battalion, who comes from Alabama.

"It will be just a nice, quiet furlough," said Sergeant Seabright of Company E, who is headed for a furlough at his home in Windchester, Maryland.

"With four children, including an eight-month old daughter I have never seen, I imagine I won't have a hard time finding something to do," remarked Private First Class Woodrow Stark of Company A, who lives in South Bend, Indiana. He added he still couldn't understand why that fourth child wasn't worth twelve points.

Last, this letter to the troops from the Regimental Commander:

TO OFFICERS AND MEN OF THE 22nd INFANTRY: The "Double Deucers" return this mid-July after approximately eighteen months overseas— more than half that time spent in combat. The Regiment has established an enviable record. Listed in its fighting history are such names and accomplishments as: D-Day assault, Utah Beach, Montebourg, Cherbourg, the Hedgerows, St. Lô Breakthrough, Paris, Landrecies, Brandscheid, Hürtgen, Luxembourg, Prüm, the Kyll River, Lauda, Bad Mergentheim, Crailsheim and Tegern See.

The face of the Regiment has changed. It sailed forth in January 1944 fresh and untried. It returns, battle-tested and proud; with a great mission accomplished—a task well done.

You, as individuals, are returning to a grateful country too bent on the furthering of the war with Japan to take time out to welcome you in the true American fashion.

Return to your families and your homes. Spend your furloughs well. Remember that your families "sweated it out," too, and that it is their furlough as well as yours.

For those of you who are to return to civil life, I wish you Good Luck and God Speed. For those of you who are to return to carry on the traditions and the name of the 22nd Infantry, I need only say, "Carry On."—And may the seas be smooth.

- John F. Ruggles Colonel, 22nd Infantry

Frank Douglas, Janesville, WI
Company F, 2nd Battalion, 8th Infantry Regiment
Who's That?

Ivan Schwartz and I caught a train out of the Northwestern Station heading for Wisconsin. He to Reedsburg, and I to Janesville. It was a "milk" train that got me to Janesville at 0400 hours. I never saw Ivan again. Like everybody else in the service, you simply knew people for a while and then moved on in your own direction.

There I was at 0400 hours, on the platform of the Northwestern Railroad Depot with my duffel bag. It was only four blocks from home and I, being an old infantryman, simply planned to walk up Academy Street to Ravine for two blocks, then to Terrace Street and finally, three houses down to 326. Mr. Yahn, a local meat market owner insisted on giving me a ride home.

"You're Fenner Douglas' boy, aren't you?" he said. "Yes, sir," I told him, and I got a ride to the front door.

Nobody can ever forget those moments of our homecoming. I had been gone over two years. When I landed on the front porch and rang the doorbell, I heard someone yell, "He's here!"

The hall light came on and everybody came down the steps. My...the hugs and kisses. Tears...all the excitement. All over America for the next year, millions of people experienced the sheer joy of homecoming. After all the hell and horror, we were once again home. These scenes occasionally had a unique side. Barbara, my little sister, was six years old. I'll never forget her standing by Yvonne and Bob and asking, "Who's that?"

Frank was somebody you got a letter from once in a while, not somebody in a strange outfit or uniform standing in your dining room. Thousands of children had never even seen their fathers. Of course, all too many never would. What a mixed bag of emotions surged through all of us. My father, normally a very reserved man, hugged me and stood there with tears in his eyes.

Never again would I or any GI, ever experience a real homecoming that great. As often as I've gone on trips, there was never such a high level of joy at coming home as there was that time. How could there ever be, after all that we had been through?

Stan Tarkenton, Virginia Beach, VA
Company M, 3rd Battalion, 22nd Infantry Regiment

Expert Rifleman

At a church social, some old biddy approached me and pointed to my Combat Infantryman's Badge (CIB) and shouted out loud, "Look, girls—here is one who has got an expert rifle shooting award!"

That teed me off. At the time, I thought that since the War was just over, she should have known better. I answered her, "Yes'm...Ah allus hits dat Bull's eye smack dab in dat Bull's ass in target practis'n... Yes'm, I sure does dat."

She said, "I see," and quickly disappeared.

Tom Reid, Marietta, GA
Cannon Company, 22nd Infantry Regiment and Company I,
3rd Battalion, 22nd Infantry Regiment

The Case of the Missing Sheets

I was in the 22nd Infantry Regiment when we came back to the
States after WWII, and this is part of that story. The 22nd Infantry Regiment closed into Camp Butner, North Carolina, in late August 1945. When we sailed from Le Havre, France, in early July, the
war was still going strong in the Pacific, and we were scheduled to
train at Camp Butner for sixty days. We received new replacements
and new equipment before being scheduled to ship out to the Pacific in late 1945. While we were on leave, the first atomic bomb was
dropped on Hiroshima.

The Japanese surrendered, and our mission was changed to one of
re-enlisting those who wanted to stay on active duty and discharging
those who didn't.

All of this took time, and as there were no family quarters on
post, there was a tremendous demand for off-post housing in nearby
towns and communities. Any room or apartment would do. Due to
wartime shortages of nearly everything, these places often lacked everyday essentials like sheets, bedding and kitchen equipment.

But not to worry…Every supply room in the regiment had sheets,
pillowcases, blankets, and a variety of kitchen equipment including
dishes, pots, pans, and silverware. It seemed like the entire regiment
took whatever was needed from the supply rooms with no account-
ing, no hand receipts, or anything to show where these things had
gone.

In those days, the company commander was responsible for all
the property issued to a company. I don't know the procedure today.
One day, on taking inventory, I learned that my company was short
a considerable number of sheets and pillowcases. What to do? An

appeal to the assembled company brought in a few sheets, but I was still short eighty sheets and about thirty-five pillowcases.

My problem: Shortage of sheets and pillowcases.

The solution: Go to the post laundry and ask for remnants of sheets, mangled beyond use in the laundry process. Sew these old pieces together to form a full sized sheet. Turn these pieces in as sheets the next laundry date and get credit for a full sheet. As for pillowcases, get a remnant piece of sheet about five feet long and eighteen inches high, fold in the middle, sew the top and bottom, then turn the pillow case inside out to hide the stitches and you have a ready-made pillowcase.

Of course, when you get clean sheets and pillowcases back from the laundry you have someone there to examine each one so that somebody's amateur textile work doesn't show up in your supply room. Problem solved.

Gene Westberg, King City, OR
HQ, Special Troops, 4th Infantry Division

Camp Butner

For whatever usefulness you may find in them, these are some of my recollections of the 4th Infantry Division's period at Camp Butner, North Carolina. The primary source of these is, fortunately, not memory but rather the product of loving parents who kept every letter and every other item of service information I sent home during that time, including orders, news clippings, division publications, etc. The secondary source is two issues of: "The Famous Fourth IVY LEAF," published by the Fourth Infantry Division, Camp Butner, NC. Vol 4, No. 11, November 23, 1945, and No. 22, February 1946. The latter is cited as the last issue, and announces War Department plans for inactivation of the Fourth. One article in this issue lists about 125 D-Day men still with the 4th Infantry Division at this time.

The earlier issue reported on one of the grandest Thanksgiving feasts ever prepared in the army. The order had gone out to give GIs all the turkey they could possibly want, to say nothing of the necessary trimmings.

The Headquarters Company mess sergeant was Staff Sergeant Archie Hall, who as mess sergeant with the 121st Infantry Regiment in Europe, had traded his skillet for a rifle and engaged in actions that resulted in his being decorated. (Purple Heart, Bronze Star, French Fourragier). He was a cook who liked to fight, the article says. On this Thanksgiving, he provided an enormous feast in a decorated mess hall. He had provided curtains, flowers, and music, mostly out of his own pocket, in addition to a family-style Thanksgiving dinner. As the first Thanksgiving following the 4th's return to the States, it was memorable for all who ate, and it remains for me, probably my most memorable Thanksgiving. I was on pass the following Christmas, but I understand he did it again.

I joined the 4th Infantry Division at Camp Butner as just one of a wave from the attrition at the Infantry School at Fort Benning, Georgia. As wartime personnel needs diminished, I was a private assigned as clerk-typist to Headquarters Special Troops. It was the end of November 1945. I do not know when the Division moved into Butner, but it was only a short time before. One of the early recollections that impressed me was an old German typewriter (beat-up) with some strange keys. More poignant was witnessing columns of German POWs in formation being marched out to embarkation ports to be returned to Germany. I understood many had no homes to return to, and some had no families or relatives who had survived the War. Many were still on site after this and made our situation comfortable by taking on the details at KP, latrine, and policing details.

Initially I was occupied with typical clerk duties: morning reports, communications to the various special troops, and typing for the CO, Major Costello, and the Executive Officer, Captain Julian Dixon. Increasingly, however, time was given to getting men that were eligible for separation on their way. A letter home on January 16, 1946, states: "...to separation centers. I have over 150 leaving tomorrow because of a drop in points, effective Jan 1."

Rumors were rampant about the eventual disposition of the Fourth. In a paper, five divisions were named that were to be held in the States as strategic reserves: The 2nd, 4th, and 5th Infantry Divisions, plus the 82nd Airborne and 2nd Armored Divisions. In a letter, I told the parents: "Camp Butner is not a permanent post, so within months we'll be moving to another location." Fort Custer, Michigan, was speculated.

On January 30, 1946, I received a promotion to T5. Three days later, because of a pending freeze of ratings, I received another stripe, courtesy of Captain Dixon. He felt my rating otherwise would be held down for too long, perhaps indefinitely, considering that the work I was doing was to his satisfaction. That was February 2, 1946. On February 5, 1946, the official word came: The Division will be deactivated as of March 5, 1946. The headlines of the final issue of "The IVY LEAF," No. 22, read: "War Department Orders Inactivation of Fourth Division—Break-up to be Complete by March 5." The editorial said: "Thirty...and Thanks."

Note: The 4th Infantry Division was created in 1917 so was completing almost thirty years of service to our nation.—Bob Babcock

This same issue reported the ceremonies at which the Division was honored by Belgium with award of the Belgian Fourragere, presented by Baron Silvercruys, that country's Ambassador to the entire Division. Several individual awards were presented by France, including the French Legion d'Honneur and Croix de Guerre with palm, to past commander of the 4th Infantry Division, Major General Raymond O. Barton, by Colonel Le Bel, 1st French military Attache' to the U.S. At the behest of my good friend Sergeant Whistler, a product of a RA (Regular Army) family, the two of us marched in the review with the color guard at this ceremony. It was generally very wet as a heavy drizzle fell throughout the parade and ceremony. About twenty junior officers were decorated, and General Courtney Hodges, Commanding General of the First Army, attached unit citation streamers to each Regimental flag.

Four of us at Special Troops Headquarters and our captain were reassigned to the Fourth Infantry Division Custodial Detachment and were occupied with closing details. My March 1, letter states: "We are busy...We've shipped 1800 men. This Monday and Tuesday, 2390 more are leaving. My charge is to turn their records over to them and see them on their way." On March 8, I wrote, "Still getting men out in small groups. We go into our custodial work this next week."

Custodial work amounted to packing and shipping Division records to the Army Records Depot at St. Louis. Actually, our part was just getting them to the 4th Service Command HQ, also at Camp Butner, who did the shipping. A March 16 letter states: "last night… had to drive into Durham to take one of the last men in to catch his train."

I left Camp Butner shortly after that. After a short delay-in-route, I reported to HQ First Army, G-1. My new assignment was at Fort Bragg, where I completed my army service.

Bill Boice, Phoenix, AZ
Chaplain, 22nd Infantry Regiment

Passing in Review

From his book, History of the 22nd Infantry Regiment in World War II

At the last formal review on the parade ground at Camp Butner, North Carolina, all sensed this was an historic occasion and certainly the last of its kind for the Famous Fourth in World War II. General Courtney H. Hodges, Commanding General of the First Army, the Belgium Ambassador to the United States, a representative of the French Embassy, Major General Raymond O. Barton, Major General Harold W. Blakeley, and Major General Melborn were guests of honor and present in the stands for the review. The Regiments formed and moved on to the parade ground, in order, the 22nd, the 12th, and the 8th, followed by the Field Artillery, Engineers, and the special troop units. The day was gloomy and there was a slight drizzle as if Nature herself were weeping to watch such an organization die. There was grumbling in the ranks among the new men who had no loyalty to the Division, but there was a stillness that mirrored an ache in the hearts of the old Fourth Infantry Division men.

Colonel John Ruggles, senior Regimental Commander in the Division, was commander of troops.

Combat streamers were awarded to the Colors of the Regiments, and there was a thrill of pride within the heart of each man as the

Regimental Colors dipped to receive the ribbons. And then the Belgium Ambassador was introduced. He was a tall, stately man who carried the dignity and the honor of brave Belgium upon his own shoulders. Scarcely had he started to speak when death-like stillness fell over the entire assembled Division. It seemed as if each soldier sensed that here was something he wanted to hear. The Ambassador spoke:

"Belgium learned to love and honor the Fourth Infantry Division in the First World War, when on the banks of the Marne the blood of your men mingled with the blood of our own, and the fierce Huns were stopped. Again, in this war, it was fitting that the Fourth Infantry Division should play so large a part in the liberation of Belgium, who had suffered so much at the hands of the cruel and ruthless enemy. We knew that you would come, and, in that knowledge, liberty still lived within our hearts.

"Belgium salutes the brave men of the Fourth Infantry Division. She salutes Lieutenant Colonel Mabry, Lieutenant Ray, General Roosevelt, and Sergeant Marcario Garcia. My country has conferred upon the men of this Division the highest honor it is in her power to bestow, and in honoring you, she honors herself. The red of the Fourragere is the blood of your men shed for the liberty and for the freedom of Belgium. The green is for the constant memory of these men and what they did, and so the Fourth United States Infantry Division will always live in the heart of Belgium. Vive la America!"

No one stirred. Somehow, it was fitting. Somehow, it was appropriate that such an honor should come to the battle-weary, exhausted, broken-hearted, proud Division and to her proud Regiments. Then came the order, "Pass in Review." The men marched stiffly and well even in the mud and drizzle, and as the colors passed by, every person snapped to attention. As each one realized that this was the last time he would march as a member of the famous 4th Infantry Division, there was a stillness and heartache, which can be occasioned only by the death of a beloved friend. "Eyes right." Heads snapped. The generals looked at the soldiers. The soldiers looked at the generals. Neither saw the other but rather the foxholes and hedgerows of Normandy, the crosses at St. Mére Eglise and Henri Chappelle, the matchsticks and mud of Hürtgen. They saw marching in ranks, in file after file with perfect cadence and deathless spirit, all of the men who were not there. Not there? Certainly they were in the hearts and minds of those who remember, never to forget, in the love of those who would never cease missing them, in the freedom of every American. And so the men marched off of the parade ground and into the cities and villages and farms, office or other army posts. And with them went the 4th Infantry Division. A dead Division? Certainly not. Not so long as a single man still lives and remembers. Sleeping, perhaps, but not dead....

In 1947, the 4th Infantry Division was again called into active service, and has served our nation continuously since then, including Cold War service in Germany in the 1950's, service in Vietnam in 1966-1970, and service in Iraq and Afghanistan starting in 2003 and ongoing as of this writing. - Bob Babcock

Stories from the World War II Home Front

While our soldiers were training and fighting, their loved ones were anxiously waiting for them, and taking on the added responsibilities associated with being a serviceman's wife or loved one during war time. Although we do not have many home front stories, the accounts included here will give you an idea of the hardships of those who stayed at home and waited.

Ethel Frances Grimes Williamson, Lakeland, FL
Wife of Bob Williamson, Company F, 2nd Battalion, 12th Infantry Regiment

The Love We Shared

When the War broke out between England and Germany, I was eleven years old and living in Liverpool, England. I was at an age where the memories of the war remain etched in my mind and will forever be in my thoughts and dreams.

It was Sunday morning, September 3, 1939, that the war was declared. I was at church with my sister Patricia. She was only six years old at the time. When we got home from church our parents told us that we were at war with Germany. My sister didn't really comprehend what war was. It was not too long after that that my sister and I eventually began to realize what war was really all about.

We had an "Anderson Air-Raid" shelter in our backyard. It was made out of corrugated steel, with part of it being dug under the ground. The part of the shelter that was above the ground had grass growing on it so that the German planes couldn't spot it from the air. There also was no door on any of the Anderson Air Raid shelters because if there had been an explosion nearby, it would cause a concussion and the shelter would disintegrate. There was only a square hole in place of a door. This is how the water and cold air got in. Before my father knew about what concussions would do to a shelter, he had tried to put a door on ours, and the authorities came around to our houses and told him to take the door off.

For the next two years, my mom, dad, sister, and I slept in that airraid shelter every night. The German planes seemed to fly right overhead around 1900 hours until 0700 hours. While we were in our shelter, we would hear the German planes going overhead and hear the bombs dropping around us. The sounds of the bombs were deafening. I lost my hearing in my left ear from the blasts of those bombs.

In the winter months our air-raid shelter would get water in it. My father had made two bunk beds on each side of the shelter for each of us to lie on. The beds had no mattresses. In the dead of winter the water would flood the two bottom bunk beds on the floor, which would leave the four of us on the top bunks all night. We would all be hunched over with no room at all to hold our heads up…cold and scared. My parents never got much sleep while protecting my sister and me throughout the night. They would always throw their arms around us whenever they would hear the bombs falling close to our house. The bombs would fall so close to us that they would make our shelter shake.

Yet, through all the pain and hardships, the morale of the British people was marvelous. They would be in their air-raid shelters, and you would hear a family during a lull moment of the German planes passing overhead, singing songs like, "Roll out the Barrel," and "White Cliffs of Dover," and other songs of WWII.

In our neighborhood, all of the families had Anderson Air-Raid shelters. One night in the winter, while one family down the street was at home, the air-raid sirens went off. The family went directly to their shelter for protection from the bombs. That night they received a direct hit on their shelter from a German bomb. The entire family was killed.

As the war continued and worsened, my father had decided to evacuate my mother, sister, and me to the countryside. We had family living in Staleybridge, England. In Staleybridge they didn't get the bombings that Liverpool got.

During this time, people in England didn't have cars of their own. People rode bikes or walked. Most people used trains, buses, and ferries as a means of travel. Our family took a train to evacuate. Our train had no sooner left Liverpool and a German bomber was spotted following us. The plane followed our train until we were out of Liverpool and then started bombing the front section of the train. Some of the coaches had been hit; yet everyone still managed to get off the train. Then the German bomber came back. Some British troops were on the train at the time of the bombing and saw that all the people were off the train. Then they told everyone to get back onto the train. Everyone started scrambling to get back onto the train with women and children who were scared and crying. A while after we were on the train, they told us to get out of the train and go to a public air-raid shelter. We ran all the way and stayed there for the rest of the night. The next day we got to see the damage the bombs had done to our train. There was no train to go back to. The railroad tracks had been demolished. There was broken glass everywhere. Most everyone started to walk.

We walked past store fronts where the windows had been blown out and broken glass lay everywhere. We couldn't avoid walking through the broken glass. Some of the Brits that had cars or trucks would pick up people walking from the bombing. The vehicles would be packed full of people, like sardines. They would feel bad that they had no more room for the women and children walking. We finally got a ride from a young man. His vehicle was small, a sports car. He still stopped and picked our family up, all four of us.

We arrived in Staleybridge exhausted. We had been through a nightmare. We were relieved to be greeted by our family. We stayed with our family for about a week, relieved not to be sleeping in an air-raid shelter. We would still hear the German planes overhead on their way to bomb Liverpool. They had an indescribable sound—a heavy humming sound—a special sound that only the German planes made.

At a distance from our home in Liverpool, you could see the sky lit up in a bright orange color from the bombs. The Germans were bombing the Liverpool docks where all the big ships would come in with supplies, and also the ships with troops on them.

Upon our return back to Liverpool, the British government decided to have compulsory evacuation of all children in Liverpool.

This was truly a sad day in my life. My mother and father took my sister and me to the train station to be evacuated. I was scared, only eleven years old and having the responsibility of taking care of my sister during the war. All my sis and I had were our gas masks, which we took everywhere, and a small bag of clothing. My mother told me to hold on to my sister's hand and not let loose.

My sister and I cried at the thought of leaving our parents. My mother was crying, and my father was fighting not to. My sister and I evacuated to Whitchurch, a small country village. We stayed with a lovely young couple, but after three weeks apart from our parents, our parents decided they wanted us back in Liverpool with them. At this time, the bombings had slowed down a little in Liverpool. To this day, I can still smell the rubber of the gas masks.

In the early 1940s, I can remember the American troops arriving in England. This really helped boost the morale of the British people. Of course, the British called the American troops "Yanks," and also GIs.

It was 1945 that I met and fell in love with one of those Yanks. He was in the 4th Infantry Division. His name was Robert Williamson. He was at a hospital in Wrexham, England, recovering from a war wound. This was his third wound. I had grown up fast during the war. I was just sixteen years old and Bob was nineteen. Bob and a buddy of his got what they called a furlough. I met Bob at a St. Patrick's Day dance. We had only known each other for nine days when Bob, my future husband, proposed to me.

But Bob still had to go back to that bloody war. A few months later, I got a letter written by a U.S. nurse in Paris at an American Hospital. She told me that Bob had been in a mine blast and had lost the sight in both of his eyes. I was devastated, even my parents told me how difficult it would be to be married to someone blind. It made no difference to me. I had promised him I would marry him someday. The war would not stop the love that we shared.

Bob was blind for three months without knowing if he would ever see again. He would have the U.S. nurses write to me while he was blind. An army doctor operated on his eyes, but could only save the sight in his left eye.

In 1946 I kept the promise that I had made to Bob and came to the United States to be his bride. I took a ship from Southampton to New York. It took me thirteen days to cross the Atlantic Ocean as we ran into storms at sea. I was seasick the whole way. My face had to be green. It sure felt like it. To this day, I'm afraid of being in a boat on the water.

Bob and I celebrated our 50th wedding anniversary in England. We went back to my home in Liverpool where I grew up, which brought back a lot of childhood memories. We stayed at a bed and breakfast in Chester, and visited some of my family while we were there. We just celebrated our 54th wedding anniversary. We now call Lakeland, Florida, our home.

We have two sons, four grandchildren, and six great grandchildren. At times, I look back to when our oldest son was eleven years old, and our youngest son was six years old; the same ages as my sister Pat and I were when the war broke out. Tears come to my eyes. I would think about a war parting us from them—to be evacuated not knowing if I would ever see them again. It was then that I would realize the actual horror that my parents had gone through.

A lot of the men from the 4th Infantry Division tell me they arrived in Liverpool before they were shipped to Europe. I look at these men who all have such a brotherly love for each other and I thank each one of them for saving my country from being invaded by the Germans. I say to myself, "Where would I be today if it wasn't for the bravery and courage of those very special men and women who gave up their freedom to fight for my country?"

I would like to dedicate my story to the memory of Sarah and Joseph Grimes, my mother and father. If not for their strength and courage, I would not be here today to write this story. I love you both with all of my heart.

Thelma Avery, Three Oaks, MI
Wife of Walt Avery, Company B, 1st Battalion, 22nd Infantry Regiment
On the Home Front

When your grandchildren talk about reading in their history book about "That Guy Hitler," you know you're old. We lived through it and their Grandpa was there.

The year was 1941. After dating three months, we married. I was nineteen; Walt was twenty-two. My family predicted it wouldn't last six months. We celebrated our fifty-ninth anniversary in March 2000. By 1944, we had two children: a boy, two years old; and a girl, just past one year old. Walt had a good job in a defense plant making 75 dollars a week with lots of overtime. Life was wonderful. We thought that with two children and his job he wouldn't be drafted...wrong.

In June of 1944, Uncle Sam called. We were in shock. How could we survive the separation? There is nothing like a war to make you grow up quickly. Walt left June 6, D-Day. My monthly allotment was one hundred dollars a month, not a great deal of money even in 1944. Walt's parents invited me to move in with them, but I was determined to be independent. Besides, what could I do with the half dozen pieces of furniture we had acquired? These dear people drove forty miles round trip, with rationed gas, to check on me once a week, bringing groceries and clothes for the children.

I was better off than many wartime wives because we were living in my hometown where I had graduated from high school. At the time Walt left, we were living in a little house that we rented for fifteen dollars per month. A short time after Walt left, I learned the house had been sold. Affordable housing was nonexistent. My dad was a hard-working farmer who was still recovering from the depression, but said if he could find something he could pay cash for (he did not want a mortgage) he would buy it and we could either buy it from him when Walt came home, or he would sell it.

Just a couple blocks from where we lived was a big, old, ugly, drafty house. Dad said, "It's good and solid" and he bought it for 3,500 dollars. I was so grateful I didn't care what it looked like. Before we were even settled I met the next-door neighbors: a wonderful, childless couple who immediately "adopted" us. They took down the old fashioned storm windows, put up screens, and did all the chores I couldn't manage. They also helped comfort and reassure me on bad days.

Walt and I wrote each other daily, but the mail was unreliable much of the time. Sometimes I would receive no mail for several weeks and then there would be a box full. One time I received a big heavy envelope. Walt couldn't find any paper, so my letter was written on pages from an old recipe book. He told me how much the boxes of goodies were appreciated, even if the cookies were often reduced to crumbs.

It is strange how clearly I remember funny little incidents. Now, I might not remember what I had for lunch yesterday, but I remember vividly the day in 1945 when I left my purse on a local bus and worried about losing twenty dollars. It was returned to me—the money was there—but the ration stamps were gone.

Or the time I walked with the children to the grocery store. On the return trip, our son saw the house where we used to live and broke away from me and ran down the middle of the street. I let go of the stroller that had a bag of groceries balanced on the back. The stroller tipped over, the baby was screaming, the grocery bag split and spilled groceries all over the sidewalk. A very kind lady heard all the commotion and helped me put everything back together again.

Most of all, I remember all the wonderful people that helped me cope: The country doctor who made a house call for two sick children and didn't charge because their daddy was in the army. And the semi-retired electrician who installed wiring for an old electric stove I bought. I worried about not having enough money to pay him. He charged fifty cents.

And of course, my wonderful neighbors. How could I feel too bad for too long when I had these great people and wonderful little children that always had hugs and sticky kisses? I was grateful they were too small to realize what danger their daddy was in.

Walt was wounded February 14, 1945. I have never been so frightened. The dreaded telegram, which I still have, said, "slightly wounded," but how did I know? I soon received a letter from Walt and he reassured me. He said because of his injury he would be discharged. He arrived back in the States in July. He didn't know where he lived, so in the middle of the night he found his home with the help of a flashlight. Today he would probably have been shot, but the 1940s were a kinder, gentler time.

We are still living in this "old ugly house." With a lot of blood, sweat, tears, and thousands of dollars, it is attractive and very comfortable. All our old neighbors are gone, replaced by younger ones, but they have been great.

I don't recommend starting a marriage this way, but I do know the experience gave us a deeper appreciation of each other and we know that if we could survive the war, we would never sweat the small stuff.

Madeline Boyle, Oceanside, CA
Sister of Chuck Boyle, 3rd Battalion, 22nd Infantry Regiment (Vietnam)

December 7, 1941 Conemaugh, Pennsylvania

At Mass that Sunday morning Father White told us that Pearl Harbor had been bombed and America was at war. I was nine years old. In school the next day, Sister Chrysantha tried to explain what had happened, how we must pray very hard now. For the next four years war news loomed—then was gone. A dark cloud that threatened for a time, then forgotten in our play, in youth's blessed innocence— yet always returning.

Of course, we kids threw ourselves into the "war effort"—saving newspapers, the silver wrappings from Hershey bars, the wrappings from chewing gum—Beechnut and Wrigley's—even the lining from old cigarette packs, lying wet and muddy in the ditches…Lucky Strike, Camels. We wrapped them all together into huge balls. Who could make the biggest ball! That, too, was going to save some soldier's life, we thought. Then there were the aluminum cans that first had to be washed, their labels removed and then crushed flat. We smashed them with our feet—an exhilarating release for emotions we had no name for. When our shoes stuck to the cans we clomped about for a while, making a game of who could keep theirs on the longest.

But school was over for the day and after a while we grew weary of this serious work and forgot the grownups gloom in our play—baseball and "caddy" and "kick the can" and "Liberty Pole" and "Let's Pretend."

Life went on...changing a little each day. We were issued food ration booklets. Sugar and butter and coffee were the difficult ones for my little addict heart. My dad found substitutes: saccharin for sugar, margarine for butter, chicory for coffee—all horrible, hideous! One morning my mother and I rose before five to stand in a long line at the tiny A&P a few blocks away. They said if you got there early enough you might get some butter. We stood in a long line of women of all nationalities: Greeks and Germans and Irish, Poles, Czechs, all stomping their feet to keep warm—smiling, patient women. We moved forward and into the store and just then the owner's voice rang out:

"No more butter! Better luck next time! We've got lots of oleo!"

I cried. My good sweet mother had done it mainly for me. We trudged home to squeeze the oleo-encased package with its orange capsule until it turned the white grease into a yellow mess—a far cry from butter. In France and all over Europe, young men were being slaughtered—and all my child's body knew was its own cravings.

Father White doubled up on church services—all that stood between us and destruction, he raged, was prayer. We Boyles were there, in Sacred Heart Church on our knees, three evenings each week, not counting daily Mass and Saturday confession. We droned the rosary, listened to Father preach about—of course I can't remember now—it was so hard to get the gist of sermons. We sang to God the Father at the top of our lungs and to Mary, His Mother, and to Saint Joseph and all the saints of heaven—for peace, an end to the war. Finally, it was over and I could hurry home for tea and toast and a warm safe bed between my mother and older sister. I could forget reality there and go off to my dreams of joy—to the Paradise all children know...If only briefly—they know. A place where humans love each other. What did it matter that the baby, Charles Justin, was crying, that the bedbugs were gearing up for a feast, that I couldn't swallow because my throat was so sore, had been raw and aching for days and even when the Communion host slid painfully past it and I prayed to blessed Jesus—now, truly present within me, now actually touching my misery, "Please make my throat better"—what did it matter? For sleep, I knew, would come. There would be the blessed haven of falling into velvet blackness and knowing nothing for a while.

It seemed there were a lot of illnesses going around then—blamed on the war for some reason. My skin grew yellow, and I was constantly nauseated, feverish. When others in the family became ill, the doctor called it "yellow jaundice—caused by the war." I was thin and pale with dark circles under my eyes and one bitter, cold morning on the recess yard, Sister Chrysantha asked, "Madeline, what time did you get to sleep last night? Must get your sleep, you know."

She knew not to nag; instead she opened her huge black shawl and hugged me to her. I felt her warm strong body pressed to my own—a memory etched forever in a place within me. She was a woman full of grace, and I loved her with all my heart.

I continued to go to the Saturday movies every chance I could. Now they were all about the war—romance and valor and death and killing—"Bataan," "Corregidor," "The White Cliffs of Dover." Always they began with our standing and singing, "God Bless America," hands over hearts, and then the Movietone News blared on in emotionless monotone about this battle and that...but then the movie started, and I was lost in its "life." As I grew to ten, eleven, twelve, at times the horror of what I saw on that small screen in that tiny, dirty, dismal theatre in Conemaugh broke through, and I knew the truth of the world I lived in. I saw actual footage of a man being blindfolded and then riddled with bullets—a scene that haunted me for a long time. It seemed it was Hitler's world, the madness of one man, his power. I left the show—too sick to my stomach to stay.

My father listened to the war news on the radio. He muttered under his breath for longer periods in the mornings—shouting out now and again "Utah Beach! Omar Bradley! Okinawa!" and at times mixing in the places he'd known as a soldier in WWI: "Verdun," "Belgium." "I was in Belgium," he'd say to himself, "in the trenches, gassed, lived on turnips for two months. I never want to see another God damn turnip!"

Boys from our town died. The little gold star flags appeared in more and more windows. One morning I went with an older cousin to see a friend off to war. The train depot was just down the hill, a few blocks away. He was a stout man—I wondered how he'd manage. Older men were being called up now—no matter their age or girth. His wife, a tiny blonde woman, wept as she embraced him, and we wept with her.

World War II, four years of my young life. It would take many years before I realized the enormous stakes before all of human civilization then. I was a mother when I read The Rise and Fall of the Third Reich. I could not read all the pages—too horrible to accept that human beings were ever so cruel to each other. What madness had managed to prevail then? How? Why?

My daughter in Arizona writes to me about her studies, about the human psyche, about its "shadow side"—the destructive element that must be seen, known, dealt with, and acknowledged. She is working toward her master's degree in family counseling. She is, all on her own, a woman of great courage. Her energies, her work, have always been focused on safeguarding, understanding, nurturing children. Sometimes when I listen to the news, to NPR, about the mind-shattering changes of today, I cannot help but think we are again engaged in a great conflict— such as the World Wars and all wars—struggling to hold on to our humanness, what is best within us. Only the heart of a child knows what that is...so recently from that other place—Heaven—they have much to teach us.

Lois (Jerry) Brown, Marshalltown, IA
wife of Wayne Brown, Company F, 2nd Battalion,
12th Infantry Regiment

Fifty-Five Year Honeymoon

Wayne and I met in June of 1943 outside an ice cream shop, introduced by a mutual friend. We talked for about an hour. Then my girlfriend and I were invited to ride along to take the mutual friend home, twelve miles away. Somehow, on the way back to town, Wayne and I ended up in the back seat while Lyle, Wayne's brother, drove. My girlfriend was up front with him. I thought, Here we go again. But Wayne was so polite, quiet, and cute.

They asked us for dates to go to Des Moines on July 4. We accepted. We went to an amusement park and historical museum that day. We dated about twice a week until Wayne entered the army at Camp Dodge in Des Moines, Iowa, in October of 1943. I was a senior in high school at that time.

I wrote to Wayne every day. He came home in February 1944 from Camp Roberts, California, where he took basic training. It was during the worst blizzard of the winter. The county plowed the road out to his folk's farm, three miles from town, but the wind drifted the snow back in so fast it was hard to keep it open for long, so he walked to town to see me. After that we knew we were meant for each other. We graduated early in April, so the boys in the class could help on the farms. That was a laugh as every one of them was taken into military service before the year was over.

I went to work at Fisher Governor Company, where they made valves and regulators for gas lines on oil wells, ships, and many other things. Fisher's Logo was: "If it flows through pipes, chances are it is controlled by Fisher." I worked in the "White Room" for a while, and we were making something secret for the war effort. They never let us know what it was for. But the whole plant received the "E" award, and we each got a pin with an E for Efficiency award in 1944 and 1945.

Wayne was wounded three times, and they never told us where or how bad, or where he was. I cried a lot but still wrote to Wayne every day. It was also hard on his mother, who kept a scrapbook of the war in Europe for him. After the war in Europe ended, he came home on July 16, for thirty days of rest and recuperation. We were married July 26, 1945. We went by train to Louisiana to visit his brother Lyle, who was to leave for the war in Japan after his basic training at Camp Claiborne, Louisiana. He did not get a leave to go home.

After that we were going on a honeymoon trip to Minnesota to visit his aunt and uncle in the same 1931 Model-A Ford we had dated in, back in 1943. When we got to Albert Lea, Minnesota, church bells were ringing, sirens were wailing, horns were honking, and people were dancing in the street. When we stopped to see what was going on, they told us Japan had surrendered. Were we happy! We honked our way through town. Wayne had told us they were going to train for the invasion of Japan after his leave was over.

Wayne went back to Camp Butner, North Carolina, and they had so many to discharge on the point system that they asked him if he wanted to go home for ten days. Of course, he said, "Yes." He returned to Camp Butner and then to Camp Croft, South Carolina, where he was discharged on the point system, October 21, 1945. He spent two years and one month in the army with fourteen of those months overseas. From our marriage, we have two daughters, one son, four grandchildren, two great grandchildren, and had our 55th Anniversary on July 26, 2000.

Luella Mullen, Bradenton, FL
Wife of Orval H. Mullen, HQ Company, 1st Battalion,
8th Infantry Regiment

The Loneliness of a War Bride

I've been asked to write and tell how it was here in the United States as a war bride while our husbands were in the war. I think the worst thing, of course, was the loneliness of having my husband so far away, and the communications were so bad. Sometimes we would not hear from each other for a month or two—and me not knowing if he were dead or alive during the heat of battle. I know I wrote to him every day, and he'd write to me saying, "How are you and why don't you write to me?" Sometimes I would receive several letters at once (that I still keep in a trunk).

I think the only time he didn't get to write was during the fighting and sometimes when he couldn't find paper to write on.

It is still so hard for me even after so many years. It doesn't seem possible that it is 56 years ago because it is still so fresh in my mind. I'm sure it is in his, also. When he has shared some of his experiences, like laying on a raincoat covering (that we still have) with half of it and the snow covering him, I just want to hug him and try to make him forget some of the bad experiences. When I think of his being in the middle of the Atlantic Ocean, seasick at the same time I was in the hospital having our first child (he was not aware of it for about a month, or whether it was a son or daughter), I still cry.

I lived with my mother in an apartment. We had a fire escape, and I'd go out there and hold my baby when it got warm and I'd cry. This almost sounds terrible to tell sad things, but people need to know how horrible war is, and that it was horrible for us loved ones back here and other people that were hurt. My husband used to say, "Please send me pictures," and I did all the time, but it took so long for him to get them. With the way things are now and how things have changed, many things go so fast.

Orval was gone for twenty-one months. We did not see each other from the time I was five months pregnant, while he was still in the States, because at that time we had no money to do things. The only time he could call was one time from New York with someone listening, and all we could really say was that we loved each other. We did not see each other again until our son was almost two years old.

I remember Orval sent me hankies from France. Another thing I'll never forget: one time when he was wounded, he wrote a letter to me and said he would write another letter and send me a watch and for me to open the back of the watch and read a note in there. (Censorship didn't allow sending much information.) It told me where he was wounded and how he was doing—he was OK. I'll bet that's the first time a wife got a love letter in the back of a pocket watch. A few days later I got a "regret to inform you, your husband has been seriously wounded in combat," letter. Did I say communications were bad?

There are so many things to remember. One of the things I've always loved him for was that when he received approximately 21 dollars per month in pay, he got soap out of that and sent the rest to me and our son. (Our son became a doctor of immunology and died of a heart attack in 1988.)

When Orval got back to the States he called me and then took a bus home, arriving about 2300 hours I didn't have a car, so I walked the two miles to the bus station and to this day, I can see him getting off that bus. He also saw I hadn't cut my hair as I'd promised him. We walked those two miles home stopping every little bit hugging and crying. When we got home I showed him his son. I'd left him naked (hoping nothing would happen) because I wanted him to see him as he came into the world. As most people then, we had a time adjusting to his being back, but it was wonderful. I got pregnant as soon as he came home. We didn't know whether he would go to Japan, but the war ended. Thank God, I didn't have to have another baby without him being there with us.

So many things pop into my mind. When he was wounded at St. Lô, he told me a little about things but I didn't learn all about it until listening to him being interviewed in New Orleans at the National D-Day Museum grand opening in June 2000. We cried more tears, and I saw more people who experienced WWII crying than we've seen in years in those few days. I talked to other wives who said they were learning things about their husbands that had never been talked about before.

I must tell something funny after all this gloom. When we walked into the National D-Day Museum in New Orleans on June 4, 2000, I saw my husband's face when he saw the Higgins Boat, and I said, "Go over and let me take your picture by the boat."

He just walked on and ignored me. About a half hour later, he was showing me the coils of wire in a stack and telling me how he laid it out for communications. (Too bad we didn't have some of that communications for us sometimes.) A cute young gal came up and started to talk to us and asked if she could take his picture.

He said, "Sure," and posed like a newborn baby without the bare butt. Needless to say, I had no more problems with him posing for me for pictures, and I got my picture of him in front of the Higgins Boat.

I really believe WWII affected so many lives of "The Greatest Generation" (as Tom Brokaw calls us). The memories are so lasting for our lifetime. We have so much to praise God for to this day, and a hope of a great tomorrow.

Reinhilde Seyboth, Troy, NY
wife of Bill Seyboth, Company L, 4th Battalion, 22nd Infantry Regiment

Growing up in WWII Germany

I grew up during World War II in Germany and was on the other side of the war. I lived in a small town called Bad Bruckenau. Wildflecken was about thirty miles away and was maneuver ground for Germany and later as well for the American soldiers. I think many GIs will remember the place.

This is where I met my husband, Bill, who served with the 22nd Infantry Regiment in Company L. When the Allies came to our town in 1945, it took just a few hits from the cannons. The mayor surrendered to save the town. The troops searched from house to house looking for weapons. We were all in the cellar. My father was dead, my brother was missing in the army. My sixty-five-year-old uncle served with the Red Cross and was not in the house, only women and children.

Here came this huge tank. One guy had his head out of the hatch, and the gun was pointing straight at the house. Four GIs came out to search the house for weapons. We were shaking in our boots, but nothing was found. My four-year-old cousin, who looked like Shirley Temple, curls and all, went up to a soldier and said to him in German, "We are not afraid of you. Our rifle and gun are well hidden." The GI laughed, patted her on the head and said something in English like, "Nice girl," and then they all left the house.

Epilogue

If you enjoyed reading the stories of these 4th Infantry Division veterans, there are plenty more, equally as gripping, in the first volume of this three-book series, *War Stories: D-Day to the Liberation of Paris.* While the first two books of this series are focused exclusively on the 4th Infantry Division's experiences in WWII, the stories could just as easily have come from any of the dozens of divisions who fought to liberate Europe.

War Stories: D-Day to the Liberation of Paris, available in both paperback and e-book from www.deedspublishing.com, starts when the 4th Infantry Division landed in France, H-Hour, D-Day, June 6, 1944. Although D-Day was relatively low in casualties for the 4ID, the fight quickly heated up as the 4ID fought its way up the Cotentin Peninsula to liberate Cherbourg. By the end of June, the 4ID had suffered more than 5,000 casualties in fierce hedgerow fighting. Remaining on the front lines, the 4ID was the spearhead of the St. Lo breakout, part of Operation Cobra, in late July 1944, and fought non-stop until they were in sight of Paris near the end of August. Although never credited with the liberation of Paris, the 4th Infantry Division was told, "To hell with prestige, tell the 4th to slam on in (to Paris), and take the liberation." And they did, led by the 12th Infantry Regiment. Learning of these orders and fearing an affront to France, LeClerc's French 2nd Armored Division mounted their tanks and burned up their treads on the brick roads to enter Paris.

To read more of the personal stories of those members of the "Greatest Generation," order your copy of *War Stories: D-Day to the Liberation of Paris,* available now from www.deedspublishing.com.

The third volume of this set, available in June 2014, covers stories from 4th Infantry Division veterans who fought in the central highlands of Vietnam in 1966-1970. *War Stories: Vietnam 1966 to 1970* continues to follow the 4th Infantry Division, but as with the World War II volumes, the stories could just as easily have been about any of the units and troops who fought in Vietnam.

About the Author

Bob Babcock has had a passion for the military and military history since he was a young boy growing up in Heavener, OK during the Korean War. He was fascinated by the troop trains and freight trains with military equipment passing through his home town. In high school, he wrote a term paper on D-Day, his first deep dive into military history.

A Vietnam veteran of the 4th Infantry Division, Bob became a member of the National 4th Infantry Division Association where he met and listened to stories of many 4ID WWII vets—those who made the history reported in this book. As a founding official partner of the Veterans History Project, Bob expanded his interest in all military history through interviews with hundreds of veterans of all ranks and all services, with a strong focus on preserving WWII veteran stories while they are still with us. In 2004, Bob led a tour of ten 4ID D-Day veterans to the 60th anniversary ceremony in Normandy, France. For two years, Bob was a Department of Defense historian, serving as the official historian of the active duty 4th Infantry Division, collecting the history from Iraq and Afghanistan as it happened and acting as the go to person on all other 4ID history.

A retired IBM executive, Bob has written six books and founded Deeds Publishing, a family owned and operated publishing company in Atlanta, GA. His spare time is spent working with veterans of all wars and preserving their stories for posterity. He is currently in his third term as President of the National 4th Infantry Division Association and continues in the 4ID historian job he has held for almost two decades.

Military Books by Deeds Publishing
Check www.deedspublishing.com for these and more books

World War II

War Stories: Utah Beach to Liberation of Paris by Robert O. Babcock

War Stories: Paris to V-E Day by Robert O. Babcock

World War II WAC by Helen Denton

Foxhole Promises by Arnold Whittaker

Barbed Wire Surgeon by Albert Weinstein, MD

A Soldier, My Dad by Neal Pizzano

A Chaplain's Duty by Rev. George W. Knapp and Gayle E. Knapp

American Veterans by LTC (Ret) James Lawrence

Vietnam

What Now, Lieutenant? by Robert O. Babcock

War Stories: Vietnam 1966 to 1970 by Robert O. Babcock

Reflections on LZ Albany: The Agony of Vietnam by James T. Lawrence

Yankee Air Pirates by C.K. McCusker

Unchained Eagle by Robert G. Certain

Dear Mark by Susan Clotfelter Jimison

Cold War

Grenada Grinder by MAJ (Ret) Michael Couvillon

Airman's Odyssey by LTC (Ret) James Lawrence

What Now, Knucklehead? by MAJ (Ret)Raymond Jones

Iraq/Afghanistan

Operation Iraqi Freedom I: A Year in the Sunni Triangle by Robert O. Babcock

Operation Iraqi Freedom 07-09: Dispatches from Baghdad by Robert O. Babcock

Siren's Song by Antonio Salinas

My Son is Alive by Roberta Quimby

Freedom Express: Caught Between Iraq and a Hard Place by COL (Ret) David Allen

Wolfhound Reflections: OIF 07-09 by JB Jaso

Task Force Regulars: Operation Enduring Freedom X-XI

CPSIA information can be obtained at www.ICGtesting.com
Printed in the USA
LVOW08s1148230414

382833LV00005B/6/P